British Asians and Football

Many British Asians play football at an amateur level, but only a very few have achieved professional status. Representing the first major study into this issue, this book examines the real-life experiences of British Asians in football, and considers the reasons for their marginal place in the British national game.

Based on original ethnographic research, this work explores key issues for debate, including:

- stereotyping, cultural assumptions and popular explanations for British Asian under-representation;
- racism in English football, the impact of 9/11 and rising Islamophobia;
- the experiences of British Asian professional players – life, lifestyle and identity;
- expressions of masculinity in young British Asian culture;
- the meaning of sport – 'race', nation, culture and citizenship; and
- institutional and policy responses to racism and inequality – clubs, governing bodies and campaigns.

Presenting original research into a largely neglected area of study, *British Asians and Football* offers new insight into what it means to be young, male, British and Asian. For students, researchers and policymakers interested in the sociology and politics of 'race', identity, social values and sport, this is essential reading.

Daniel Burdsey is Senior Lecturer in Sociology of Sport and Leisure at the University of Brighton.

Routledge Critical Studies in Sport
Series Editors
Jennifer Hargreaves and Ian McDonald
University of Brighton

The Routledge Critical Studies in Sport series aims to lead the way in developing the multi-disciplinary field of Sport Studies by producing books that are interrogative, interventionist and innovative. By providing theoretically sophisticated and empirically grounded texts, the series will make sense of the changes and challenges facing sport globally. The series aspires to maintain the commitment and promise of the critical paradigm by contributing to a more inclusive and less exploitative culture of sport.

Also available in this series:

Understanding Lifestyle Sports
Consumption, identity and difference
Edited by Belinda Wheaton

Why Sports Morally Matter
William J Morgan

Fastest, Highest, Strongest
A critique of high-performance sport
Rob Beamish and Ian Ritchie

Sport, Sexualities and Queer/Theory
Edited by Jayne Caudwell

Physical Culture, Power, and the Body
Edited by Jennifer Hargreaves and Patricia Vertinsky

British Asians and Football

Culture, identity, exclusion

Daniel Burdsey

 Routledge
Taylor & Francis Group

LONDON AND NEW YORK

First published 2007
by Routledge
2 Park Square, Milton Park, Abingdon, Oxon, OX14 4RN

Simultaneously published in the USA and Canada
by Routledge
270 Madison Ave, New York, NY 10016

Routledge is an imprint of the Taylor & Francis Group, an informa business

© 2007 Daniel Burdsey

Typeset in Goudy by Swales & Willis Ltd, Exeter
Printed and bound in Great Britain by Biddles Ltd, King's Lynn

British Library Cataloguing in Publication Data
A catalogue record for this book is available from the British Library

Library of Congress Cataloging-in-Publication Data
Burdsey, Daniel, 1976–
British Asians and football: culture, identity, exclusion/Daniel Burdsey.
p. cm. – (Routledge critical studies in sport)
Includes bibliographical references and index.
1. Discrimination in sports – Great Britain. 2. Asians – Great Britain. 3. Soccer – Great Britain. I.
Title. II. Series.
GV706.32.B87 2006
796.3340941 – dc22

2006015262

ISBN 10: 0-415-39500-3 (hbk)
ISBN 10: 0-203-96686-4 (ebk)
ISBN 13: 978-0-415-39500-7 (hbk)
ISBN 13: 978-0-203-96686-0 (ebk)

Contents

Series editors' preface

In 1996, the 'Asians Can't Play Football' report hit the desks of the football authorities. If British football was to live up to its claim to be at the forefront of combating racism and the embodiment of multi-culturalism, it was acknowledged that something had to be done to open up the pathways to professional football for aspiring young British Asians. But in the 10 years to 2006, although there were improved opportunities for some British Asians in different areas of life and culture, there was no significant increase in their numbers in professional football. During that period, a generation of British Asian football hopefuls passed through their formative years as the early teenagers of 1996 became the twenty-somethings of 2006, but in spite of the many projects and initiatives aimed at eliminating discrimination and nurturing inclusion, an upsurge of British Asians in the professional game simply did not take place. This situation is the focus of Dan Burdsey's timely and important book, *British Asians and Football: Culture, Identity and Exclusion*. In his analysis, Burdsey places the question of the low level of British Asian football players firmly within the social and political milieu of the time, taking account of the particular problems and uncertainties facing British Asians following the political backwash from the 11 September 2001 attacks on New York and Washington and 7 July 2005 bombings in London, the intensification of Islamaphobia, and a generalised atmosphere of suspicion towards all the diverse British Asian communities. In his book Burdsey addresses the highly sensitive and complex dynamics of 'culture, identity and exclusion' that are relevant to professional football in Britain as well as to broader society.

Through meticulous fieldwork, including numerous interviews and participant observations, Burdsey was able to spend time listening first hand to the experiences of British Asian football players at different professional and amateur levels of the game, to 'get under their skins', and to represent them through his text. He also interviewed administrators of the game and those in leadership positions in the anti-racism football movement. As a result, he has produced a book that interrogates assumptions about under-representation, is interventionist through the telling of previously untold stories, and is innovative by way of a very detailed development of previous academic arguments about football and anti-racism that includes original material and sophisticated analysis.

The British Asian participants in his book were keen for Burdsey to 'tell their story', to expose the myths about an ethnically-based disinterest in the game and to explain the reasons for their strong feelings of exclusion based on racial discrimination. They recognize that they do not have an 'official' voice in the places where decisions are made about football development and that this book can provide an alternative, non-establishment, more honest and accurate version of the situation. As Series Editors we share these views. It is a vindication of one persons' privileged position being used to progressive effect. Although Burdsey is not authentically 'part of' the culture that he investigates, he has chosen to use his authoritative 'speaking position' as a white academic to articulate the needs and desires of those whose voices have generally been ignored.

We hope that this text stimulates interest amongst researchers, lecturers and students and is given requisite space on the curriculum in the expanding disciplinary field of Sport Studies. We also hope that it will act as a catalyst and encourage a new generation of British Asian scholars to undertake research into sport. And most of all, we hope that the book will kick-start a radical debate based on the actual experiences, needs, and wishes of British Asian footballers themselves, as well as reigniting discussions about the need for change in the football industry that was promised a decade ago but not delivered.

Jennifer Hargreaves and Ian McDonald
University of Brighton
Series Editors

Acknowledgements

Huge thanks are due to the following people whose assistance and encouragement have been invaluable in the production of this book:

Jennifer Hargreaves and Ian McDonald for inviting me to write a book for their series and for their ideas, encouragement and support in bringing this to fruition; Gary Armstrong who, along with Jennifer Hargreaves, supervised the doctoral thesis on which this book is based – their support and advice were invaluable throughout, especially in helping me to think differently and critically about social phenomena; Les Back and Ian Robinson who examined the thesis and offered some very helpful comments and advice on how to turn a Ph.D. dissertation into a book; friends and colleagues in the international research group on Anti-racist Discourses – Mark Alleyne, Hemant Shah, Ingrid Lehmann, Liesbet van Zoonen, Jairo Lugo, Karina Horsti, Sagrario Cruz Carretero, Felicidad Góngara Berlín, Sylvanna Falcón, Nakisha Nesmith, Floris Müller and Laurens de Roode, who have provided constructive comments and ideas that feed into this book, and a supportive, scholarly environment in which to develop my research, in Madrid, Atlanta, Dresden and cyberspace; Aarti Ratna, for her friendship, and for her thoughts and continuing discussions on the issues included in this book; colleagues at the Chelsea School, University of Brighton who continue to make going to work such a fantastic experience and particularly Alan Tomlinson who gave me the opportunity to work full-time in academe; Iain Moir, Charles Jenkins, Patrick Murphy, Ken Sheard, Ivan Waddington, Dominic Malcolm and Martin Roderick, my undergraduate and Masters tutors who introduced me to, and were central in developing my love of, the sociology of sport, and who convinced me that I could make a career out of teaching and writing about it; Samantha Grant and Kate Manson for providing great editorial support; and the three anonymous academic reviewers who made very helpful and constructive comments on the original book proposal.

Thanks must also go to my mum Margaret, dad David and brother Tim for obvious reasons.

Most gratitude goes to the British Asian footballers who gave up their time to participate in the research and shared their stories, thoughts, attitudes, aspirations, desires and criticisms with me. This book could not have been written without them. It is these players, therefore, to whom this book is dedicated.

I am grateful to both Sage Publications and Taylor and Francis for permission to reproduce previously published material. Earlier versions of Chapter 4 and Chapter 5 can be found in: Burdsey, D. (2004) '"One of the lads"?: dual ethnicity and assimilated ethnicities in the careers of British Asian professional footballers', *Ethnic and Racial Studies*, 27, 5: 757–79 (<http://www.tandf.co.uk/journals/titles/01419870.asp>); and Burdsey, D. (2006) '"If I ever play football, Dad, can I play for England or India?": British Asians, sport and diasporic national identities', *Sociology*, 40, 1: 11–28 (reprinted by permission of Sage Publications, © BSA Publications Ltd, 2006). Other parts of this book also contain modified material from: Burdsey, D. (2004) 'Obstacle race? "Race", racism and the recruitment of British Asian professional footballers', *Patterns of Prejudice*, 38, 3: 279–99 (<http://www.tandf.co.uk/journals/titles/0031322X.asp>); and Burdsey, D. (2006) 'No ball games allowed? A socio-historical examination of the development and social roles of British Asian football clubs', *Journal of Ethnic and Migration Studies*, 32, 3: 477–96 (<http://www.tandf.co.uk/journals/titles/1369183X.asp>).

1 Introduction

Kick-off

On Saturday 5 April 2003, the scoresheet for the Nationwide Division One match between Burnley and Watford included an unfamiliar name: Chopra. In fact it was listed not once, but four times. Michael Chopra, a nineteen-year-old striker, had achieved the remarkable feat of scoring four goals in a single match as his team romped to a high-scoring victory over their Lancastrian opponents. The reason why Chopra was unknown to the footballing public at large was because he had only made his professional debut a week previously, having been loaned to Watford by Newcastle United to gain match experience. Yet the most unusual thing about this game was the sight of a South Asian surname on an English professional football teamsheet. Chopra's mother, Sharon, is white, but his father, Minty, is Indian. With only a handful of players of South Asian background having ever played professional football in England, he is thus an extremely rare commodity.

Since his goalscoring feat, Chopra – who, following a spell back at Newcastle United and periods on-loan at Nottingham Forest and Barnsley, now plays for Cardiff City – has been joined in the professional ranks by a handful of other British Asians: Zesh Rehman – whose brother Rizwan narrowly missed out on joining him in the game – plays for Fulham, and has also enjoyed loan spells with both Norwich City and Brighton and Hove Albion; Adnan Ahmed has begun to make his mark at Huddersfield Town; Harpal Singh has spent periods at Leeds United, Bury, Bradford City, Bristol City and Stockport County; and Shahed Ahmed has made a handful of appearances for Wycombe Wanderers. Although these British Asians are not the first to play professional football in England, they are the first to make a significant breakthrough for the best part of two decades. However, whilst their presence is hugely encouraging, the tendency for their clubs to loan them to lower division sides reflects the fact that none of them has become a household name. One must, therefore, be extremely careful not to overstate the wider repercussions of this breakthrough or to paint an overly benign picture of increasing inclusion of British Asians in the professional game. In short, these players are the exceptions to the rule. British Asians remain heavily under-represented in the game in proportion to their numbers in the overall population and there is much more that needs to be done to overcome their exclusion.

About the book

This book is about Michael, Zesh, Adnan, Harpal and Shahed. It is also about those British Asian players who have had fleeting periods at professional clubs without ever quite making the grade (such as Anwar Uddin who, after captaining West Ham United to FA Youth Cup success in the late 1990s, had brief spells with Sheffield Wednesday and Bristol Rovers before joining semi-professional side Dagenham and Redbridge) and those youngsters currently registered at academies or centres of excellence with dreams of making the final, and most significant, stage of progression. It is about their participation and experiences, their aspirations and desires, the issues and problems that they encounter, and their feelings of inclusion and exclusion as British Asian footballers in an occupational culture in which they have traditionally been regarded as 'outsiders'. Some of these players tell parts of their stories here. They are not, however, the only characters in the tale. They may be the most well-known, but the supporting cast runs into tens of thousands. The other players will be completely unknown to the majority of readers for they are not professional footballers. Their faces are not seen on television, and their names are not printed in matchday programmes, club websites and newspapers, or heard on the radio. Those who speak within the pages of this book are, for example, businessmen, students, call-centre workers, landlords, football coaches, sports administrators, civil servants, caterers, waiters and taxi-drivers. Their common denominator is a passion for football that dominates their leisure time, in their capacities as players, coaches, referees, and/or in other off-field administrative roles that are intrinsic to the existence of amateur clubs and competitions. These players have never played and will never play professionally although, as this book suggests, for some it was not due to a lack of talent.

This book, therefore, is comprised of two main threads of narrative: one from those (contingently) inside the professional game and one from those outside. Despite the vicissitudes of their footballing careers, many of the players come from similar backgrounds, some even from the same specific local communities. For others, the only thing they have in common is a mutual – yet vague and nebulous – status of 'Asianness'. Combining these two threads of narrative and elucidating the similarities, differences, complexities and nuances both within and between them, this book sheds light on the factors that have conspired historically and contemporarily to exclude British Asians from English professional football. Accordingly, the analysis seeks to overcome the poverty of knowledge about the involvement of young British Asian men in English football; to investigate the discrepancies between amateur and professional levels of participation, and the factors that contribute to exclusion from this latter sphere; and to analyse the specific relationship between constructions and articulations of British 'Asianness' and the cultures of football. In this sense it is a book about football and a book about young British Asian men.

The subtitle of the book is *Culture, Identity, Exclusion* – concepts that help to explain the relationship between British Asians and professional football; moreover, concepts that contribute to the fact that despite their passion for the game and considerable involvement at amateur level, British Asians are significantly under-represented as professional footballers in proportion to their numbers in the overall population. As the last (2001) census recorded, out of a total population of just under 59 million people in Britain, there are 1,053,411 Indians, 747,285 Pakistanis and 283,063 Bangladeshis. A government agency or painstaking period of research is not needed to calculate the number currently playing professional football; they can be counted on a single hand.

Werbner (2005: 747) argues that within the social sciences 'culture has come increasingly to be seen as a concept that essentialises, reifies, stereotypes, orientalises, racialises, Others, exoticises and distorts the subjects of anthropological research'. As this book demonstrates, this approach to minority ethnic groups, especially British Asians, is also widely evident in English football and the associated institutions that represent it, such as the media. This book aims to challenge this state of affairs by illustrating the heterogeneity of British Asian communities and cultures, and the myriad ways that they approach and interact with professional football. The analysis progresses from the belief that culture is a process: something that is dynamic, mobile, unfinished, both enabling and restricting, fluctuating throughout time and space, and does not exist or operate outside the individuals that construct and are shaped by it. As Stuart Hall (1992a: 225) states, 'cultural identity . . . is a matter of "becoming" as well as of "being" . . . cultural identities come from somewhere, have histories. But like everything that is historical they undergo constant transformation . . . subject to the continuous "play" of history, culture and power'. Furthermore, following Gilroy (1992), the idea that cultures are hermetically sealed units, experientially unique and mutually impermeable, is likewise rejected. Cultures are part of social fields of interaction and are not the property or possession of particular groups (Alexander 2005: 206). In terms of English football, again, it is incorrect to talk of a dominant culture in the singular. Yet at professional level, in particular, there are certain patterns of norms, values and attitudes that form a cohesive set of dominant structures, activities, behaviours and networks which reflect and promote the interests of some groups, yet marginalize and discriminate against others.

Identity refers to the way that the politics of identity and representation are constructed, contested and articulated by British Asian players in relation to football. On one hand it is about the importance of the game in reflecting ethnic, national, diasporic and hybrid identities. On the other it refers to the implications or outcomes that arise when these identities come into contact with those that are dominant, and are inexorably related to boundaries of inclusion/exclusion, in the professional game: opposition, conflict, co-existence, assimilation, manipulation, resistance. The central paradox is that the game of football is a key social arena for intercultural dialogue and exchange, and an arena for British Asians to articulate their identities, but it is also a social space in which these identities are met with some of the most severe forms of discrimination and examples of contemporary racisms. In this sense 'identities become open ended, unpredictable and often ambiguous in the ways they appear and are lived through' (Alexander 2006: 269).

The concept of *Exclusion* refers to both a state and a process. The current situation with regard to British Asians in professional football can be described as one of exclusion – a term that characterizes the processes, structures and attitudes that have denied, and continue to deny them the opportunity to participate at elite level. Exclusion operates in overt ways through acts of blatant racism and the reproduction of racial stereotypes, but also in much more subtle, complex and less 'visible', yet equally ingrained, ways by influencing who are 'insiders' and who are 'outsiders', what is 'normal' or 'traditional', what are regarded as desired cultural traits, and how one becomes involved in the professional game. With this in mind, this book argues for shifting the analysis away from seeing British Asian communities as the problem, as is often purported in dominant discourses, to examining how football's clubs and institutions construct and maintain racial inequality and disadvantage.

To summarize the central argument in this book: whilst a handful of British Asian players have broken into the game and there is a gradually increasing presence of British Asian supporters on the terraces and in the stands of the nation's stadia, this is not sufficient. The job is not done, the game is not won. As the *Asians Can Play Football* report, the most recent analysis of this topic, states:

> It might feel like the game is changing, and initiatives in the sport may be multiplying, but all the evidence confirms that change in behaviour at the highest levels of the game still lags lamentably behind any real change in attitude or in stated policy. We have had nine years of 'change' in the game since [the] Asians Can't Play Football [report] but are things really that different?
>
> (Asians in Football Forum 2005: 6)

Although the need for change is recognized, at least publicly, by an increasing number of agencies, the problem lies in the fact that despite the rhetoric espoused, and the promises made, by professional clubs, governing bodies and anti-racist football organizations, these are generally not being reflected in the construction and implementation of appropriate policies. The intransigence and resistance that traditionally has met demands for these institutions to work more proactively towards overcoming the exclusion of British Asians from the professional game may have begun to slowly erode, but an equally problematic state of affairs may be occurring: one of complacency. For example, a British Asian player interviewed for this book described an exchange with a prominent and well-known member of the anti-racist football movement: 'We went to a conference the other week and [he] was asked a question on why there are no Asian footballers. He turned round and said, "Oh, it's a boring subject". Not the answer I would be looking for' (interview with British Indian amateur player, 27 June 2002).

The existence of such attitudes has contributed to what, according to the subtitle of the *Asians Can Play Football* report, might be seen as 'a wasted decade' in attempts to overcome the exclusion of British Asians from professional football. This lack of action is not universal though and the last ten years have certainly not been wasted by British Asian players and clubs, as this book and the afore-mentioned report demonstrate. Yet the same could be said about every decade since the 1960s as British Asian football clubs have built a thriving football scene despite little recognition, intervention or assistance from the professional game, county associations or local leagues. The current state of affairs is one where, whilst some of the relevant issues and problems have been acknowledged, little concrete action has been implemented to deal with or remedy them. It is this factor that represents, at the very least, wastage, but arguably also widespread institutional failures.

Those looking for an unequivocal answer or a magic solution will not find it here. One book cannot provide a universal resolution to such an inveterate problem and, like football, academe is a game of opinions. Nonetheless, it is hoped that this book will challenge some of the orthodoxies that characterize dominant explanations of the relationship between British Asians and professional football and, in this regard, will contribute to identifying the solutions (in plural) that are required to overcome the exclusion of these players.

The fieldwork

This book stems from doctoral research undertaken between 2000 and 2004. The investigation involved a process of in-depth ethnographic fieldwork based around interviews and observations with British Asian footballers. Interviews were under-taken with four main groups: professional, ex-professional and semi-professional players; amateur players; members of anti-racist football organizations; and staff from the academies/centres of excellence – special development centres designed to coach and train talented players aged between seven and nineteen – at English professional football clubs. The interviews were often lengthy affairs, generating large amounts of rich empirical data. These exchanges created strong bonds between me and the players, resembling more what Burgess (1984: 102) labels a 'conversation with a purpose', and were often supplemented by *ad hoc* contri-butions from interested and enthusiastic team-mates, friends or family members who were in attendance.

Interviews only provide a partial representation – a snapshot – of the lives and identities of the players in the study, and so the data generated by this method were complemented by a series of observations. These were undertaken with four British Asian clubs: a predominantly Punjabi Sikh team in Greater London, two Bangladeshi Muslim teams in Inner London and one Pakistani Muslim club in Inner London. Observations were not strictly of the participant variety as, despite frequent invitations, my own limitations in ability and fitness meant that I turned down the chance to don my kit and boots. Instead, observations involved watching matches with supporters, and interacting with players, coaches and club members before and after games and training sessions. These occasions provided the opportunity to watch, listen, enjoy stories, share in the joys and sorrows of a game, and recognize the special exchanges and rituals intrinsic to football. At some clubs, 'access all areas' was permitted on matchdays, enabling close-hand involvement in the complete match experience. This provided not only the chance to mix with players, but also to witness their interactions and dialogues – footballing banter and conversations about their social lives – thus delineating the context and ways in which British Asian footballers articulate and construct their identities in relation to the game.

Matches also provided the opportunity to meet other key club members, especially those with off-field responsibilities, and members of British Asian football federations; to observe the interaction between British Asian players and white or African-Caribbean teams; and to gauge the attitudes and behaviours of referees, opposing teams and visiting supporters. Invitations were also gratefully accepted to important social occasions, for example, the chance to participate in a ceremony at one club's local *gurdwara* (Sikh temple) to honour the birthday of Guru Nanak, the founding father of Sikhism. This involved presenting the trophies that the club had won during the previous season to the congregation leader, and receiving a blessing and the *langar*[1] in return. As well as being a proud and enriching personal experience, it was a further means of contextualizing the research, in terms of how South Asian ethnicities and traditions are fused with twenty-first-century British football cultures and lifestyles. On another occasion, players were accompanied to the re-opening of a local community centre, whilst trips with players to some of east London's finest curry emporia were especially enjoyed. Gratitude towards players for their role in the research was repaid on an informal *quid pro quo* basis. This ranged from helping to put up the goalposts or doing matchday chores, to assisting in other activities, such as giving players lifts to matches or taking family members to football training. Further observations were carried out during two matches featuring the Indian national team, against Fulham at Craven Cottage in July 2000 and against Brentford at Griffin Park in July 2001. The objective of attending these matches was to gauge 'mainstream' supporter reactions to, and interpretations of, participation by South Asians in football. The research has also been informed and influenced by my involvement (between 1998 and 1999) in the inaugural steering group for the *Foxes Against Racism* initiative at Leicester City Football Club.

Voices, epistemologies and Critical Race Theory

> I think what we sometimes resent, perhaps more than anything else, is people who become patronizing in saying to Asians, 'Well, you don't actually know what your needs are, we need to articulate your needs for you'.
>
> (Interview with British Indian amateur player, 23 April 2002)

Traditionally, the authoritative voice, i.e. the 'knower', within discourses of 'race', ethnicity and sport has been the white (male) academic, policy maker or anti-racist activist. Specifically, whilst football is the most researched and written about sport in Britain, British Asian players systematically have been excluded from contributing to analyses of the game. *Their* accounts of their exclusion from professional football have not been listened to or integrated into official reports or publications. Consequently, a key objective of this book is to overcome the 'silencing' of these players. Their experiences, attitudes, opinions, aspirations, accounts and stories are crucial to the generation of knowledge about 'Asianness' and football, and to understanding the reasons for their absence from the professional game. Therefore it is vital to position them as 'knowers'. As Bryman argues, 'The most fundamental characteristic of qualitative research is its express commitment to viewing events, actions, norms, values... from the perspective of the people who are being studied' (cited in Prior 1997: 64). Similarly, Young Jr points out that:

> Researchers must always acknowledge and assert the cultural complexity of the people whom they study, and they must strive to capture and represent the voices of these people to their best ability, given that they are the ultimate creators of the statements being made about them.
>
> (2004: 200)

This book also seeks to contribute towards an understanding of contemporary manifestations of 'Asianness' and the manner in which the identities and lifestyles of young British Asian men are articulated in the early twenty-first century. Therefore, it centralizes the use of oral testimonies and life stories, and attributes high status to the accounts provided by British Asian players themselves. Listening to their stories is crucial to challenging solipsistic and ethnocentric ways of seeing the world (Delgado 1989).

In his powerful ethnography of magazine vendors, scavengers and panhandlers in New York's Greenwich Village, Duneier (1999: 352) makes the point that, 'as an upper-middle-class white male academic writing about poor black men and women, who are some of the most disadvantaged and stigmatized members of my own society, I have documented lives very different from my own'. This book is written from a similar standpoint: as a white middle-class academic writing about British Asian footballers, many of whom come from the lower socio-economic strata, I am writing about players from backgrounds very different from my own. The players experience forms of discrimination, prejudice and exclusion that I do not. This is a distinction that cannot be ignored for, as Andersen (1993: 41) points out, 'The problems of doing research within minority communities are compounded by the social distance imposed by class relations when interviewers are white and middle-class and those being interviewed are not'. However, Back (1996: 24) rightly argues that, 'although it is profoundly true that whites cannot fully comprehend the experiential consequences of racism, we do experience the transmission of racist ideas and formulae'.

In terms of the research process itself, debates have existed for a considerable time about the correlation between a researcher's ethnicity and insider/outsider status (for further discussion on this in relation to this study see Burdsey 2005b). However, not only is the insider/outsider dichotomy much more fluid and contingent than has often been recognized, but also it is premised on a series of problematic assumptions. For example, as Alexander argues:

> The ideology of 'race matching' in research pivots on the assumption that 'native' researchers occupy an innate 'insider' status that places them apart from the oppressive regimes embodied by mainstream White, middle-class, male 'professional' academics and guarantees access to the hidden 'Truth' of experience.
>
> (2004b: 141)

She points out that this standpoint has progressed from being the preserve of radical critics of 'white sociology' to forming part of commonsense approaches to research methodology, but argues that it is problematic in the way that it essentializes notions of community and authenticity, homogenizes group experiences, and underplays the subtleties and complexities of achieving access (ibid.: 142; see also A. Shah 2004). Ethnic differences between researchers and their participants are by no means unassailable, but in research of this nature, a failure to recognize their significance would demonstrate methodological and epistemological naivety. I concur with Duneier (1999: 354) that 'perhaps the best starting point is to be aware that a different social position can have a serious effect on one's work, and these differences must be taken seriously'. Both the research and writing stages have involved a continual process of reflexivity, and an acknowledgement of the importance of critically scrutinizing, challenging and interrogating how our ethnicities impinge on the research process.

Throughout the research for this book, players spoke openly on a range of topics, either within interviews or during casual conversations. Every attempt has been made to ensure that this emphasis on oral evidence is reflected within the narrative, through the inclusion of British Asian players' testimonies, many of which are of substantial length. However, whilst verbatim interview transcripts are used with the objective of representing players in as accurate a manner as possible, as Clifford (1986: 7) points out, 'ethnographic truths are . . . inherently *partial* – committed and incomplete'. By utilizing the method of oral testimony, I have adopted the position not only of narrator, but also that of interpreter (von der Lippe 2000: 181), and what is written remains a *personal* interpretation.

I do not claim to speak *for* British Asian players; this book is merely a forum for some of their testimonies. Back (1996) and Sharma *et al.* (1996), for example, are rightly suspicious of those who claim to possess some kind of insider status, particularly those who claim to speak for the people they are researching. Nevertheless, Hargreaves (2000: 11) reminds us that 'bell hooks . . . has insisted that those of us who are privileged have an obligation to support and facilitate those from minority groups. . . . Providing research and knowledge is one way to do this'. If this book achieves one thing, it is hoped that it will generate information that is beneficial, useful and enabling for the individuals it is written about.

In this sense, it embodies a commitment to critical social research, whereby 'researchers not only seek to highlight forms of inequality and injustice, but also view the research act itself as constituting a challenge to the status quo' (McDonald 2002: 101). This book aims to open up a hugely important issue to a wider audience, both inside and beyond academe, but more importantly it represents a commitment to challenging racism and an attempt to contribute towards overcoming the exclusion of British Asians from the professional game.

In order to centralize the voices of British Asian players, the analysis incorporates aspects of Critical Race Theory (CRT). Originating in the USA and in the discipline of legal studies, CRT has received minimal recognition in the UK and, in particular, until Hylton's (2005) seminal contribution, there were no significant applications to the study of sport. According to Parker and Lynn (2002: 10), CRT has three main objectives:

1   to centre storytelling and narrative as legitimate approaches through which to examine 'race' and racism in social institutions (such as sport) and the wider society;
2   to combat racial subjugation whilst, at the same time, acknowledging that 'race' is a social construction;
3   to highlight the relationship between 'race' and other forms of oppression.

All are influential in this book, but in terms of methodology, the first factor is most significant. CRT insists on acknowledging the experiential knowledge of minority ethnic groups when analysing sport and society. It represents a methodological and epistemological tool to assess the ways that 'race' and racism affect the footballing experiences of British Asians, and to define, expose and address the problems that they face. The use of oral testimony, life history and storytelling is crucial in generating knowledge in this area for they help to 'uproot the dysconscious racism or uncritical and distorted ways of thinking about race that have led to tacit acceptance of the dominant White norms and privileges' (Singer 2005: 370). Employing CRT is particularly important for the arguments raised in this book for it enables us to understand that dominant claims that football is 'colour-blind' or meritocratic are actually a means of sustaining white hegemony in the structures and subcultures of the professional game.

Alongside the role of tenets of CRT, it is also important to maintain a critical approach to players' stories and testimonies, and to not take what players say as unequivocal 'truths' or the reflection of an external reality that exists outside of representation. It is our role as sociologists to persistently approach the data that have been generated with a critical eye, but it is also essential that players' 'voices' are not deafened by the machinery of sociological analysis. In this regard it is important to point out that this book is not about the representation of a 'voice'; rather it is about 'voices'. The notion of a single, unified 'voice' not only essentializes British Asian identities, but it also homogenizes the myriad discourses and narratives that are, at various times, similar, different, conflicting and corroborating. Similarly, by elucidating their multifarious nature, it can be demonstrated that despite commensurable issues and occurrences, there is no singular British Asian football experience; rather there are a range of experiences that emanate from the intersections between ethnicity, class, religion, generation and participation in the game.

Notes on terminology and the issue of gender

Sayyid (2006: 4) points out that 'there is a continuing debate about the most appropriate way of describing and labelling those settlers that hail from South Asia'. This book employs the term 'British Asian' to refer to those British citizens who trace their ancestry to, or who themselves migrated from, the Indian subcontinent. The term 'Asian' as a form of categorization has been subject to considerable debate and contestation. As Kaur and Kalra (1996) point out, its use is inconsistent, both throughout history and in different geographical locations. For example, whilst in the British context 'Asian' predominantly has been used to refer exclusively to those people from the Indian subcontinent, in the USA its usage is far broader (and more literal/logical) to include those from the rest of Asia, including China and the Far East. Furthermore, Sharma argues that:

> The term 'Asian' marked as an ethno-cultural category in both popular and academic discourses has so far been confined to the simplistic describing and subsuming of specific national, ethnic and religious identities. Those accounts that have attempted to explore the category 'Asian' in more political terms have only served to reassert an essentialist and culturalist understanding of Asian identity formation.
>
> (1996: 33)

Kaur and Kalra (1996) argue that the notion of 'British Asian' can also be problematic, not only by essentializing the component identities, but also by prioritizing the British signifier. Sayyid (2006: 7) adds that 'the use of British as prefix or suffix establishes a superficial relationship between Asian and British. The identity of British or Asian is not radically transformed by being conjoined'. Instead, these authors (and others, see e.g. Ali *et al.* 2006) propose use of the intriguing concept of 'BrAsian', which probably represents the best attempt (so far) to overcome these problems, through its recognition of the problematic connotations of 'Britishness' for many minority ethnic people and its capacity to destabilize West/non-West binaries.

The term 'British Asian', it might be argued, possesses decreasing explanatory power due to the heterogeneity of the groups and the diversity of identities, lifestyles and experiences represented within it, and the problematic connotations of the prefix. However, it is retained here (with reservations) as a form of general categorization. First, this is because it was the term used by the players involved in the study to describe themselves – except when referring to very specific aspects of their identities – and also when asked what anonymous label they wished to be used in published material. Second, it reflects a clear trend for these young footballers to assert a hybrid identity that simultaneously celebrates their South Asian heritage and asserts a sense of British citizenship (see, in particular, Chapter 5). Players are described in this chapter who are of, for example, heterogeneous British Bangladeshi, British Indian or British Pakistani ethnicities. Where appropriate, these classifications are employed yet, when referring to more general trends and issues, it is more logical, although by no means ideal, to use the wider category of 'British Asian'.

The term 'South Asian' is used to describe populations physically resident in the Indian subcontinent and migrants in the period *before* their migration to Britain. This is not to suggest that they necessarily felt or feel themselves to be British as an automatic corollary of migration, but it is used to reflect (in most cases) their changing citizenship rather than a conscious identity choice. It is also necessary to make a clear distinction between the terms 'British Asian' and 'Anglo-Asian'. The former relates to people of South Asian background who, through birth/residence in Britain, are – even if they choose not to promote this aspect of their identities – afforded British *citizenship*. The latter refers to ethnicity and applies to individuals of dual white and South Asian heritage. The term 'black' is used to refer to people of African or African-Caribbean heritage and not those other groups that, at various times, have been included under this banner as a political identity (see Chapter 6).

Notions of, for example, 'Asianness', 'Muslimness' or 'Englishness' are displayed in quotation marks to demonstrate that they are social constructions and subject to differing interpretation, definition and contestation, both temporally and spatially. Similarly 'race' is placed in inverted commas to demonstrate that it is the *idea* of race that is being referred to and the fact that it has no biological validity. In terms of all the categorizations employed, this book 'in no way accept[s] that these identifications relate to natural communities, or that one notion is more politically legitimate than others' (Bulmer and Solomos 2004: 9). As Gunaratnam (2003: 38) points out, definitions are simply a 'temporary moment of closure'.

To maintain anonymity, the names of interviewees and participant clubs have been removed from the text. In order to distinguish them, despite the wider social trend for an increasing prioritization of *religious* signifiers, players are referred to predominantly by their ethnic identities. This reflects the fact that whilst their faith is important for some players, it is much more marginal for others. This commitment to anonymity inevitably results in a degree of depersonalization. The focus is, after all, on 'voices' and these emanate from a person, a personality, an identity. Consequently, where appropriate, extra portraiture is included to try to depict the myriad identities and experiences of British Asian footballers. This necessarily has to be restricted though because, with very few British Asians playing (or having played) professional football, providing any more detail would compromise anonymity and confidentiality. Players are referred to as 'professional' if, at some stage of their career, they have been registered at a professional club. In some cases, at the time of interview they had not (yet) played for the first-team.

This title of this book refers to British Asians, yet it specifically focuses on

Asian *men*. This is not to say that many of the issues do not apply to British Asian women as well, for there are a number of parallels in terms der articulations of social identity and experiences of racism, inclusion and lusion, both in sport and in the wider society. The focus of the book is on men because the project is specifically about the relationship between British Asian footballers and the *professional* game. This is a sphere that is not only exclusively male in its playing personnel, but is also predominantly male in other areas, such as management, administration and governance.

In respect of the amateur clubs represented in this book, whilst they had a number of sides spanning age groups and playing abilities, none fielded girls' or women's teams. Furthermore, generally speaking, there is very little auxiliary involvement of women in British Asian men's football. Unlike the situation with many white amateur men's clubs (experienced through my own Sunday League playing career), there were no British Asian female supporters at the matches that I observed during this research, and they were not involved in off-field roles either, for example, as secretaries or treasurers. As a result, this particular ethnography focuses on an exclusively male social space. There is some evidence of increasing involvement of young British Asian girls and women in amateur football (BBC Radio 2005b; Ratna 2005; Scraton *et al.* 2005) but, echoing wider trends in the social sciences, issues of gender and women's football traditionally have been interpreted through the experiences of white women, and the participation of minority ethnic groups has been seen as the preserve of men. Analyses of sport have thus tended to reinforce the subordinate position of minority ethnic women as 'a "blind spot" in mainstream policy and research studies that talk about women on the one hand or ethnic minorities on the other' (Mirza 2003: 121). In the popular imagination, any mention of British Asian women and football continues to conjure up visions of Gurinder Chadha's 2002 hit movie *Bend It Like Beckham* (Giardina 2003). The film has certainly raised the profile of the women's game, but should not preclude focusing on the *realities* of participation by girls and women of South Asian heritage both in the Indian subcontinent (Majumdar 2003; J. Mills 2006) and in Britain (Ratna 2005). British Asian women have arguably made a greater breakthrough at elite level than their male counterparts and, indeed, the first British Asian to represent the full England national side was a young woman, Aman Dosanj.

Overview of the book

Chapter 2 provides a socio-historical analysis of popular representations of British Asians as the non-sporting 'Other' and 'commonsense' explanations of their under-representation as professional footballers. Two contrasting branches of explanation are analysed: those that focus on social structures (i.e. ideologies of physicality, religion and diet); and those that cite the role of British Asians as determining agents (i.e. consciously deprioritizing careers in professional sport). It is argued that hegemonic images of British Asian physicality in contemporary professional football need to be located firmly within colonial ideologies, in particular, taking account of the role of scientism in constructing alterity. The chapter then outlines current challenges to these dominant images, with reference to the 'special case' of Sikhs, the gradual increase in the number of British Asians in certain elite sporting activities, and the involvement of young British Asians in incidents of urban unrest. The ubiquitous stereotypes regarding the supposedly inhibiting influences of South Asian cuisine and religions on playing football are also discussed. The second half of the chapter examines popular claims that British Asians prioritize educational and economic achievement ahead of sport but, by examining issues of generation and parental attitudes, suggests that such claims are no longer accurate. The chapter concludes with an analysis of the social significance of football for young British Asian men.

Chapter 3 examines the continuing presence of racism in English football and highlights the ways in which it serves to exclude British Asians from the professional game. The broad premise for the chapter is that professional football traditionally has been characterized by a widespread and ingrained denial of the existence of racism, which has made it increasingly hard for individuals in the game to identify it, admit culpability and actively challenge it. The analysis covers broad patterns of discrimination and exclusion, such as the ways in which the backlash against British Asians since the terrorist attacks in the USA on 11 September 2001 (henceforth 9/11) has manifested itself in the realm of football fandom, and the repercussions of the court trial involving Lee Bowyer and Jonathan Woodgate following their involvement in the vicious assault of the young British Asian man Sarfraz Najeib. The analysis then moves to the processes and practices by which players are recruited into the game. It argues that widespread claims of meritocracy and 'colour blindness' ignore the ways that British Asians are excluded, and are actually a means of maintaining white hegemony in the professional game. In this regard, the chapter also identifies the problems faced by, and the stigma attached to, those players who speak out against racism. By extending the analysis to *amateur* football, the chapter demonstrates how racism at all levels of the game combines to exclude British Asians and to restrict their opportunities and pathways to becoming professional footballers. The final part of the chapter considers the rise in contemporary Islamophobia and assesses its implications for British Asians in English football.

Chapter 4 examines the extent to which those British Asians who have been involved in professional football have sought – and, at times, managed – to become 'one of the lads'. Specifically it examines the manner in which British Asian players have actively modified their identities to gain (contingent) inclusion in this occupational culture. Using a diverse theoretical framework ranging from Bourdieu – namely the concepts of 'cultural capital', 'habitus' and 'field' – to Fanon's 'white mask', this chapter uncovers three significant trends regarding the identities and lifestyles of these players. First, historically speaking, the majority of British Asians who have played for professional clubs have been Anglo-Asians, i.e. they have had one white parent. Second, in direct contrast to wider shifts in the politics of identity and representation, British Asian professional footballers appear to consciously deprioritize their ethnic identities and seek to share the dominant habituses of their white and African-Caribbean team-mates. Third, many British Asian players believe that those players who have experienced Anglicized processes of socialization will possess more of the specific cultural capital needed to make the professional grade. The final part of the chapter demonstrates the ambiguous status of dual ethnicity players, within British Asian communities, the anti-racist football movement and the media.

The focus of Chapter 5 is on the complex interplay between 'race', nation, culture and citizenship in contemporary British society, and the ways in which the identities that are created by British Asians in relation to these are articulated within the global sports arena. The first part of the chapter traces the origins of the notion of 'cultural racism' in post-war Western Europe and examines its manifestations and effects in late twentieth-century Britain, particularly in relation to the migration and settlement of South Asians. It highlights how entrenched racism and xenophobia, and socio-economic transitions, have contributed to increasingly ethnically exclusive notions of 'Englishness' and 'Britishness'. The analysis then illustrates how these trends are articulated in relation to national sport teams, primarily in football and, by way of comparison, in cricket. By highlighting the contrasting patterns of support and affiliation in these sports, the chapter shows how these trends influence and reflect the racial, generational and spatial subjectivities of young British Asians, and reflect the nuanced and complex nature of twenty-first-century diasporic lifestyles and identities. The final section situates these trends theoretically within the concept of 'diaspora' and argues that the sporting allegiances of young British Asians enable them to celebrate their traditions and histories, whilst also articulating their British citizenship and hybrid, 'glocal' (Robertson 1995) identities.

Chapter 6 is the first of two chapters that investigate institutional approaches to anti-racism and the issue of British Asians in English professional football. This chapter provides a broad outline of shifting ideologies and political strategies of anti-racism in Britain during the late twentieth to early twenty-first centuries. It traces the shifting sands of anti-racist resistance, from a focus on difference and diversity to a belief in the need to prioritize sameness and solidarity (and back again), together with the way that British Asians have been positioned within these respective discourses. These main themes are then discussed in the context of English football. It is proposed that any anti-racist strategy aimed at overcoming the exclusion of British Asians must possess an appreciation of both the specific issues that they face and the wider racial dynamics that permeate the game. The dominance of 'official multiculturalism' ahead of more radical anti-racist measures as a way of trying to increase the participation of British Asians in the game is also critiqued. The final part of the chapter examines wider socio-political developments around issues of social inclusion and community cohesion, and their influence in placing British Asian footballers so prominently on football's equity agenda.

Chapter 7 offers an in-depth, empirical critique of the contemporary policies and activities undertaken by professional football clubs and anti-racist football organizations with regard to increasing the participation of British Asians in professional football. It examines some of the most prominent issues facing British Asian footballers, and the problems, inconsistencies and misrepresentations that they perceive to characterize many dominant, institutional responses. The chapter argues that a widespread failure of professional clubs and anti-racist football organizations to consult young British Asian footballers or include them in decision-making processes means that they are often out of touch with their identities, lifestyles, attitudes and desires. Consequently, current attempts to overcome their exclusion from the professional game are inexorably limited. In this regard, the following areas are examined: the manner in which professional football clubs and anti-racist football organizations attempt to engage in 'community consultation'; the significance of ethnicity in coach–player relations; the implications of collaboration with the police in anti-racist projects; the use of matches between British clubs and teams from the Indian subcontinent as participation-raising initiatives; and the effects of media publicity on young British Asian professional players.

The concluding chapter draws together the trends, issues, problems and arguments identified and analysed throughout the book, and assesses their wider social and political significance for contemporary Britain. Fundamentally, it reinforces the call for sport and football, in particular, to be taken seriously in sociological studies of ethnicity, racism and identity. It examines contemporary debates surrounding integration and details how football is becoming increasingly implicated in wider political rhetoric around community cohesion, 'shared values' and 'norms of acceptability'. This chapter also provides a further reflection on the nature of contemporary young, male, British Asian identities and the role of football in their construction and articulation.

2 Myths, stereotypes and discourses surrounding the exclusion of British Asian professional footballers

Introduction

> I went to [a trial] at [a Premier League] football club. I was chatting to a guy across the road who's got friends that work there, that come from [that city]. I asked them for directions to this place. They were laughing at the fact that an Asian lad had trials with [that club]. They found it such an amazing [thing], you know, *how can it be*?!... So you can see how much of a big thing it was, not just for myself, but for people outside.
>
> (Interview with British Pakistani ex-professional player, 20 February 2002)

> It was funny once because we were playing [the] Derby [youth team]. Obviously my mates and the club itself, you know, they all knew about my background and so on. This young lad ran out with a turban on and we were playing against him. And the lads started laughing because it was, you know, their first impression, probably the first time they'd ever seen that . . . I don't think it was racism, I think it was just the unknown really because they'd not seen that before, you know. And the lad could play. The lad was a good player. But even to myself I'd never seen that before. I don't know where he's playing now or if he still plays, but it was one of them things where, you know, it could have been classed as racism, but I knew my friends close enough to know that it wasn't that, *it was just probably the unexpected of seeing that on a football field*.
>
> (Interview with British Indian ex-professional/semi-professional player, 5 March 2002)

> [We are] unaware of any Asian communities that actually play football.
>
> (Premiership football club cited in Commission for Racial Equality 2004: 12)

Today the under-representation of British Asians in professional football generates heated and polemical debate in academe, the media, sports governing bodies and anti-racist pressure groups, and also notably in football changing rooms, social clubs and public houses up and down the country. This has not always been the case. For a long time the debate was restricted to British Asian communities themselves. In dominant discourses it was 'their fault' and 'their problem'. Unsurprisingly the feelings of frustration, despair, anger and resentment that were articulated by British Asian players about their exclusion were rarely acknowledged or reciprocated outside their communities. Times have changed, however, and so have the parameters of interest, concern and action. During the process of researching and writing this book many friends, family, colleagues and students were keen to discuss the issues and engage with the debates, often confidently asserting their own explanations for, or proposed solutions to, this inveterate problem. Some people supported the contention that the lack of research into British Asian footballers represents a significant lacuna in both sport sociology and ethnic and racial studies, and that, for some time, there has been considerable need for academic contributions to this area. One only needs to survey the proliferation of, for example, studies into the relationship between young British Asians and popular music, or the history and popularity of football in India, to recognize that research about British Asians and sport is under-developed by comparison. Conversely, for others, the significance of this investigation has been less apparent. For them, the reason is clear: the under-representation of British Asians in professional football is simply a manifestation of a historically grounded, diametrically opposed relationship between British Asian communities and sporting participation.

Minority ethnic groups in Britain share a common historical experience of racialization and subjugation within Western sporting ideologies, yet the components on which images and discourses are based differ considerably. Whilst African-Caribbeans traditionally have been seen to possess physical capabilities that make them 'natural' sports people (Hoberman 1997; Entine 2000; St Louis 2003), British Asians have been categorized as the non-sporting 'Other'. In 'commonsense' ideologies (St Louis 2004), the African-Caribbean body is perceived to be the epitome of athletic prowess and, indeed, genetically predisposed for success. Conversely, sport is viewed as an arena in which British Asians lack both the competence and desire to participate (Fleming 2001). The roots of these stereotypes can be traced back to colonialism, empire-building and slavery during the eighteenth and nineteenth centuries (see below), but they have been substantiated by and, in turn contributed to, three more recent developments. First, the differential inclusion of minority ethnic groups at elite level, for example, in football – where although approximately twenty-five per cent of all professional players are of African or African-Caribbean heritage (Kick It Out 2005), there were only five British Asians playing professionally during the 2005–06 season – is seen to corroborate this dichotomous model of sporting proficiency. Second, employing a Cartesian mind–body separation, and adhering to the notion that intellect and physical prowess co-exist in a zero-sum relationship (St Louis 2005), there has been a tendency for many school teachers to endorse popular beliefs regarding the different educational and sporting abilities of African-Caribbean and British Asian pupils. This has led to the former being channelled towards sporting activities, whilst the latter have been encouraged to concentrate on more academic disciplines (Hayes and Sugden 1999; Ismond 2003). Third, these perceptions are underpinned by a media fetishization of the powerful, athletic African-Caribbean male body (S. Hall 1998; Carrington 2000) and, Amir Khan notwithstanding (Burdsey 2005a), the absence of positive British Asian male sporting imagery.

It is often assumed that the act of stereotyping a group is simply a form of categorization. However, processes of stereotyping are inextricably linked to power relations and are undertaken not simply to demarcate, but also to undermine and stigmatize the subject group. Stereotyping is always related to a specific context, period or location, and representations of the 'Other' require a simultaneous construction of the 'Self', for this is the model that is seen to represent normality and is the position from which degrees of 'Otherness' are gauged. In terms of racial stereotyping, Ross (1996: 4) points out that it is a case of 'the dominant looking at the subordinate: how *they* are different from us rather than how *we* are different from them... where whiteness is taken as the profoundly unproblematic norm against which all 'others' are measured'. The stereotype thus acts as a means of control, limiting the freedom and progression of individuals within a given context (Fiske 1993).

Ismond (2003: 183) correctly points out that analysing issues of 'race' and racism must progress from the notion that specific ideologies are constructed in relation to deeply rooted issues of power. West (1999: 261) argues that minority groups tend to suffer from a 'relative lack of [cultural and political] power to present themselves to themselves and others as complex human beings, and thereby to contest the bombardment of negative, degrading stereotypes put forward by White supremacist ideologies'. In particular, British Asians lack both the specific sporting success and, more generally, the socio-political power required to overcome and contradict dominant propositions regarding their suitability for football. Their relative powerlessness, and their inability to break into the professional sphere, means that they have been unable to challenge definitions and manifestations of 'tradition' and 'normality', and the consensus on desired physical and cultural traits at all levels of the game. As Sampson (1993: 13) points out, 'the Other cannot be permitted to have a voice, a position, a being of its own, but must remain mute or speak only in the ways permitted by the dominant discourse'. Hegemonic representations of British Asians as the non-footballing 'Other', accordingly, have continued to receive widespread corroboration. As the testimonies at the beginning of this chapter elucidate, traditionally they have been regarded as both antithetical to, and incompatible with, the structures and cultures of English football.

Due to a pervasive, yet erroneous, belief in the meritocratic nature of British sport, and a widespread failure to acknowledge how racial power relations influence patterns of inclusion and exclusion, the under-representation of British Asians in professional football frequently is perceived to be a result of a lack of participation at lower levels of the game. In other words, it is widely believed that there is an insufficient pool of talent – both in terms of quantity and quality – from which potential professional players can be drawn. However, this represents a huge misconception. A passionate and, in some parts of the country, numerically significant British Asian amateur football culture has existed since the migrations of the 1950s and 1960s, and British Asian communities have been providing generations of talented players ever since. Yet this remains a 'hidden' history, excluded from dominant accounts and stories of the nation's rich footballing past. British Asian clubs are often affiliated to associations and leagues that are organized on a predominantly – if not exclusively – British Asian basis, and hegemonic social histories of amateur football rarely have extended beyond the white, male game. This state of affairs is sustained by sections of the mainstream media who give little serious attention to football in these communities, preferring instead to provide what are seen as 'humorous', yet what are actually irreverent or offensive, portrayals.[1] Few people outside the British Asian amateur football scene are aware of its existence, scope or social significance, and so stereotypes about a lack of interest and aptitude in football by British Asians continue to receive widespread verification. Consequently, the question that is often asked is: 'Why do British Asians not play football?' Instead, the real issue is the massive imbalance between levels of participation by British Asians in amateur and professional football, and so the question that requires investigation is: 'Why do British Asians continue to be excluded from the professional game?'

This chapter examines how representations and explanations of the relationship between British Asians and sporting participation have manifested themselves within both the popular imagination and the context of professional football. Popular 'explanations' of the under-representation of British Asians in professional football can be divided into two broad categories: one that might be labelled 'structural' and another that relates more to 'agency'. The former category includes arguments about inappropriate physicality and the constraining influences of dietary and religious practices. The latter body of explanations cites the role of individuals as determining agents and purports that whilst British Asians are *capable* of playing football, they are either uninterested in the game or prioritize achievement in other areas, such as education or business. The final part of the chapter argues that, in reality, football is not simply a popular sport for young British Asian men (and increasingly women), but it also possesses considerable social significance.

Racial science, the body and the role of football in British colonialism in India

The racialization of physical body types provides a primary ideological foundation for certain schools of thought in attempts to rationalize and justify the dominance of particular ethnic groups in sporting endeavours. This notion – which not only lacks scientific rigour, but is also underpinned by implicitly racist assumptions – can be traced back to the British Empire and particularly the rise of 'racial science' in nineteenth-century Europe. This discipline involved the affirmation in popular, scientific and political discourses that humanity could be divided into distinct groupings whose members possessed common physical and biological characteristics (K. Malik 1996; Banton 1998). As Carrington (2004a: 84) points out, 'the disciplinary power of Western science was central in produc- ing alterity' and various attempts were made to classify, understand and, most importantly, subjugate indigenous populations within the British Empire.

Dispatches and reports from the Indian subcontinent frequently cited the perceived physical and biological inadequacies of the indigenous population. For example, in 1903, writer and Oxford alumnus, Cecil Headlam, informed British visitors that soon after arrival they would 'cease to be surprised at the resemblance of human beings to monkeys, when you see them altruistically picking at each other's heads, and otherwise behaving like their cousins in the Zoo' (cited in Williams 2001: 18). He added that one also needs to understand that:

> You must be very careful how you hit a man in India. Nearly every native suffers from an enlarged spleen, and any blow to the body is likely to prove fatal. . . . It is best to carry a cane and administer rebuke therewith upon the calves or shins, which are tender and not usually mortal.
>
> (Ibid.)

It is not coincidental that the burgeoning interest in racial classification and constructions of the Indian[2] 'Other' took place contemporaneously with the establishment of British colonial rule. On a micro level, British people were brought into direct contact with the indigenous Indian population for the very first time. It is also the case that the processes of modernization and empire building that were intrinsic to the colonization of the subcontinent were unequivocally connected to dominant European theories of racial and cultural difference.

Colonialism and, in particular, the establishment of the Raj in India, allowed the British – who viewed themselves as modern and civilized – the opportunity to contrast themselves with those populations that they perceived to be backward and inferior. As Said argues:

> Race theory, ideas about primitive origins and primitive classifications, modern decadence, the progress of civilization, the destiny of the white (or Aryan) races, the need for colonial territories – all these were elements in the peculiar amalgam of science, politics, and culture whose drift, almost without exception, was always to raise Europe or a European race to dominion over non-European portions of mankind.
>
> (1985: 232)

The dominant ideology underpinning these processes was 'Orientalism'. Through its construction of the world as a longitudinally divided binary unit, Orientalism 'was ultimately a political vision of reality whose structure promoted the difference between the familiar (Europe, the West, 'us') and the strange (the Orient, the East, 'them')' (ibid.: 43). One can observe, therefore, a historical manifestation of what has been described in more recent times as a 'clash of civilizations' (Huntingdon 1997) or 'the west versus the rest' (Scruton 2005). Such binaries allowed the British to categorize themselves as a 'healthy race', for they believed that they possessed characteristics such as bravery, courage, physical strength and vigour – the very attributes necessary for establishing and maintaining a global empire. Conversely, the Indian 'race' was seen to be bereft of such qualities. The British were, therefore, able to contend that this disparity reflected the fact that their own level of civilization was a consequence of their superior sophistication, and more rational thought and behaviour (Pickering 2001). The colonizers used these differences to justify both their position in the racial hierarchy and the need to subject indigenous peoples to a civilizing Western influence (Dimeo 2001b). In fact, the civilizing of other 'races' was not simply seen as necessary; it was believed to be a religious *obligation* of the colonizing powers.

Central to this civilizing mission was the moralization and Christian religious indoctrination of the Indian colonial subject. These processes attributed great importance to the 'games ethic', and the hegemonic role of sport and physical education in seeking to legitimize British rule and to create populations that were conducive to the colonial project (Mangan 1998). Beliefs about physicality and representations of the body therefore operated as primary agents in colonial constructions of the Indian 'Other'. This was especially the case with football. For example, a 1909 issue of *The Illustrated Sporting and Dramatic News* reported that:

> Association football as a regimental game in the native Army of India is in its infancy, and is only just beginning to find favour. The reason for this is probably that the sepoy [Indian soldier], as a rule, has not the build necessary for a first-class player. . . . The recruit, when he first emerges from the jungle or village, has rather less control over his legs than a newborn camel, but in a surprisingly short time he learns how to kick and run.
>
> (Cited in Vasili 2000: 156)

As Mills and Dimeo (2003: 118) point out, football was a sphere 'in which evidence of the flawed nature of Indian bodies was manufactured'. This is unsurprising for, as Benson (1997: 123) argues, 'the body is . . . the *medium* through which messages about identity are transmitted'. Similarly Alter (1994: 24) points out that sporting images are not just *allegories* of wider racial ideologies, for the sporting body 'may be seen, not simply as a signifier of meaning, but as a subject actor in a larger drama of culture and power'. In particular, it was after the Indian Mutiny in 1857 that football began to assume wider social significance in the subcontinent. Whilst this military uprising had been instigated by Bengali officers, Punjabi soldiers remained loyal to the British. This led to a binary construction of 'martial' and 'non-martial' 'races', the former comprising Punjabis and Gurkhas, and the latter Bengalis. This model was literally played out within football as players were stereotyped as either too weak or, if physically adept, still too undisciplined to play the game as well as their colonizers (Mills and Dimeo 2003: 115–18). It is important to point out, however, that whilst – for a variety of reasons – Indians were believed to be incapable of playing football proficiently, participation was viewed by some to be beneficial and was thus encouraged. In this regard, it paralleled the role of cricket which, as Williams (2001: 28) points out, was 'believed to encourage non-whites to accept the white English qualities of sportsmanship and fair play, which in turn would convince them of the beneficence of British rule'.

'We shall fight like lions'[3]: the special case of the Sikhs

Whilst Indians generically were placed beneath Europeans in dominant racial hierarchies, there was significant internal differentiation. The primary criterion for this classification was again physicality, with the capacity to play football not only differentiating 'colonizer' from 'colonized', but also acting as 'an idiom in which ideas about the different types of Indian bodies were constructed' (Mills and Dimeo 2003: 118). Bengalis, for example, were constructed as weak and effeminate (Dimeo 2002a). The nineteenth-century journalist G.W. Steevens claimed that:

> The Bengali's leg is either skin and bones; the same size all the way down, with knocking knobs for knees, or else it is very fat and globular, also turning in at the knees, with round thighs like a woman's. The Bengali's leg is the leg of a slave.
>
> (Cited in Talbot 2000: 22)

In contrast, the Sikhs of the Punjab were lionized due to their perceived qualities as both formidable warriors and loyal British subjects (Singh 1999). These corporeal classifications were heavily influenced by dominant eighteenth-century beliefs regarding the effects of environmental factors on human genetics and evolution. Due to the cold weather and difficult terrain that they endured, northern Indians were believed to be hardier and more courageous than their southern counterparts who, because of the sub-tropical heat of the southern states, were perceived as weak and indolent (Dimeo 2002a). Perceptions of Punjabi physicality were further substantiated after the near defeat of the British Army in the Anglo-Sikh wars, which reinforced Sikh designation as a 'martial race' and awarded them a privileged position within the British Army.[4] Sikh soldiers subsequently joined the Allied Forces for the First and Second World Wars, enhancing their image of being physically adept and loyal to the British regime. This status was achieved predominantly through their venerable role in warfare, but it was also complemented by the fact that their residence in army garrisons enabled them to learn and play football. For example, an officer serving with a Burma-based Punjabi regiment of the British Army reported that 'there is always some sort of game [of football] going on every afternoon, and everybody gets an opportunity of playing' (cited in Mills and Dimeo 2003: 117–18).

Historical representations of the South Asian body clearly have influenced contemporary sporting imagery and there are specific threads of continuity.

Evidence suggests that Sikhs warrant particular attention because they are central to modern manifestations of these historically based stereotypes. In parallel to their reputation during the Empire, Sikhs differ from other British Asian groups because they *are* sometimes seen to possess the requisite physicality for contact or strength-requiring sports. For example, England's 2002 Commonwealth Games wrestling squad included two Sikhs, Jatinder Singh and Amerjit Singh Tutt, whilst the 105 kg weightlifting bronze medal was won by British Sikh Gurbinder Singh. Furthermore, many of the British Asian players that have been involved in professional football have also been Sikhs, e.g. Jaswinder Juttla, Nevin Saroya, Amrit Sidhu, Bobby Singh, Harpal Singh and Shinda Singh. Significantly, dominant perceptions about Sikh physicality are also reproduced by members of these communities themselves. Ismond (2003: 98) notes the importance attached to male physical strength in Punjabi culture, and the opinion also exists amongst many Sikh players that they are more likely to become professional footballers than other British Asians. Their involvement is perceived to be a consequence of not only their substantial involvement in amateur football – where, incidentally, it is quite common for Sikh football clubs to include some form of martial reference in their name, e.g. Sikh Hunters or Khalsa Warriors – but also a result of advantageous *genetic* factors. For example, one (Sikh) British Indian amateur player stated that:

> The Sikhs, together with the Muslims, are the [physically] dominant Asians really. You'll find that the Sikhs and the Muslims are stronger than, say, the Hindus, you know, physically and more alert. The Hindus, you'll find, would tend to go towards more educational [pursuits]. That way the Sikhs and the Muslims are more sport-orientated. I think to myself, hang-on, you've named these [British Asian players] and you're right, you know, amongst them they are mainly Sikhs. . . . *To me that looks as if they are the stronger breed.*
> (Interview, 5 February 2002)

Other players added that:

> In terms of the biological thing, there is possibly evidence of, you know, the Singh name is a lion,[4] we are lion-hearted and yes, our physical build is a lot bigger than the Bengalis or the Muslims and so forth.
> (Interview with (Sikh) British Indian ex-semi-professional player,
> 19 March 2002)

If I have any thoughts on that, it's got to be around saying that there's probably a cultural issue in that Sikhs as a caste [sic] are actually regarded as warriors: fearless, defenders of human rights, justice, equality. . . . They're certainly more prone to be sort of a fearless race in terms of when it comes to competing, physically, in a game, and football is a contact sport. Whereas there is a stereotype that perhaps those of Bengali origin – because of the part of India they come from – tend to be manual labourer-orientated and that perhaps makes them less, you know, willing to take risks and be more obedient.

(Interview with (Sikh) British Indian amateur player, 23 April 2002)

These testimonies demonstrate the manner in which racialized groups often inadvertently endorse and reproduce the racial hierarchies that were constructed by dominant groups during the Empire to subjugate and control them. They highlight that colonial racial hegemony was achieved by indoctrinating subaltern groups about the logic and legitimacy of these categorizations to the extent that they permeated social relations not just between colonizer and colonized, but also *within* the latter category. Locating the comments of the above players in this context is crucial when one considers that they appear to support the scientifically-discredited, yet still socially significant and perturbing, notion of 'race', based around the belief that different groups possess distinct biological and physical characteristics which are transmitted genetically between generations. In this regard, what is also apparent about these statements is their conflation of religious and cultural identity with racial difference. The latter testimony, in particular, purports an ethnic absolutist notion of culture (Gilroy 1992) in which a group's cultural traits are perceived to be distinct from all others' and directly related to their physical composition. Further evidence of the reproduction of hegemonic racial stereotypes can be detected in contemporary Indian football where beliefs regarding the physical abilities of different ethnic groups, and particularly their ability to play professional football, are prevalent. For example, the success of the black Nigerian striker Chima Okorie in Indian football during the 1980s and 1990s was in part related to his muscular style of play. This led to a trend amongst many Indian clubs of identifying big, strong, foreign (often African) strikers based at Indian universities and trying to tempt them away from their studies by offering lucrative contracts (Kapadia and Kundu 2001).

The extent to which these specific categorizations have directly influenced those involved in recruiting potential professional players in Britain is difficult to measure. Nevertheless, British sport undoubtedly continues to operate as an arena for the articulation of dominant racial ideologies which, due to sport's inherent power relations, are also reproduced by minority groups (see Fleming 1995 and Ismond 2003 for further examples). It also demonstrates how social hierarchies within British Asian groups are based not only on class and caste, but also, through their associations with health and poverty, issues such as physicality.

Fighting back? Challenges and changes to representations of British Asian physicality

During the later decades of the twentieth century, the families of the South Asian men who had settled in Britain since the 1960s came to join them and subsequently a large number of second-generation migrants began to enter the British education system. In Physical Education, in particular, inveterate colonial stereotypes started to re-emerge. Physicality was again a key issue and the following claims were widespread: 'Asian children have low ball skills, low co-ordination and are weak'; 'Asian...children dislike the cold'; 'Asians are too frail for contact sports'; 'Asian children dislike contact sports but excel in individual skill sports such as badminton'; and 'Asian boys generally prefer non-contact games' (cited in Fleming 1995: 38–9). Thus British Asians were believed to be physically unable to compete in 'traditional', 'manly' school sports such as football or rugby. They were, however, seen to have a 'natural' ability to play cricket and racquet sports, because they possessed the wile to become successful spin bowlers, whilst they were also 'wristy' and able to rely on timing, agility and placement, rather than strength, when batting or playing racquet shots (Malcolm 1997: 267).

Stereotypical images of British Asian physicality and sporting competence soon began to permeate the sphere of professional sports as well, and a perceived lack of physicality and masculinity amongst British Asian men began to form the basis of 'explanations' for their under-representation in professional football. The exclusion of British Asians on the basis of perceived physical traits alone should not come as a surprise when one considers the significance of Back *et al*.'s (2001b) 'structure of antipathy'. This schema contrasts the player attributes that are perceived by 'traditional' supporters to be ideal for participation in English professional football with those that are seen to be anathema. The 'normative preference' is for players to be 'unpretentious, practical, tough and masculine', whilst an aversion is shown to players that are seen to be 'effeminate, weak, pretentious or fancy' (ibid.: 131). Whilst this dichotomy ignores the popularity of players who fit into the latter category and is certainly less applicable than it was in the past, a strong emphasis on physical toughness and overt displays of masculinity remains amongst British players and coaches in English football, especially in the lower echelons.

Racial stereotypes in football have undergone significant contestation and transformation during the last thirty years (Back *et al*. 2001b; King 2004a), yet the belief that British Asians lack the physical competence to participate remains popular. For example, Branigan (2001) contrasts the position of British Asians with African-Caribbeans. She argues that whilst the stereotypical attributes associated with the black male body – muscularity, strength, aggression and toughness – are now seen to epitomize the credentials needed for participation in professional football, British Asian bodies continue to be regarded as anathema. She states that:

> In popular racist mythology, Arab and Asian men are weak, effeminate, unmanly. If the black 'crime' is to be aggressively and uncontrollably male, the eastern equivalent is to be insufficiently so.... It is no coincidence that Asians have failed to prosper in football, the sport that now espouses masculinity for British men.
>
> (Branigan 2001: 18)

Perceptions of physicality have been a common and constant source by which minority ethnic groups in general have been marginalized and discriminated against in English professional football. It is ironic that, despite the different ways in which British Asian and African-Caribbean bodies have historically been racialized, many of the stereotypes associated with British Asians were promoted in the 1970s and 1980s in relation to the breakthrough of black players. Similarly, the physical attributes of African-Caribbeans were also correlated with cultural or behavioural dispositions, and it was often argued that they were not sufficiently tough, disliked playing in the (cold) British climate, lacked determination and were lazy. They were subjected to a process of 'stacking', in that they were rarely selected for central positions (Maguire 1991) – in terms of both the pitch and in relation to leadership – enabling white hegemony to be sustained in the face of an increasing black presence in the game. However, as Ismond argues:

> Sport is an area of contested and shifting ideologies, rather than a consistent and functional ideology working in the interests of a dominant group. Therefore, the possibility exists that racialised perceptions about playing and managing can be overturned through time.
>
> (2003: 93)

Accordingly, generations of talented black players have been able, gradually yet certainly not universally, to erode these stereotypes. Other stereotypes are far more resistant, though, particularly those that are articulated about groups who lack the power or are denied the opportunity to challenge them. Therefore, due to their non-involvement in the professional game, British Asians have been less successful in combating dominant imagery and so they are often still believed to lack the necessary tough, masculine qualities. For example, the Director of the Youth Academy at a Premier League club stated that:

> I do put some substance behind the belief that, physically, certain types of people are more suitable to certain sports than others . . . I think that Afro-Caribbean players are particularly suited to be footballers. Whether Asians are, or not, I don't know, but I've yet to see evidence.
>
> (Interview, 16 January 2002)

British Asian players – like black coaches and managers – are thus in a Catch 22 situation. Their exclusion is based, in part, on an inability to substantially subvert pervasive racial stereotypes, but the space where they can best challenge them and prove them to be erroneous – the professional game – remains one which they cannot access.

Minor shifts in stereotypes about British Asian footballers can be detected within certain groups, but there is little sign of the seismic changes needed within dominant discourses to overcome the exclusion of these players. There is evidence though that the belief that British Asians are less suited for contact sports may be becoming increasingly residual in some sections of the wider sports community. Predominantly this is the result of the achievements of a handful of successful British Asian athletes who have been able partially to challenge the hegemonic consensus about their innate abilities in particular activities: Ikram Butt playing rugby league for England; Jawaid Khaliq winning the IBO world welterweight boxing title; Zaf Shah representing England at Tae Kwon-do; Kuljit Singh Degun winning the British national heavyweight title in full-contact San Shou; Sikhs wrestling for England in the Commonwealth Games and, in 2006, the emergence of teenage wrestler Sandeep Rai; plus, perhaps most significantly, Amir Khan winning the lightweight boxing silver medal at the 2004 Olympic Games. The wider effects of the small band of British Asians playing football remain, at this stage, to be seen.

A further challenge to conventional representations of British Asian physicality and masculinity has come from outside the world of sport, although its repercussions may be felt within it. It has emanated from the urban unrest involving young British Asian men during the spring and summer of 2001. Britain is no stranger to violent rebellions by its minority ethnic populations yet, with the notable exceptions of outbreaks in Southall (in 1979 and 1981) and Manningham, Bradford (in 1995), these have predominantly involved African-Caribbeans. However, the involvement of British Asians in violent incidents during 2001 has led to a wider shift in dominant perceptions of young British Asian men in early twenty-first-century Britain. Key elements within this popular re-positioning are notions of physicality and masculinity, as these groups – particularly Bangladeshis and Pakistanis – move from being seen as the victims of racist violence to being viewed as hyper-masculine and prone to criminality and wanton disorder (Goodey 2001; Glynn 2002; Macey 2002; Alexander 2004a; Burnett 2004; Back 2005). As Bhattacharyya (2005) points out, young British Asian men have been constructed as 'dangerous' because they are perceived to have rejected dominant social values in favour of alternative ones, such as religious extremism and sexual harassment of vulnerable white – and, according to the allegations that prompted the violence between young black and Pakistani men in Birmingham in October 2005, African-Caribbean (Muir and Butt 2005) – girls, and they have congregated in large numbers in prominent public spaces. Stereotypes that have traditionally been associated with African-Caribbean men have re-emerged to stigmatize and legitimize discrimination of different racialized groups, namely British Asians. It will be interesting to observe the implications of these changing representations. Will shifting perceptions of physicality and masculinity mean that British Asians are seen as fulfilling the 'normative preferences' of English football identified by Back *et al.* (2001b) to a greater extent? Conversely, to what extent might such a shift increase existing racial antagonisms and inequalities? It is too early to fully gauge the implications of these trends for the inclusion of British Asians in professional football, although some of the repercussions are discussed in the next chapter.

Food for thought? Perceptions of diet and religion as impediments to participation

In recent years there has been a fundamental change in the ideology under-pinning popular explanations for the under-representation of British Asians in English professional football. Parallel to the wider transition from biological to cultural racisms in late twentieth-century Western societies (see Chapter 5), explanations that revolve around perceived cultural, rather than physical, con-straints have tended to receive greater credibility. As the belief in physically distinct 'races' becomes increasingly, although not universally, residual, cultural reasons are generally seen to be more plausible and, significantly, less racist. This shift demonstrates not only the fluctuating and contested nature of dom-inant racial discourses in English football, but also the way that stereotypes of British Asians as 'outsiders' are modified and reconfigured to maintain white hegemony.

The two main factors that have comprised cultural explanations have been diet and religion. Both discourses possess an inherent essentialism in that they refer to *the* British Asian *community* and locate British Asians as a homogenous, monolithic entity that possesses a single, common culture. As T. Turner (1993: 411–12) points out, 'the tendencies to reify the 'cultures' of ethnic minorities, to stylize pseudo-biological categories into communities, and to appeal to popular biological conceptions of culture are not difficult to substantiate in British politics and media'. Raval (1989) and Fleming (1994) examine this tendency in sport and leisure and, appropriating the concept from Eisenstein (1984), suggest that representations of British Asians are characterized by a 'false universalism'. As Fleming (1994: 164) argues, this 'typically occurs when the process of logical induction is applied inappropriately, and on the basis of limited evidence huge generalizations are made'. The factors that influence the sporting participation of one individual, therefore, are seen to be representative of all British Asians. Yet, as Hutnyk points out:

> To extrapolate from one or two cases of some behaviour or other to then ascribe that behaviour to a cultural, national or ethnic group as a whole would be an error. The imaginary god-like observations that declare that 'Muslims are X' or 'Sikhs do Y' is as unacceptable as the old anthropological attributionism of 'Nuer think . . .', 'Nuer say . . .'.
>
> (2005: 437)

Dominant explanations are also characterized by what Baumann (1996: 1) calls 'ethnic reductionism'. This approach traditionally has been present in both pop-ular accounts and academic studies of British Asian communities, contributing to a situation where:

> Whatever any 'Asian' informant was reported to have said or done was interpreted with stunning regularity as a consequence of their 'Asianness',

their 'ethnic identity', or the 'culture' of their 'community'. All agency seemed to be absent, and culture an imprisoning cocoon or a determining force.

(Baumann 1996: 1)

The factors that are perceived to inhibit the participation of British Asians in professional football are seen to be specifically a result of their 'Asianness', even though individuals from any ethnic group could be affected. For example, if a player states that his parents discouraged him from playing football, this is believed to be exclusively because he is British Asian, and other factors that might have influenced this standpoint are not acknowledged. This leads to a reification of British Asian 'culture' whereby all attitudes and behaviours are reduced to the product of ethnicity. Consequently, explanations for the under-representation of British Asians in professional football become tautologous: they are under-represented *because they are British Asian*.

The food of the early South Asian migrants was a key source of their 'Otherness' in the eyes of the British population, as the introduction of a cuisine consisting of previously unfamiliar ingredients and emitting a pungent odour was deemed to be extremely alien. The dietary and nutritional habits of these migrants were also believed to correlate directly with the perception that South Asians were physically underdeveloped. Unsurprisingly, a 'commonsense' belief pervaded professional football that the absence of British Asians was a result of abnormal dietary practices. For example, in 1995, Sheffield United manager Dave Bassett argued that, 'the Asian build is not that of a footballer. . . . It may well be that Asian ingredients in food, or their nutrition that they take, [are] not ideal for building up a physical frame' (cited in Fleming 2001: 114). Similarly, former Luton Town coach Terry Westley claimed that, 'their eating habits are also a problem' (cited in Bains and Patel 1996: 6).

Such arguments are so preposterous that it is hard to believe that they ever achieved legitimacy, yet the fact that they received widespread adherence highlights the level of ignorance about, and discrimination towards, British Asians in professional football. In particular, the way that terms such as 'diet' or 'nutrition' are referred to in their singular forms is enlightening. The implicit perception is that *all* British Asians enjoy only their own common, standardized cuisine, reflecting broader hegemonic implications that British Asians are ghettoized in hermetically sealed units that deny them access to 'Western' commodities. Their lives are interpreted as being structured predominantly (even exclusively) by the cultures, traditions and religions of the subcontinent, not only denying their roles as determining agents, but also ignoring their position as members of a dynamic, eclectic diaspora that is influenced by (and increasingly influences) British and wider global practices and consumer cultures (see e.g. Din and Cullingford 2004). Ironically, by the end of the twentieth century, 'going for a curry' was one of the most dominant British social culinary practices for white under-50s (Basu 2003), with the group Fat Les reminding us that 'We all love vindaloo' in the chorus of their 1998 hit record.

Religion is similarly perceived to be a constraining factor that universally inhibits British Asian participation in professional football yet, as is the case with diet, arguments tend to be of an anecdotal, and extremely dubious, nature. For example, a senior (unnamed) official at West Ham United claimed that, 'You hear about Asians stopping practice to say their prayers' (cited in Bains and Patel 1996: 6). Many of the religion-based 'explanations' assume that there is a singular British Asian religion and, parallel to wider social trends, this is normally constructed from stereotypical ideas about Islam and Muslims. In certain instances, specific religious dogma can (seek to) inhibit sports participation, particularly in the case of girls and women (Hargreaves 2000). For example, in 2005, supporters of *Muttahida Majlis-e-Amal*, an Islamic political alliance, targeted female runners competing in a mixed marathon in Pakistan (Walsh 2005). Similarly, Hamad Al Mohannadi, a leading Bahraini politician claimed that the Muslim female runner, Maryam Yusuf Jamal, was 'disrespecting Islamic precepts and offending local values' by wearing what were perceived to be revealing athletic outfits (Mackay 2005), whilst Muslim cleric Haseeb-ul-hasan Siddiqui stated that the clothing of eighteen-year-old Indian tennis star Sania Mirza was 'unIslamic' and 'corrupting' (Ramesh 2005). However, in contrast, there is increasing evidence in Britain that Islamic extremists are using football to promote their teachings and to indoctrinate young British Muslims, as demonstrated by the football tournaments organized by *Hizb ut-Tahrir* (Malik, Shiv 2005).

The influence of religion is unclear, accentuated by the inconclusive nature and conflicting findings of many empirical studies (e.g. Carrington *et al.* 1987; Carroll and Hollinshead 1993; De Knop *et al.* 1996; Dagkas and Benn 2006), together with the Eurocentric orientation of pioneering researchers in this area. (see Siraj-Blatchford 1993 for a critique.) In reality, the degree to which any religion restricts participation in football or other leisure pursuits is related to individuals' personal religious preferences and the degree of secularization in different families and communities. In Turkey, players often wear swimming trunks in the showers in order to avoid contravening Islamic regulations about bearing the body in public, but this obviously does not restrict their participation in football. In recent years, the Islamic nations of Iran, Saudi Arabia, Senegal and Turkey have all qualified for the World Cup, with the latter two progressing to the quarter- and semi-finals respectively in 2002. It is also the case that many dominant accounts assert that Islam is solely the preserve of South Asia and the Middle East, thus failing to acknowledge the large number of *African* Muslims currently playing in Britain. Being a Muslim clearly has not restricted the participation of these players. For example, Arsenal's Ivory Coast international Kolo Touré states: 'My religion is just one part of my life . . . I pray when I can, when I have time. It's not as if I'm in the dressing room and get down and pray' (cited in M. Walker 2003c: 2). Indeed, Egyptian striker Mido, formerly of Tottenham, cites his Islamic faith as an important influence on his career. He adds that:

I will be fasting during Ramadan[5] and to be honest, I never had any problems with it – it's not as difficult as people think, it's very easy. I eat early in the morning and your body gets used to it, it's difficult for the first few days, but it becomes easier and I never had any problems during games or training.

(Cited in Kick It Out 2005: 6)

However, despite such proclamations, popular stereotypes persist, fuelled by anecdotes about the negative influence of religion, especially Islam, on participation by British Asians. For example, in 2004, a mixed-ethnicity boys club was expelled from the Bury and Radcliffe Sunday League in Lancashire after contesting a punishment meted out in response to its failure to fulfil fixtures during Ramadan, when Muslim players were attending the mosque (*Asian News* 2004).[6] The following year, referees in the county reported a Muslim club from Preston to the FA for wearing longer shorts than those usually sported by players (Kelso 2005). These examples illustrate the fact that it is often British Asians themselves who are seen to be the problem rather than the intransigent nature of the game's structures. In reality, perceptions about the inhibiting influences of religion are often matters of inflexibility, Eurocentrism or racism by clubs and governing bodies.

Talking about my generation: parental attitudes towards playing football

The discourses analysed so far claim that British Asians are *unable* to play football, either because they lack the requisite physicality or because of various constraining cultural factors. The other branch of explanation acknowledges the role of British Asians as agents and proposes that they actively choose to avoid involvement in the game. In particular, it is believed that British Asian parents consciously try to steer their sons away from a career in professional football, whilst participation in a recreational capacity is deprioritized behind other extra-curricular activities. For example, in their study of British Asian schoolboys in Greater Manchester, McGuire and Collins (1998: 82) conclude that, 'Quite simply, the overriding factor which prevented the boys from pursuing either extra-curricular sport or careers in sport was not racism but parental influence, especially at the secondary age level'. However, not only does this analysis underplay the significance of 'race' and racism in leisure spaces and in excluding British Asians from professional sport, but also it arguably overstates the significance of parental influence and demonstrates insufficient appreciation of the nuances of generational difference.

In the period following the first mass migrations from the Indian subcontinent there was some degree of accuracy in the claim that many British Asians valued academic pursuits above sporting ones. Irrespective of the previous qualifications of migrants, racist employment practices meant that they were mostly restricted to the lowest-skilled sectors of manual work. Accordingly it was perceived that through educational achievement and success in the labour market, it was possible to improve socio-economic status. Thus the idea of youngsters spending time outside school playing football – a pursuit in which they were also likely to encounter frequent racist abuse and violence (see Chapter 3) – rather than studying, was not seen as supporting this long-term objective. Worse still, the idea of pursuing a career in professional sport was seen as precarious and short-term. Not only did professional football represent a realm in which British Asians had little realistic chance of obtaining inclusion – African-Caribbeans were still heavily under-represented at this stage – but, in comparison to today, the modest financial rewards the game offered were unlikely to justify the risk of prioritizing sport above education. Furthermore, as R. Ballard (1994b: 9–10) points out, long-term migration is primarily an 'entrepreneurial activity' and the South Asian migrants of the 1960s had held a 'middling [social] status' in the subcontinent. It is possible that they eschewed careers in professional football because it was viewed as a working-class activity and, despite their low social status in Britain, they possessed middle-class aspirations.[7] The following testimonies demonstrate this perspective:

> My parents certainly weren't supportive. . . . Things when I was growing up were somewhat different. My parents were very cautious about football and very cautious about the community out there, you know. There was a lot of fear. When I was at school my PE teacher actually suggested that he could put me forward for a trial at Arsenal, just for a training session. When I came home and told my parents about it, it was a no-go area, you know. They kind of referred to so many people who had broken limbs and, you know, had never made anything out of football really. And football wasn't seen to be a profession, it was just a pastime. It was something that you did when you were young, really to keep yourself busy. So support from my parents never really arrived.
>
> (Interview with British Bangladeshi amateur player, 16 March 2002)

> To be honest, family-wise, I had very little support. I've got to be really honest. I don't think my parents ever watched me play. I think my mum came to see me play when I was about 36/37! My first cup final and she came to see me play! So they never had an interest.
>
> (Interview with British Indian amateur player, 5 February 2002)

These players are approaching the end of their playing careers and the sons of first generation migrants. However, with more recent generations, attitudes appear to have changed. Indeed, a number of professional players specifically cite the support of their parents as the *main* influence on their careers (see Ismond 2003 for similar examples from other sports). For example, Harpal Singh states: 'I have had the backing of my family, that is the number one reason why I am where I am today [as a professional player]' (cited in Bhatia 2003c). These sentiments are echoed by the following players who have also reached the professional ranks of the game:

> My family [have supported me] definitely because, like, they made a lot of sacrifices, like getting me boots and all sorts of football stuff. We were a bit

short for money, but they still stuck by me and got me stuff. So mostly my family supported me.

(Interview with British Pakistani professional player, 11 February 2002)

I think [my family] have [been supportive], because we weren't really well off or nothing and they bought me the boots and that. My sisters' [needs] were sacrificed. Me and [my brother] used to get boots and shinpads and stuff like that. But now is the time I can, like, pay them back, know what I mean? My dad always said that he wanted us to be footballers. We didn't think we were going to be footballers, but [when we were] about fourteen/fifteen he really pushed us. He never really said that, 'You've *got* to play football'. He said, 'Do what *you* want to do' and it went from there.

(Interview with British Pakistani professional player, 20 March 2002)

To be perfectly honest the supportive [people] have been my parents. They've certainly encouraged me to do what I felt was right and if football was the thing that I wanted to do then they've been right there supportive of it. I wish other people would actually come in and see that kind of scenario and set-up. They're saying that Asian parents aren't supportive and yet, you know, I wouldn't be where I am without that support.

(Interview with British Indian ex-semi-professional player, 19 March 2002)

Current players replicate this support towards the potential involvement of *their* sons, as the following statements testify:

If somebody says, 'I want to be a professional footballer', my father would have said, 'Don't be silly', you know. Whereas if my kid said to me I want to be a professional footballer I'd say, 'Yes, have a try'. That's the generation gap.

(Interview with British Indian amateur player, 5 February 2002)

I think you have to see it in terms of the third or fourth generations here. I've got a young lad – he's twelve now – and if anybody tapped him up I'd be pushing him to go, you know, with a balance still to maintain education. But if somebody said to me, 'Right, we want him to train for [a professional club]', I'd encourage that. Absolutely, no problem at all.

(Interview with British Indian ex-semi-professional player, 19 March 2002)

These statements suggest that it is more appropriate to view the issue as a case of progressive generational *difference* (which is reproduced and re-imagined through all subsequent generations) rather than inter-generational conflict (between essentialist, monolithic migratory and British-born 'second' generations) or parental constraint. Previous opposition to a career in professional football needs to be placed in the context of a recently migrated population that possessed alternative, more long-term priorities when settling in this country. Attitudes towards a career in professional football were influenced by specific historical factors and immediate post-migratory conditions, such as prevalent racial discrimination in football and in the wider society. These beliefs are certainly neither a universal British Asian trait nor evidence of a 'culture clash'. Whilst Baumann's (1996: 154) cautionary note that 'one should be wary . . . of playing a sociological generation game, as if the forging of an *Asian* post-immigration *culture* were the preserve of youngsters alone' is acknowledged, it is apparent that more positive attitudes towards football have developed predominantly within more recent generations of British Asians. Whilst the habituses of first-generation migrants may have undergone little significant modification since their migration, those of younger British Asians need to be located in relation to their lives as young people growing up in Britain. Their relations with older generations form only one of a number of factors, such as age, gender, class, locality and global youth cultures, contributing to their British Asian identities, and they are increasingly willing – although, due to racism in the labour market, not necessarily able – to emulate the career patterns of their white peers rather than those of their parents and grandparents.

Issues of class and socio-economic achievement also need to be considered within this analysis. Traditionally it was perceived that British Asians would experience a 'Jewish future', i.e. one of economic success and cultural conservatism (Kundnani 2002b). However, whilst this has been the case for some British Asian groups, others have continued to suffer socio-economic disadvantage. Indians and African Asians have attained considerable economic success, to the extent that somewhat simplistically they have been labelled 'white in achievement and black in discrimination' (Modood 1992b: 41). Conversely, the social mobility of Bangladeshis and Pakistanis has been far more limited. They are more likely to suffer from material deprivation, to be unemployed, and to work in manual trades, and less likely to reach management positions (Mason 2003). This contextualizes, and repudiates, the popular stereotype that British Asian parents primarily want their children to be doctors or lawyers. The salary and status of these professions make them very attractive, but to *all* ethnic groups. What has become apparent is that, just like other ethnic groups, they are feasible careers for some British Asians yet not for others. For those in the lower socio-economic groups, when the only other viable options may be limited to working in restaurants – one third of all British Bangladeshi men work as cooks or waiters (D. Walker 2002) – or mini-cabbing (Kalra 2000), a career in football is clearly an appealing alternative.

Towards an understanding of the social significance of football for young British Asian men

YOUNG MAN: This lot are unbeaten on this tour so far
OLDER MAN: How many games have they played before this?
YOUNG MAN: None! [cue laughter amongst all]

This exchange was overheard during the match between Brentford and India at Griffin Park in July 2001. It took place within a group of four 'respectable-looking' white men and formed part of the 'banter' amongst the home supporters, who were generally expressing their amazement that football was actually played in India. In another incident, one man asked, rhetorically, 'What game is it they play? Kabaddi? They'll be bloody knackered holding their breath for ninety minutes!'[8] As Brentford striker Lloyd Owusu scored his team's third goal of the match, another supporter exclaimed, 'Stick to fucking cricket!' Common to all of these exchanges is the belief that Indians and, by implication British Asians, do not play football and that sports that are more closely associated with the Indian subcontinent, such as cricket or kabaddi, are preferred. Bizarrely, the notion that British Asians, like other groups, might enjoy more than one sport is incongruous to these supporters. However, as was discussed earlier in this chapter, it is also the case that stereotypes about sporting competencies are reproduced by the targeted groups themselves. Consider the following brief conversation that I (DB) had with a British Asian newsagent in Osterley, west London:

[DB approaches counter to buy a copy of the weekly British Asian newspaper *Eastern Eye*]

NEWSAGENT (INQUISITIVELY): *Eastern Eye*?

DB: Yes, it's for my research. I work down the road at the university.

NEWSAGENT: What are you researching?

DB: The under-representation of British Asian professional footballers.

NEWSAGENT (WITHOUT IRONY): It's 'cos they're all shite mate! [followed by laughter]

The above examples demonstrate the lack of knowledge about British Asian involvement in football that exists in the wider society but also, it should be remembered, sometimes within British Asian communities themselves.

However, although British Asians remain significantly under-represented as professional footballers in proportion to their numbers in the overall population, these players represent simply the tip of the iceberg. Throughout Britain, football has become an extremely popular and widely played leisure activity amongst young, male (and increasingly female) British Asians. The first major study to highlight this trend was Bains and Patel's (1996) seminal – and ironically titled – *Asians Can't Play Football* report. In particular, it showed that the participation of young, male British Asians – particularly Bangladeshis – is greater than that of many other ethnic groups. A further account of the game's popularity is provided by Bains and Johal (1998) who pay specific attention to a number of well-established British Asian clubs, and the prestigious and sizeable British Asian football tournaments that are staged during the summer months.

Whilst the most significant developments in British Asian football – in terms of the establishment of federations, competitions and the achievements of particular teams – have taken place in the relatively recent past, a number of clubs have existed since the 1960s and 1970s. These include Guru Nanak FC (Gravesend), Paak United FC (Nelson), Albion Sports (Bradford) and Coventry Sporting FC. The establishment of football clubs by South Asian migrants was influenced by the specific social conditions they experienced in the immediate post-migration epoch. Rather than being undertaken to escape poverty, the act of migration was seen as a means of career advancement. Originally it was intended that settlement in Britain would only be temporary and so the first South Asian migrants of the 1960s were almost exclusively adult males. The money they earned would be sent home to their families in the subcontinent to contribute towards housing improvements or buying agricultural machinery, thus improving their standing in the local social hierarchy (R. Ballard 1994b). The men planned to work until they had earned sufficient income and then return 'home' to reap the benefits of their short, but assiduous, residence in Britain. Consequently, at this stage, it was not envisaged that their wives and families would join them. Playing football together was thus an accessible social activity for these young, 'single' men. It was a way of socializing with fellow migrants in a recreational capacity that required little economic or cultural capital (Bourdieu 1984).

However, for significant numbers of South Asian migrants, settlement in Britain eventually became permanent for, as R. Ballard (1994b: 12) points out, 'the longer they stayed, the more rooted and at ease they felt in their new British environment'. When their families came to join them there was thus already an inchoate British Asian football culture for their sons to participate in. For example, one British Indian amateur player stated that:

> I came to this country when I was three years old. My father came here first, then me and my mother came here a year after . . . I went to a local school, just up the road from here and on this road there used to be quite a large population of Asians. I started playing football at about [age] nine, you know, mainly at school. . . . There's a plot of land down the bottom of the road and all our mates would get together and start kicking a ball around, and that used to be, like, the highlight, basically, of our day. We used to call it our 'mini Wembley'. Fifth year is when I started playing for [my British Asian club]. In the last form I'd play football for the school on Saturday morning, then I'd play football for [my British Asian club] in the afternoon, then I'd play football for [my British Asian club] on Sunday, you know. In between there would be training on Tuesdays and Thursdays!
>
> (Interview, 5 February 2002)

Another player added:

> My dad came over when he was quite young anyway. He played football back home [in India] and he played football over here as well, so when me and my brother were tiny we used to go and watch him and kick the ball about

ourselves. . . . My dad's slightly older now, but I mean he was playing until he was forty-two. Nowhere special, just a Saturday team, but he loved it.
(Interview with British Indian ex-professional/semi-professional player, 28 January 2002)

Not only was football established as a popular leisure activity amongst many British Asian men, but it also began to play a key role in post-migratory male lifestyles. For example, the following two interview transcripts point to the belief among some amateur players that football played an integrative role for many British Asian men:

We started the [British Asian] football club in 1965, because we wanted to promote, if you like, ourselves as a culture and also at the same time, we actually wanted to go out into the community and say, 'Look, we can be part of you *through football*'. And we used to get lumps knocked out of us by the local teams! They'd say 'Paki', 'wogs', 'go home' or 'you couldn't kick a ball straight'. But we learned to live through that and what it did was it made us much, much stronger and now what we've got is a football club of over thirty-five years old that actually is respected by the whole community because not only can they play football, but they can actually articulate what their views are and they can actually live with the best. And they drink after the game. The players won't be huddling together as ten, twelve Asians in the corner of a bar and drinking. No, they'll be drinking with the team they've just played, who happen to be all white, but they're all mates and they'll respect each other for what they bring to the sport.
(Interview with British Indian amateur player, 23 April 2002)

I was born in India, and obviously we came over here when I was about seven and it was a new sport to me totally. I'd never seen it in India. So I became familiar with the game just through primary school really. It was a good way of being part of the crew as well, you know, being accepted more easily.
(Interview with British Indian amateur player, 5 February 2002)

These statements refer to men who started playing football in the 1960s and 1970s, shortly after the first waves of subcontinental migrations. The game (and associated activities such as post-match drinking) clearly had an important integrative function for these men, although it is important to point out that integration was always contingent and operated alongside pernicious racism in the amateur game (see Chapter 3).

If the contemporary British Asian football scene is considered, it is evident that the game still serves a significant social function (Burdsey 2006). In particular, this is embodied by the role of British Asian football clubs. These clubs are often cited as 'evidence' of the self-segregating nature of British Asian communities, yet their formation results in no small part from the exclusion of British Asian players from mainstream teams, leagues and facilities (see Chapter 3). It is also the case that these clubs represent an important social space and a means of cultural resistance (Carrington 1998b). Shaw (2000) highlights that the settlement of South Asians in Britain consisted of a process of 'chain migration' involving specific *biraderi* (kinship networks). Migrants that were already resident in Britain provided the loans, accommodation and employment contacts for friends and family leaving the subcontinent. Thus, even in an era of rapidly fluctuating urban geographies, a particular local British Asian community can usually trace its roots to a specific village or district in the subcontinent. Consequently, it is common, yet by no means universal, for British Asian clubs to possess a distinct ethnic, religious and/or regional identity, operating as key representatives of locality and community. Some British Asian clubs are affiliated to religious institutions or cultural associations, whilst the names of others are chosen to explicitly celebrate their backgrounds and identities. Taking, for example, those clubs affiliated to the Sikh-based Khalsa Football Federation, referents include Sikh gods, e.g. Guru Arjan Dev Khalsa Sports Club (in Derby); the original point of migration, e.g. Punjab United (Wolverhampton); revered Sikh martyrs, e.g. Baba Deep Singh (Birmingham); and the notion of Sikhs as a 'martial race', e.g. Khalsa Warriors (Birmingham). Despite their role as important signifiers of identity, it should be noted that the implications can be problematic. As Carrington and McDonald (2001c: 54) demonstrate with cricket, there is evidence that some white clubs discriminate against teams with British Asian names when choosing who to play in friendly fixtures.

This chapter has demonstrated that the stereotypes associated with British Asian footballers are erroneous and that, instead, football is an extremely popular and socially significant activity for increasing numbers of young British Asian men. However, challenges to sporting stereotypes do not necessarily result in a reduction in other forms of prejudice and discrimination, and their gradual erosion should not be extrapolated uncritically to suggest an overly benign picture of progress and change. To revisit the distinction made at the beginning of the chapter, it is clearly not a case of, 'Why do British Asians not play football?' It is a question of, 'Why are the large numbers who participate at amateur level not making the transition into the professional game?' This question is addressed in the next two chapters, covering both the subtle and overt ways in which 'race' and racism serve to either exclude British Asians from the game completely, or to discriminate against them within it, by dictating conditions of entry and the forms of capital that are valued in the occupational culture. Chapter 3 examines the continuing influence of racism in the game and Chapter 4 analyses the responses made by British Asian players to the dominant racialized cultures that exist within it.

3   Racial discrimination and white privilege in English football

Introduction

In seeking to understand why British Asians have failed to make the transition from amateur to professional football, one of the most important issues to consider is racism. Whilst racism cannot, in isolation, explain the absence of British Asians from professional football, it must be placed at the centre of any analysis, for it influences patterns of inclusion and exclusion, belonging and marginalization, in a variety of ways. Thus the present analysis supports Hylton's (2005: 84) argument, in his persuasive call for use of Critical Race Theory (CRT) in examining social relations in sport and leisure, that 'race' and racism must be given prominence, whilst at the same time linked to other forms of subordination and discrimination.

In 'commonsense' explanations, it is often argued that the under-representation of British Asians in professional football cannot be due to racism because other 'non-white' players – black Britons and migrants from Africa, South America and the Far East – have gained inclusion in the English game. However, the suggestion that the presence of black players and increased global recruitment signifies the disappearance of localized racisms is empirically erroneous. It also ignores the fact that the global and commercial dimensions that now permeate English professional football rarely extend beyond the Premier League and so are less likely to influence processes of selection at more parochial, lower division clubs. These explanations revolve around a black–white dualism, which positions all minority ethnic groups as achieving common levels of inclusion/exclusion because of their 'non-whiteness'. Whilst their common status as racialized groups means that British Asians and African-Caribbeans frequently experience forms of oppression and exclusion commensurably, it is also the case that they often receive and interpret racial prejudice in different ways (see Chapter 6) and achieve contrasting degrees of acceptance in various social spaces and subcultural spheres (e.g. Back 1996, 2005). Thus the representation of one minority ethnic group in professional football does not necessarily result in the inclusion of all others or signify that racism is no longer an issue. Furthermore, it should be noted that claims that racism does not restrict British Asian participation reflect a long history of denial in the game. As Back et al. state:

The typical 'public' response of football clubs and individuals associated with the game to allegations of racism has historically been one of denial: denial that the problem exists at any significant level at individual clubs or amongst players, denial that there is a problem within the game more generally and, on occasions, denial that racism exists itself as a problem in society.

(2001b: 164)

As this chapter demonstrates, these refutations emanate from individual prejudices, a failure to appreciate the increasing complexities of contemporary racisms, and dominant occupational cultures that create and sustain an environment where speaking out against racism is often discouraged.

Whilst a growing number of academic accounts have examined the ways in which African-Caribbeans are subjected to racism in English football (Back *et al*. 2001b; Garland and Rowe 2001; Ismond 2003; King 2004a), very few have considered how racism impacts directly on British Asians. More specifically, there has been a marked dearth of analyses that have looked at how racism actually influences the recruitment of British Asians at elite level. In order to overcome these lacunae, this chapter examines the manner in which racism permeates processes of inclusion and exclusion, together with associated developments and events that have contributed to discrimination against, and the marginalization of, British Asians. In focusing specifically on the transition of players into the professional game, there is a need to consider both wider manifestations of contemporary racisms and the specific micro-relations that characterize and affect patterns of recruitment and selection. Racism in football operates in increasingly complex, subtle and nuanced ways, to the extent that it often goes unrecognized, and subsequently unchallenged, in the game. The contention here is that, although the exclusion of British Asians from professional football has many causes and many solutions, it is necessary to shift the analysis away from seeing British Asian communities as 'the problem' to actually getting under the skin of the institutions that construct and maintain racial inequality and disadvantage. This chapter initially examines broad patterns of discrimination and exclusion – both physical and symbolic – and feelings and experiences of fear, intimidation and threat that emanate from professional football and its institutions. It then narrows the focus to consider how racism serves to maintain unequal access paths for players of different ethnic backgrounds seeking to move from amateur to professional level. The final part of the chapter considers the rise in contemporary Islamophobia and assesses its implications for the involvement of British Asians in English football.

English professional football and racial exclusion

In examining the influence of racism on the involvement of British Asians in professional football, one needs first to consider broad, general patterns of racial exclusion. These may be tangible barriers which physically restrict involvement or symbolic ones which serve to maintain unequal inclusion by dictating which groups (do not) feel acceptance and belonging. Despite the efforts of the anti-racist football movement in challenging terrace racism, many English football stadia continue to be hostile environments for minority ethnic groups. As a result, British Asians, among others, remain an all too infrequent presence as live supporters. This exclusion is obviously a problem in itself, yet it possesses further consequences. First, it can construct stadia as alien, unwelcoming environments for emerging minority ethnic players. Second, because racism is one of the factors that traditionally has excluded British Asians from stadia, paradoxically, *direct personal* experiences of football-related racism are most likely to occur outside the grounds, in the local vicinity.

Following the 'white-flight' from the inner-cities to the suburbs that occurred in the latter half of the twentieth century – in response to deindustrialization, urban regeneration and the rise of new technologies and forms of employment – vacated districts became home to recently migrated Caribbean and South Asian populations. Whilst the economically more prosperous Indian and East African Asian communities eventually were able to replicate this suburban migration, the more deprived Bangladeshi and Pakistani communities have remained in inner-city areas. Consequently, these populations are well-represented in the local communities immediately surrounding a significant number of professional clubs. For many of these residents, home matches represent a fortnightly 'invasion' by thousands of predominantly white football fans – from other areas of the town or city and beyond – into their territory. British Asian residents have experienced discomfort, fear, verbal abuse, intimidation and violent assault (Holland 1995; Pinto *et al.* 1997; Bradbury 2001b).

Taking this into account, it is unsurprising that the (often violent) racist backlash that occurred against British Asians in the aftermath of 9/11 and the urban unrest in 2001 has also been enacted in football. For example, in April 2001, before Oldham Athletic's match against Stoke City, hooligans from both sides joined together and fought street battles with British Asians in the Westwood district of Oldham. The rallying cries of 'We hate Pakis' and 'If you all hate Pakis, clap your hands' were continued inside the Boundary Park ground (Howard 2001). The following month, members of Oldham Athletic's hooligan firm, Fine Young Casuals, together with members of neo-Nazi groups attacked British Asians in the Glodwick area of the town (Kundnani 2003), whilst two British Asians were attacked by a gang of thirty Middlesbrough fans outside Bradford City's Valley Parade ground (Wainwright 2001). In June 2001, a group of fifty right-wing extremists, including members of the Burnley Suicide Squad hooligan firm carried out racist attacks on British Asians in the town's Daneshouse district (Campaign Against Racism and Fascism 2001). Also that month, intelligence from the anti-fascist magazine *Searchlight* suggested that Aston Villa hooligans were planning to attack Pakistani supporters at the England versus Pakistan one-day cricket international at Edgbaston (Bans 2001). Plymouth Argyle hooligans have clashed with British Asians in Luton as well (Lowles 2005a). These attacks are in no small part due to the close links between the British National Party (BNP) and certain hooligan groups (ibid.).

They also demonstrate a shift in racialized representations of British Asians and responses by local white communities. Whilst British Asians traditionally have been seen as passive targets for indiscriminate racist abuse and violence, changing perceptions of the physicality of young British Asian men, and the associated challenges to masculinity, community and identity that are felt by certain white groups, mean that they are now seen to represent a significant source of threat that needs to be combated. Football provides the setting where an increasing 'white backlash' (Hewitt 2005) manifests itself as racist violence. These developments accentuate the fragility of the relationship between professional football, its clubs and their local British Asian communities, and sustain the sense of exclusion felt by British Asian players and supporters.

The denigration of British Asians has also been a central tenet in attempts by white football fans to celebrate their own, and contest rival supporters', racialized masculinities. For example, since the 1990s, the chant 'You're just a town full of Pakis' has been frequently sung by some white supporters to fans of clubs based in areas with significant British Asian populations, such as Bradford and Leicester. Similarly, in order to challenge the position of West Ham United fans as 'real', i.e. white, Londoners, some followers of Millwall (from *south* London) have chanted 'East London is like Bengal' (Back *et al.* 2001b: 63). The fact that the British Asian population in the borough of Newham is predominantly Pakistani, and thus has only a tenuous link to Bengal, is irrelevant to the chanters; it is a space that is 'Asian' and therefore 'non-white'. Whilst the chants centralize the 'Paki' as the despised 'Other', the primary aim is to question the 'whiteness' – and, in turn, the 'Englishness' – of rival supporters and their towns (ibid.). Another variant is 'I'd rather be a Paki than a Scouse' (or other identity), which seeks to disparage the target group by suggesting that being a universally reviled 'Other' is still better than being born, for example, in Liverpool (see Back *et al.* 1998). On some occasions, travelling fans have sung 'You're just a town full of *taxis*' (Thorpe 2002: 28). As Keith (2005: 30) points out, 'Racism at times works by a process of substitution, a coding of phrases and terms which conveys racist meaning without specific reference to explicitly racist beliefs'. In this case, this alteration also enables the perpetrators to escape prosecution yet, by referring to taxi-driving, which is a major source of employment for working-class British Asian men, the racist implications of the chant remain clear. The centrality of British Asians in chants aimed at almost exclusively white audiences is hugely symbolic as it requires both the *singers* and the *recipients* to possess a negative (and in many cases racist) perception of British Asians and to see them as anathema to professional football culture.

'Bowyer-gate', racial violence and the symbolic exclusion of British Asians

In recent years, the single event that has most problematized the relationship between British Asians and professional football has been the 'Bowyer-gate' affair.

In January 2000, Sarfraz Najeib, a British Pakistani student from Rotherham, was viciously assaulted as he left the Majestyk nightclub in Leeds, suffering a broken nose, cheekbone and leg. His assailants included white Leeds United star players Lee Bowyer and Jonathan Woodgate, and reserve team player Tony Hackworth (along with two of Woodgate's friends). Despite the victim's claim that the assault was racially motivated, the prosecution insisted that this was not the case and declined to seek such a conviction (Campaign Against Racism and Fascism 2002). In December 2001, a retrial – called after the original proceedings had to be halted in light of an article published by the *Sunday Mirror* that was considered prejudicial against the defendants – convicted Woodgate of affray and sentenced him to one hundred hours' community service. Bowyer and Hackworth were acquitted of all charges. In November 2005, after a long-running legal battle, Bowyer agreed an out-of-court settlement with Sarfraz Najeib and his brother Shahzad – who had also been present at the assault – reported to be worth £170,000 (Keely 2005).

In January 2003, Bowyer joined West Ham United and Woodgate moved to Newcastle United. The players were briefly reunited in May 2003 when Newcastle signed Bowyer on a free transfer, before Woodgate left for Real Madrid in 2004. Having previously remained steadfastly silent on his involvement in the assault, Bowyer made his first public comments in August 2003. He stated that:

> I'm no racist. I have never been and I never will be. . . . I was brought up in a mixed community in London and all my friends and schoolboy pals were of different nationalities. . . . I have always supported Keep Racism out of Football [sic] when I was at Charlton with my pal Carl Leaburn and at Leeds with Lucas Radebe. It's something I've always supported – but people seem to forget that these days.
>
> (Cited in Oliver 2003)

Similarly, the (then) Newcastle United manager Bobby Robson spoke out on behalf of Woodgate, citing his friendship with three players of dual African-Caribbean and white heritage. He stated that 'Jonathan is a close friend of Kieron Dyer, Jermaine Jenas and Rio Ferdinand, and that speaks for itself. If we had any inkling that he harboured racist thoughts we wouldn't have signed him at this club' (cited in M. Walker 2003a: 36). The 'some of my best friends are black' rhetoric is a common form of defence used by individuals accused of racism. It is one of a range of denials used in dominant discourses, including blame-shifting and claims of reverse racism, to distance perpetrators from allegations of deliberate and conscious prejudice (van Dijk 2002). With these particular examples, the (spurious) line of reasoning claims that having a minority ethnic friend would preclude any act of purposeful racism towards another individual. Any racist action or epithet is thus seen to be purely a mistake or accidental, literally an aberration on one's usual good character (van Zoonen *et al.* 2005). Irrespective of the veracity of these claims – and, in Bowyer's case, in particular, previous offences, including assaulting a British Asian employee at a McDonald's restaurant, do seem to cast doubt on his anti-racist credentials – the assault of Sarfraz Najeib has had considerable repercussions for the players involved and the way that their respective clubs are viewed by British Asian communities. In this regard, the following discussion does not seek simplistically to label certain clubs as more (or less) racist than others (Back *et al.* 1998: 72); rather it aims to examine the ways in which minority ethnic groups are symbolically excluded and situated as 'outsiders'.

Leeds United has been associated with terrace racism for a number of years, with the National Front recruiting amongst its fans in the 1970s (Phillips 2002). This trend was met with resistance from other fan groups within the club, such as Leeds Fans United Against Racism and Fascism (Thomas 1995). More recently, the club has attempted to forge links with its local British Asian and black communities (Brown 2006), but the 'Bowyer-gate' affair has threatened to undermine their work in this capacity. By continuing to select – up to and after the trial – players that were involved in an assault with indubitable racist undertones, not surprisingly the club's commitment to anti-racism has been questioned by local minority ethnic communities. This was acknowledged belatedly by a senior (unnamed) figure at the club following the transfer of Bowyer to West Ham. He admitted, 'Is there relief at Leeds to see Lee Bowyer go? Yes, of course. Does it make it easier for Leeds to extend its work in the community? Yes, of course' (cited in M. Walker 2003b: 2). The club's relationship with British Asian communities was further damaged after a performance by 'comedian' Stan Boardman at a social function held at the club's Elland Road stadium in 2002. During his act, Boardman portrayed a scenario in which Bowyer and Woodgate leave a nightclub and, in discussing where to go for some food, one says to the other, 'I could murder an Indian'. Steven Thomas, a British Asian guest and long-term United supporter, called Boardman 'a disgrace', to which Boardman replied, 'Fucking hell, I'm being heckled by Pakis now! Why don't you go back to your curry house or shop in Bradford? Your elephant's waiting outside' (cited in *Eastern Eye* 2002b).

It is ironic that, in the years succeeding the Najeib assault, one of the most promising young British Asian players, Harpal Singh, came through Leeds United's youth ranks and signed as a professional. It is difficult to gauge how the involvement of three of his team-mates in the assault of a young British Asian man affected Singh's position and development at the club, yet the fact that he never played for the first-team is perhaps revealing. For his part, Singh states that, '(I) blocked the whole thing about Bowyer out of my mind' (cited in Bhatia 2003b). Whether British Asian supporters and other young players have been able to do the same is questionable, and Singh's potential to enhance Leeds United's profile within British Asian communities clearly plummeted as a result of its associations with the Najeib case. British Asian players and supporters have been further marginalized and excluded from the club (and professional football in general) by the behaviour of some fans who eulogized Bowyer and Woodgate in football chants. For example, travelling home from a match in December 2001, in the immediate aftermath of the retrial, a group of supporters sang: 'Jingle bells, Sarfraz smells, Woody got affray, oh what fun it is to see Bowyer get away' (*Observer* 2002: 2). Blackshaw and Crabbe (2005: 335) report a similar chant: 'Johnny Woodgate is our friend, is our friend, is our friend, Johnny Woodgate is our friend, he hates Pakis'.

Bowyer and Woodgate both left Leeds United in January 2003, but the controversy surrounding them continued. When Woodgate joined Newcastle United, the club was 'inundated with hostile e-mails and telephone calls' from supporters who were angry about the signing (M. Walker 2003a: 2), although it is unclear as to whether this hostility was due to his criminal conviction or the allegations of racism. However, despite his acquittal, it is Bowyer who has been subject to most criticism and public opprobrium. This suggests that opposition to Bowyer takes into account his previous misdemeanours and perhaps the fact that whilst Woodgate appeared penitent throughout the trial, Bowyer remained brazen, with the judge stating that his police interviews had been 'littered with lies' (Blackshaw and Crabbe 2005: 336). At the time of the case Bowyer was on the fringes of the England squad and Gloucester MP, Parmjit Dhanda, argued that his selection for the national side would alienate and exclude British Asian supporters (Blake 2002). This standpoint was widely reiterated when Bowyer joined West Ham. A number of British Asian supporters publicly denounced the signing, arguing that it contradicted the club's anti-racist work in the borough of Newham. Particular concerns were raised about the repercussions for the club's groundbreaking Asians in Football project, an initiative that provides coaching for large numbers of British Asian youngsters in East London. Journalist and season ticket holder Shekhar Bhatia argued that, 'West Ham will risk consigning years of good work in furthering relations with Newham's Asian community to the dustbin' (Bhatia 2003a: 24). Suresh Grover, chairman of the National Civil Rights Movement, added that:

> Over the past few years West Ham United Football Club has done much to distance itself from racism. It has also worked with local partnerships and secured funding to involve both the local Asian and black communities and young people. However, all its good work will now be undermined by securing Lee Bowyer as one of its players.
>
> (Cited in Brodkin 2003b: 26)

Film director and West Ham fan Suri Krishnamma claimed that he was 'outraged at hearing of the signing of Bowyer.... It is probably the lowest moment in recent West Ham football history. It is worse than the prospect of relegation' (cited in Kaur Grewal 2003a). Another British Asian season ticket holder stated that, 'I can't believe they've done it. I really don't know what my reaction will be when I see him in the claret and blue. I certainly won't cheer when he scores – and that'll be a first for me' (cited in Chadband and Low 2003). However, not all British Asian West Ham supporters were against the transfer. For example, one fan stated that:

Well, he [Bowyer] wasn't found guilty was he? Jonathan Woodgate was found guilty. If the court system found [Bowyer] not guilty why are people turning around and saying there's a problem? He may be a thug, but he's also a footballer. He's not coming here for his lifestyle. I won't be joining in the protests.

(Cited in Kaur Grewal 2003b)

The most public protest was held on the day of Bowyer's debut, in January 2003, organized by the spontaneously formed West Ham Fans United Against Racism group outside the club's Upton Park ground. A small number of demonstrators distributed leaflets stating that they were 'appalled' by the signing and calling for the club to 'reaffirm its total commitment to anti-racism' (Brodkin 2003a: 2). Some white West Ham supporters spat at and abused the protesters, labelled them 'white Pakis' and tore down their banners (Kaur Grewal 2003b). Significantly, the protesters were mainly white supporters. The absence of British Asians highlights the fact that they do not have the comforting protection of 'whiteness' into which they can retreat after such public protests, both within the football ground and in wider society.

It is too early to gauge the wider, long-term repercussions that Bowyer's presence has had for West Ham's relations with its local British Asian communities. He was injured for a large part of his brief period at the club which took much of the heat out of the immediate situation. Nevertheless, for many British Asians, his presence represented a form of symbolic exclusion and was perceived to cast doubt on the club's anti-racist work. This demonstrates that the generic positioning of professional footballers as role models can have negative consequences that extend far beyond the individuals themselves. Furthermore, Bowyer's signing allowed racist elements of the West Ham support a new platform to celebrate their white, Cockney identities. In their eyes the white, working-class, East End boy had come home. In what is becoming an increasingly multi-ethnic part of London, Bowyer and West Ham United were perceived to represent an enduring bastion of white, working-class identity and masculinity, in which British Asians were unequivocally 'outsiders'.[1]

Racism and player recruitment in professional football

The previous sections demonstrate that racism – threats, abuse, violence and symbolic events – serves to construct professional football (as an occupational sphere) and the stadium (as a space) as out-of-bounds for British Asian players and supporters. However, whilst the effects of the examples discussed so far are quite clear in terms of British Asian supporters, to understand how racism affects the recruitment of players, further analysis needs to be undertaken at a micro level on the degree to which racism permeates the personal relations and interactions between managers, coaches, scouts and players.

In their pioneering study, Bains and Patel (1996: 30) state that three-quarters of British Asian footballers believe that their under-representation at professional level is a result of racial discrimination by professional clubs. Of those players who have had trials at professional clubs, one-fifth state that they received racist abuse from coaches (ibid.: 28). In a similar, although smaller-scale, study, McGuire *et al.* (2001: 75) found that 9 out of 10 British Asian players believe that their absence from the professional game is due to institutional racism. In the past, a number of personnel at professional clubs have harboured overtly racist beliefs about British Asian players, and some probably still hold these views. However, most professional club coaches and scouts now state that ethnic background is not a factor in the recruitment of players. For example, the Education, Welfare and Technical Advisor at one Premier League club stated that:

> Because we're an excellence programme we scout from schools, local Sunday clubs and community programmes. We're really picking the best boys, you know. Whether that's an Afro-Caribbean, a white boy, a Chinese boy, an Asian boy, it doesn't really matter to us, we just want to get the talent into the club.
>
> (Interview, 1 March 2002)

Similarly, two other academy staff argued as follows:

> We identify the strongest leagues and go and scout them. . . . If there happens to be Asian teams and schools participating in them, I ain't got a problem. If they've got a player, we'll try and get him.
>
> (Interview with Youth Development Officer at a Premier League club, 14 November 2001)

> I don't know of any club that would not recruit Asians just because they're Asian. I'm sure there may be one or two people in every walk of life, at every club, that may not fancy Asian kids for one particular reason or another, but we would recruit Asian kids if they were good enough.
>
> (Interview with Director of Youth Academy at a Premier League club, 16 January 2002)

It is often suggested by those in the game and in the media that 'race' is no longer an issue in player recruitment and that any institutional barriers have been dismantled. Literally football 'sees no colour' or is 'colour blind'. This position is particularly prominent in elite activities such as professional football for, as Long and McNamee (2004: 415) point out, 'there seems to be a presumption that self-interest (the success of the team) will override any racism and ensure that players from minority ethnic groups gain the opportunities they deserve'. Similarly, 'the playing field is a context in which athletes are typically socialized to believe race does not matter' (Brown *et al.* 2003: 163). Conversely, more critical voices have suggested that such sentiments are merely bogus claims of racial equality and are really public cover-ups of inherent institutional racism in the scouting and recruitment networks of professional clubs.

The former argument reflects a widespread and inveterate denial of racism in English football. However, this denial operates in spite of clear evidence that racism is deeply rooted and pervasive in the game. This reluctance to acknowledge racism has contributed to a failure to eradicate it, for the fact that many people inside the game do not believe that it exists or that it is a problem means that they are not inclined to challenge or eliminate it. Long (2000: 121–2) suggests that there are four main reasons why, despite the profile of, and lobbying by, anti-racist campaigns in sport, racism might not be dealt with. He argues that individuals may be: i) informed, but ill-inclined to act; ii) informed, but unable to recognize racism; iii) uninformed; or iv) actively opposed to taking such action. Examples of all four cases could probably be found in elite football. Nevertheless, taking the oral testimonies cited above, they appear to reflect the second category most closely. All of these coaches were aware of the various campaigns and publicly supportive of anti-racism, yet they appear unable to recognize that certain acts and processes that comprise elite recruitment and selection – whether it be the leagues that they scout, the location of coaching projects and academies/centres of excellence, the way that they communicate with players' families, or the intermediaries they use to identify talent – continue to maintain racial inequality and disadvantage in terms of access to the game. This is particularly the case in football where arguably there has been a general shift from blatant, overt acts of racism to more subtle, nuanced, complex and contradictory manifestations. In this regard, the exclusion of British Asians from professional football often represents what Essed (1991) calls 'everyday racism', through the way that racism is integrated into everyday situations through systematic, recurrent, familiar practices that activate underlying power relations. Professional coaches and scouts often make statements alluding to the fact that a player's ethnicity is irrelevant, but they do not appreciate that such rhetoric is a long way from making clubs inclusive institutions, breaking down barriers and making recruitment a 'level playing field'. This is why Critical Race Theory is so important to analyses in this area. Not only does it foreground the experiential knowledge of minority ethnic groups in analysing social institutions, but it also challenges 'dominant . . . claims of neutrality, objectivity, color [sic] blindness, and meritocracy and posits that these claims are camouflages for the self-interests of the powerful entities in society' (Singer 2005: 369).

Not only is it the case that many people involved in professional football are unable (or unwilling) to recognize acts of racism, but they also do not understand that whilst they might perceive themselves to be non-racist and may not necessarily engage in purposefully racist acts, the outcomes of their behaviour can be characterized as racist. In other words, they do not see themselves as being accountable for racial inequality in the game. In this regard it is useful to refer to Feagin and Vera's (1995) notion of 'sincere fictions'. These describe the processes by which individuals employ a view of society that denies the existence of racism and construct self-definitions of themselves as innocent of possessing any form of prejudice, yet simultaneously engage in behaviours that reproduce racial stereotypes and maintain inequalities. Thus:

Whites generally use these fictions to define themselves as 'not racist', as 'good people', even as they think and act in anti-Black ways. It is common for a White person to say, 'I am not a racist', often, and ironically, in conjunction with negative comments about people of color [sic].

(Ibid.: 14)

These sincere fictions often hide everyday realities and, consequently, a failure to change structures and processes of recruitment so that they are more accessible to all ethnic groups is not recognized as a form of racial discrimination. In other words, because they do not necessarily involve a conscious desire to select players based on their ethnicities, this is not recognized in dominant interpretations as representing racism (van Zoonen *et al.* 2005). Established recruitment procedures are seen as normal or traditional, and therefore it is those groups that are unable to access them, rather than football itself, that are seen as the problem. However, irrespective of intention, these procedures are evidently a means of maintaining racial disadvantage and upholding white privilege. This suggests that in seeking to understand and analyse racism in professional football there is a need to move away from a simple correlation between intention and outcome, and the notion that racism is simply an individual problem, to understanding instead the subtleties, gradations, complexities and contradictions of contemporary racisms (Back *et al.* 2001b; Long and McNamee 2004).

It is also significant that British Asian players themselves often do not cite racism as the most significant factor inhibiting their involvement in the game. In particular, those players who have been involved with professional clubs do not attribute their eventual failures to racism. For example, with reference to his release from his professional club, one British Indian ex-professional/semi-professional player stated that, 'I honestly don't think me being released was down to the colour of my skin; just that the opinions that mattered didn't think I was quite up to it' (interview, 28 January 2002). Another player argued that:

I would say that it was purely football. White players get released, you know. Chinese players get released. I never looked at it that I've got an Asian background, that race was anything to do with it. . . . And I still stand by that.
(Interview with British Indian ex-professional/semi-professional player,
5 March 2002)

Similar testimonies were provided by two other British Asian players who have experienced the same fate:

I think [that] if it was my race, I wouldn't have been there in the first place. They wouldn't have offered me a YTS [Youth Training Scheme contract] if they thought it was my race. That didn't come into it. . . . I got released and [my British Asian team-mate] got signed on so I wouldn't say it's down to colour. He was good enough and I wasn't at that time.
(Interview with British Indian ex-professional player, 11 March 2002)

I look at it and I was standing next to [the team manager]. He's a black man. So how can I look at a black man and think he's racist to me. Do you see what I'm saying? And I'm not saying I can look at a white man and think he's a racist, I don't think like that. But if ever at any time it occurred to me, not one bit did I ever think it was racism. It never crossed my mind.

(Interview with British Pakistani ex-professional player, 20 February 2002)

These trends reflect those identified by Long *et al.* (1997b: 34) in their study of racism in local league cricket, where 'accusations of racism were not the first resort of cricketers trying to justify themselves'.

The above testimonies portray the selection and recruitment procedures in professional football as being 'colour-blind', yet as this chapter demonstrates, this is rarely the case. Why, therefore, might British Asians corroborate the dominant denial of racism in professional football? Long (2000: 130) proposes four reasons why minority ethnic sportspeople endorse hegemonic claims that racism in sport has decreased: i) they are correct; ii) they may feel that if the situation has not improved during their careers they might be seen (by themselves if nobody else) to be partially responsible; iii) they are now established stars and thus less likely to encounter petty jibes and behaviour; or iv) they have become hardened to it. There are factors specifically related to professional football that may influence this situation as well. First, the players simply may not have experienced racism at their clubs. In some instances, this might be influenced by the fact that those British Asians who have made the professional grade have tended to come from dual heritage or Anglicized backgrounds (see Chapter 4). Their 'Asianness' is less distinctive than with other potential players and perhaps less likely to form the basis for prejudice. Second, as the above testimonies imply, the inclusion of African-Caribbean and, in some cases British Asian, team-mates may be interpreted (mistakenly) as evidence that racism does not, or cannot, exist. Third, because racism in football increasingly manifests itself in informal, subtle and sometimes unintended forms, its existence is not always easy to detect. This is particularly the case with the use of derogatory verbal epithets which, if they do not include overt, crude, universally acknowledged terms, may not be recognized as racist. Furthermore, certain behaviours and discourses may be regarded by some as part of the 'culture' of football and thus not worthy of discussion. As King (2004b: 25) points out, 'black players may find it difficult to identify racism and to hold white men accountable, when racist "industrial language" is seen as a legitimate form of competition between men and as a normal part of being a professional soccer player'. Finally, those African-Caribbean players who have spoken out publicly about racism often have been accused of being 'over-sensitive' or 'having a chip on their shoulder' (Moran 2000). British Asian players may be trying to distance themselves from such an accusation. There is also evidence that those players who 'accept' racism as 'part of the game' are seen as 'less troublesome' by some managers and coaches, and are more likely to succeed (King 2004b). As Puwar (2005: 53) points out: 'In most professions there is a taboo attached to naming racism, let alone organizing against it. Those who openly take it up as an internal issue, in one way or another, mark themselves out as potentially risky bodies'.

Extending analyses of 'race' and racism in football to grassroots amateur level – an arena where overt prejudice is arguably more prevalent (Long *et al.* 2000; R. Jones 2002), yet one that has received considerably less attention – helps to further establish why British Asians are failing to make it as professionals. One of the main factors inhibiting their progression from amateur to professional level is the fact that significant numbers play for British Asian clubs in all-Asian leagues. By playing exclusively in these competitions these players remain extremely unlikely to be identified and recruited by professional clubs. In seeking to explain why this is the case, it is necessary to examine both why British Asian clubs and all-Asian leagues have been established, and the procedures by which professional clubs recruit talented young footballers.

As Chapter 2 highlighted, it is often the case that British Asian football clubs are centred around a particular ethnic/ancestral regional group (e.g. Bengali Muslims) or religious institution (e.g. a gurdwara). Similarly, many organizations have a specific British Asian emphasis, such as the UK Bangladesh Football Association and the Khalsa Football Federation. Due to the pervasive nature of contemporary political and public discourses about integration and community cohesion (Alexander 2005; McGhee 2005), it is often suggested that that these clubs and organizations embody the perceived self-segregating tendencies of British Asians. However, not only has this wider belief been proved to be a demographic myth (Dodd 2005b), but also this claim ignores a number of other factors intrinsic to amateur football. Analogous to dominant interpretations of racialized geographies that apportion segregation to minority ethnic groups, the large number of white-only clubs playing amateur football up and down the country is not regarded as a problem or believed to contribute to racial divisions. Furthermore, despite the importance of British Asian clubs as symbols of ethnic identity and community, membership is rarely exclusive and, although most clubs are dominated by a particular ethnic group or religious denomination, they are, at the very least, pan-Asian institutions.

Perhaps most importantly, dominant discourses fail to appreciate the influence of racism in the trend for British Asians to play together in the same teams. As Johal (2001: 162) states in relation to the pioneering British Asian clubs, 'with the indigenous white community harbouring a great deal of hostility and manifest resentment toward any foreign immigrants, penetrating into the ranks of local all-white teams was a near impossible and often perilous endeavour'. However, in the early stages of the post-migration epoch, there were not sufficient teams to form their own competitions and so British Asian football clubs competed in predominantly 'white' amateur leagues. Although some degree of integration was occasionally achieved (see Chapter 2), amateur football also operated as one of the primary outlets for manifestations of wider societal racism, with players frequently encountering verbal and physical racist abuse from opposition players and supporters (Bains and Johal 1998). One British Indian amateur player describes his experiences in the 1970s as follows:

> When we first went into the county league some teams hadn't heard of us and obviously didn't know the background. One or two teams, to be honest, were a little bit racist possibly in their remarks when they turned up at our ground because adjacent to our ground we've got an education centre where they teach Punjabi on Saturdays and Sundays, and on occasions there have been weddings down there, so there have been a lot of Asians down there. So you always obviously got, you know, racially motivated remarks coming from [visiting players].
>
> (Interview, 5 February 2002)

Racism remains deeply rooted and pervasive in contemporary amateur football. Many British Asian amateur players state that the worst incidents of racism occur when their clubs play matches against teams from countryside villages or semi-rural areas, which possess almost exclusively white populations. The population of minority ethnic groups in rural areas is far less than in urban areas, yet the rate of racist attacks in England is much higher in rural locations (Ray and Reed 2005). A team-mate of the above player spoke about his experiences coaching young players at his club:

> What I've found is that if you play against a team from, say, out in the countryside, they will throw racist remarks at you. . . . They haven't got many Asians living there so they've all sort of got their own little village and their own little families there and that's it. Whereas football teams [in this area], they go to school with the Asian kids, their next-door neighbours are Asian, they shop at an Asian newsagents and that's why you'll find you get people swearing, racially, more in the countryside than you will, you know, locally. . . . I found that when I was playing football and I found that now when I'm taking the kids. Take an occasion two seasons ago. The under-13s were playing a team from just outside [x], in the countryside and even the kids were swearing at our players! 'You black this', 'You black that', you know, language like that! I'm thinking, hang on, that's disgusting really, but in the end their manager threatened to beat my assistant manager up. My assistant manager was running the line where their supporters were standing. [My assistant] is an honest guy, right, and he is not one that would cheat, especially with kids, you know. He flagged for offside, the referee's given it – we're beating this team – and [the opposition manager] started an argument with him and he's sworn at him. And then this guy has pulled his head back and gone to sort of headbutt him!
>
> (Interview with British Indian amateur player, 5 February 2002)

Similar occurrences continue to take place, particularly with urban British Asian clubs that are (one of) the only minority ethnic representative(s) in otherwise exclusively white suburban/village leagues and associations. In both 1997 and

1998 players from Essex-based club Bari FC were verbally and physically assaulted by opposition teams, resulting in one player being beaten unconscious (Lindsey 1997; Kick It Out 1999), whilst in April 2002, players from GNG in Leicester were attacked by a mob of skinheads wielding baseball bats and bottles (*Times* 2002).[2] Incidents such as these have been central to the development of all-Asian leagues. Rather than being deliberate forms of ethno-cultural segregation, they are environments where British Asians can play without fear of racist abuse or violence. As Johal (2001: 165) argues, 'There is an almost Machiavellian tautology that operates whereby South Asians are forced into creating their own mono-ethnic football teams in order to protect themselves from racial abuse and still partake of the sport'.

Anecdotal evidence – raised, for example, by a number of delegates at *The Future for Asians in British Football* conference in 2005 – suggests that racism in local football is compounded by the failure of local county football associations to challenge it and their concomitant discriminatory treatment of minority ethnic clubs (see also Lusted 2005). This relates to what McDonald and Ugra (1998: 29) – in their study of amateur cricket – refer to as a 'culture of exclusion', through which the normalization of 'whiteness' and white privilege permeate the structures of amateur football. This process subtly discriminates against minority ethnic groups, marginalizing their interests and silencing their 'voices'. All-Asian leagues ensure that individual clubs are treated equitably, that they are represented in administrative structures and committees, and that specific interests, issues and problems are acknowledged.

However, despite the function served by all-Asian leagues, they represent a significant obstacle in terms of the progression of British Asian players from amateur to professional football. This is because those players who play in all-Asian leagues are not likely to be spotted by professional clubs. In the majority of cases, professional clubs recruit players from a small selection of established amateur leagues and rarely extend their observations beyond them. This is the result of four main factors. First, some coaches and scouts are ignorant of the reasons why British Asians often play outside 'mainstream' leagues. They believe that if a player is good enough, he will be participating in one of the leagues that they already scout. The barriers that prevent players from participating in these competitions are not acknowledged. Second, many coaches and scouts believe that any 'specialist' league is unlikely to be of a sufficient overall standard to make scouting it a worthwhile activity. For the majority, this is the case regardless of the dominant ethnicity of a particular league, yet for others stereotypes of 'Asianness' are more central. For example, the Academy Director at one Premier League club stated that:

> As far as recruiting from Asian leagues directly, one of the hardest things would be the standard of football and actually being able to say that that football is of a sufficient level to demonstrate that players have sufficient talent to come into the higher level. The trouble is also that if players only play at that level then they are not going to improve from that level and

that's an added issue. That's, I think, really why we wouldn't seek to actively scout an Asian youth league, if it started up in [this city].

(Interview, 21 November 2001)

Third, and relatedly, many small clubs do not have the resources to designate scouts to watch what are ostensibly 'specialist' leagues. For example, the Centre of Excellence Director at one League Two club reported that whilst a neighbouring Premier League club could deploy up to forty youth scouts, his club only possessed four, all of whom were part-time. It has been suggested that professional scouts could observe the best British Asian players by attending the national tournaments that take place over the summer yet, again, anecdotal evidence suggests that, despite invitations from organizers, most clubs have failed to attend. Fourth, most all-Asian leagues tend to be based predominantly around *adult* football and so the majority of players are too old to have a realistic chance of making it as a professional (see Chapter 7).

The implications of playing in all-Asian leagues are widely acknowledged by British Asian players. They feel that they preclude competing against the best players and teams, and thus they are an impediment to their progress into the professional game, as highlighted in the following quotations:

Why separate Asians and English [whites]? If you want to better yourself as a footballer you've got to go and play against the best players and with the best players, you know. Whatever your ability level is. Now, if you're a good Sunday league player, why be stuck playing with, you know, an Asian league? You've got to mix and play at the best Sunday level that you can. And that's going to be a mixed level. Whatever race you are.

(Interview with British Indian ex-professional/semi-professional player,
5 March 2002)

It is *absolutely* important that we play in mixed leagues. It is a way backwards for us to play in the Asian league. It is a way of us saying indirectly to the white mainstream, 'We accept what you say'. So what are we going to do? We are going to hide in a corner, we're going to build our own league, we are going to stick to ourselves.

(Interview with British Pakistani ex-professional player, 20 February 2002)

I think it's really important [to play in mixed leagues]. It's one of the disadvantages at the moment, especially for Asians, because they just play amongst themselves, you know, local teams, Asian teams. But they need to broaden their knowledge, definitely, by playing with whites, blacks, everyone, because if they just think about themselves, then I'm afraid, you know, there's a long way to go still for us to get our mentality right, then to get the experience, especially for the youngsters. They need to broaden their horizons as early as they can and eradicate from their mind this mentality of racism.

(Interview with British Bangladeshi semi-professional player, 11 May 2002)

What is particularly significant about this last transcript is the way that it inadvertently corroborates dominant discourses of denial and actually serves to underplay the existence of racism, by suggesting that it often exists purely in players' minds and that its effects can easily be overcome.

An increasing number of British Asian clubs are now playing in mixed-ethnicity leagues, and many have been successful in these environments. Building on these foundations is necessary to ensure that appropriate structures are in place to enable British Asians to progress from amateur to professional level. Of course, players in mixed leagues still experience problems and these competitions have not facilitated a sizeable breakthrough of British Asian professional players, yet all the professional players interviewed for this book previously played in such environments. It is crucial to distinguish, however, that the situation in football should not be conflated with wider political calls for greater integration between British Asian and white communities, which is seen to be the central tenet of community cohesion. It is the prerogative of any group to play football with whom they want, yet it becomes an issue when doing so is enforced due to discrimination in 'mainstream' settings, and/or prevents progression to elite level. Both these scenarios currently characterize the participation of British Asians in football. This chapter has identified the need for what are being labelled 'midfield players' (with the pun intended), i.e. individuals and agencies who are able to help span the chasm between British Asian amateur clubs and the professional game, and can ensure that nationally implemented policy actually disseminates down into the grassroots. There is a pressing need for anti-racism and equity policies to be implemented at *all* levels of the game, for whilst British Asian players acknowledge the need to play in 'mainstream' leagues if they are to have a chance of making it as a professional, for many, these remain uncomfortable or dangerous spaces.

They think it's all *fatwa*: Islamophobia, British Asians and football

Since the turn of the twenty-first century, a number of key events have occurred that have problematized the position of Muslims in contemporary British society: 9/11 and its global repercussions, the Blair–Bush coalition's 'war on terror', urban unrest in northern England in 2001, and the London transport bombings of 7 July 2005 (hereafter 7/7). These events have fuelled a widespread and historically entrenched (Said 1985; Miles 1989; Ansari 2004) vitriolic denunciation of Islam and Muslims in Britain. Consequently, the citizenship, identities and national affiliations of British Muslims have become subject to rigorous political and public debate (Abbas 2005; Bunting 2005; Modood 2005; A. Malik 2006). The current increase in Islamophobia (Runnymede Trust 1997) has significant implications for British Asian Muslim footballers – at professional and amateur levels – in terms of both their inclusion and the degree to which they choose to articulate/celebrate their 'Muslimness' and/or 'Asianness'. Parallel to wider social trends, it is also possible that British Asian players of other religious denominations will be affected.

In examining modern manifestations of Islamophobia, one needs to go back to 1988, the year that British-based Indian novelist Salman Rushdie published *The Satanic Verses*. In the book, Rushdie made a number of references that were perceived by Muslims to be blasphemous against Islam and derogatory to their communities. The following year, the author was issued with a *fatwa* (a religious declaration, in this instance a death sentence) by the Iranian religious leader Ayatollah Khomeini (officially renounced in 1998) and was consequently forced into hiding. Whilst the majority of British Muslims were offended by the book and supported calls for its withdrawal, many opposed the *fatwa* (Shaw 2000). However, many young, militant, Mirpuri (Kashmiri) youths in Bradford, in particular – a city with a history of British Asian political mobilization, for example, following the arrests of the 'Bradford Twelve' in 1981 and as part of the backlash against local head teacher Ray Honeyford in the early 1980s[3] – issued a demand that the decree be enforced in response to the damage that Rushdie had inflicted on their *izzat* (honour). Support for the *fatwa* in Bradford saw Muslims throughout the whole of Britain sensationally attacked by both a Eurocentric British press and the main political parties (Appignanesi and Maitland 1989).

For many people, this episode confirmed their perceptions that Islam was incompatible with, and a threat to, British society. To a modern, libertarian state such as Britain, which claims to champion individuals' rights to free speech, groups that call for someone to be killed because of what they have written are anathema. Demotic interpretations of nationhood and British citizenship were reconstructed along religio-cultural rather than racial demarcations. The crude 'white/black' or 'white/Asian' binaries and categorizations that had been commonly articulated in previous decades were rapidly replaced with 'British/Muslim' (Asad 1990; Samad 1992). As Modood points out:

> The more distant an individual or group is from the norm of white middle-upper class British Christian/agnostic, the greater the marginality and exclusion. The hostility of the majority is likely to be particularly forceful if the individual in question is a member of a community (and not just a free-floating or assimilated individual) which is sufficiently numerous to reproduce itself as a community and has a distinctive and coherent value system which can be perceived as an alternative and possible challenge to the norm.
>
> (1992b: 54)

Re-employing historical stereotypes, Muslims have since been constructed and represented in dominant discourses as a homogenous, static group, and characterized as backward, uncivilized, threatening and a danger to national security. As Goldberg (2006: 346) succinctly points out, 'The Muslim image in contemporary Europe is one of fanaticism, fundamentalism, female (women and girls') suppression, subjugation, and repression'. They are viewed and treated with suspicion and hostility, and, unlike other religious denominations, their loyalty to Britain is frequently questioned. Surveillance of Muslims by the state and its intelligence/security apparatuses has increased, and rapidly implemented anti-terror legislation manifests itself in ever more Islamophobic ways. Clearly, in the eyes of many, the line between Islamic extremists involved in global terrorism and the Muslim communities of Britain has become increasingly blurred. Like other forms of prejudice, contemporary Islamophobia is regularly exhibited through violence. In the immediate aftermath of 9/11, a number of mosques and Islamic cemeteries and schools were vandalized whilst, according to figures compiled by Islamic organizations, attacks on British Muslims increased to a rate thirteen times higher than that of a typical year (Herbert and Burrell 2002). This pattern was repeated following 7/7, with similar incidents taking place throughout the country.

British Muslims have also become the primary target for certain Far Right groups. In the aftermath of the urban unrest in 2001, the British National Party (BNP) quickly targeted the towns and cities where the violence had taken place – Bradford, Burnley, Leeds and Oldham – for electoral support. A central tenet of the BNP's campaign is their contention that it is Muslims, rather than minority ethnic groups *per se*, who represent a threat to Britain's social cohesion and stability. The party has labelled Muslims 'the enemy within' and hold them directly responsible for the social problems that exist between white and British Asian communities in many areas of northern Britain (Allen 2005). Chairman Nick Griffin stresses unequivocally that people should:

> Stop saying Asian. It is not a question of Asian versus white. This is a Muslim problem. There are Hindus in Oldham who have been burnt out of their houses and pushed out. There are West Indians who have been pushed out of their houses as well. This isn't an Asian problem. *This is a Muslim problem.*
>
> (Cited in BBC TV 2001a)

The Far Right is by no means the only political stratum to contribute to the present climate of Islamophobia in Britain. Such is the pervasiveness of anti-Islamic discourses in twenty-first-century Britain that even left-wing politicians are espousing such rhetoric. For example, David Blunkett, Ann Cryer and Denis MacShane have all spoken of what they believe to be an inherent incompatibility between Islamic and British values.[4] As Said argues:

> Malicious generalizations about Islam have become the last acceptable form of denigration of foreign culture in the West; what is said about the Muslim mind, or character, or religion, or culture as a whole cannot now be said in mainstream discussion about Africans, Jews, other Orientals, or Asians.
>
> (1997: xii)

What, therefore, are the implications of increasing Islamophobia for the involvement of British Asian Muslims in English football?

Clearly identifiable Islamophobia in English football, as opposed to more generalized racism, is a relatively recent phenomenon. This is a result of two main factors. First, the absence of British Asian and, until the late 1990s, migrant African players in English professional football has meant that a Muslim 'Other' has not been present as a target for anti-Islamic sentiment. Second, the England national team never play South Asian countries and very rarely play Middle Eastern ones. Until recently, the only Islamic nations (or those with significant Muslim populations) that England have played – with the exception of Saudi Arabia – have been African nations: Cameroon, Egypt, Morocco, Nigeria and Tunisia. In such instances, little reference is made to players' religious denominations and, with sub-Saharan nations, media discourses have instead tended to focus on crude *racial* stereotypes based on the notion of the overtly physical yet undisciplined black African footballer. The situation in football thus contrasts directly with cricket, in which English–Pakistani relations have a long, acrimonious and often Islamophobic history[5] (Williams 2003).

However, since the beginning of the twenty-first century, a new source of antagonism has been added to the equation – the growth of anti-Turkish sentiment in English football. This is the direct result of the murder of two Leeds United supporters, Christopher Loftus and Kevin Speight, by a Turkish man, Ali Umit Demir, during clashes in Istanbul before a UEFA Cup semi-final match against Galatasaray in April 2000. Anti-Turkish songs have become prominent amongst some England supporters and many of these have begun to adopt an anti-Islamic, as opposed to simply an anti-Turkish, content. For example, chants during the European Championship qualifying match between England and Turkey in Sunderland in April 2003 included 'Die Muslim die' and 'Kill all Muslims' (Bailey 2003; Kelso 2003). Coaches transporting Turkish supporters to the match were also attacked by English hooligans. Similarly, travelling supporters of English club and national sides have often been involved in violence with Turkish communities in cities in Belgium and Holland (see e.g. Nicholls 2002).

Whilst it is perhaps too early to measure their wider implications for English football, there is clear evidence that the aforementioned occurrences have resounded significantly in localized football settings. For example, in the aftermath of the Rushdie Affair, some Leeds United supporters were reported to have chanted 'Rushdie is a Leeds fan' as a means of expressing their opposition to the (re)actions of Muslims in West Yorkshire (Fleming 1995). In July 2005, hooligans from Arsenal, Crystal Palace, Millwall and West Ham were found to be communicating over the internet regarding the need to put aside club rivalries and form a London-based front against Muslims. Subsequently, a match between Millwall and Iran, as part of the latter's UK tour, was called off due to fears that it would be targeted by Far Right extremists[6] (Muir 2005). Later that year, Tottenham's Egyptian striker Mido was taunted with chants of 'shoe bomber' and 'your mother's a terrorist', the former a reference to Richard Reid, the British Muslim man jailed for attempting to blow up an aeroplane using explosives concealed in the soles of his training shoes (Jacob 2005).

Up to the present time, anti-Islamic sentiments in football have not been directed towards British Asian players, for they have not been present in professional football as a significant 'Other'. However, in one particularly ominous example, one (Muslim) British Pakistani professional player recounted an exchange that he had with a teenage academy player in the aftermath of 9/11:

> One of the kids at [my club], he was late for football and I said, 'What are you late for?' And he went, 'Shut up you terrorist!' He called me a terrorist! And I just thought, like, you ignorant little kid. I was going to actually whack him. It was on a Saturday when a match was on, but I just ignored him. I told my manager and he got a bollocking. I just felt like hitting him. On the pitch sometimes, they say, 'You Paki', and this and that. It gets to me sometimes.
>
> (Interview, 20 March 2002)

With regard to *amateur* football, the research for this book did not uncover any specific incidents of Islamophobia, although it exists in a variety of other British sporting spheres. For example, in August 2003, British Muslims playing for St Chad's in the amateur Wetherby Cricket League (in Yorkshire) were racially abused and labelled 'al-Qaeda members' by opposition supporters (Wainwright 2003). As this book has highlighted, Muslim clubs are well represented within the sphere of British Asian amateur football, which would suggest that Islamophobia inevitably occurs here as well.

One of the corollaries of the upsurge in Islamophobia is that non-Muslim British Asians have also been implicated and targeted. Following 9/11 and 7/7, a significant number of other British Asians, particularly Sikhs – because of the fact that Osama bin Laden, the person believed to be responsible for orchestrating the attacks on the USA, wears a form of turban – were victims of verbal and physical racist attacks (Shah and Das Gupta 2001; Birt 2006). In football, following the death of the Leeds United supporters in Istanbul in 2000, the (then) club chairman, Peter Ridsdale, claimed that reports of racism at their Elland Road stadium increased and that, in particular, a number of British Asians were assaulted in the vicinity of the ground (Football Unites Racism Divides 2000). A widespread public inability to distinguish between different British Asian groups means that current manifestations of Islamophobia in football could affect the inclusion/exclusion of *all* British Asians, not simply Muslims, at both amateur and professional levels. A related current trend is for non-Muslim groups to endorse dominant perceptions of the Islamic 'Other' and to try to construct divisions between themselves and Muslims. For example, after the urban unrest in 2001, many British Asians sought to avoid being implicated in an anti-Muslim backlash by actively distancing themselves from Muslims (Kundnani 2002a). By highlighting their difference and aligning themselves with white players and supporters against the mutual Muslim 'Other', Hindus and Sikhs could potentially gain a degree of contingent inclusion in 'mainstream' player and supporter subcultural collectivities.

Whatever the specific, immediate repercussions of Islamophobia, anti-Muslim sentiment will have further, long-term consequences and, most likely, will sustain the marginalization and exclusion of British Asians from professional football.

The next chapter examines some of the consequences of, and reactions to, racism and Islamophobia. Specifically, it examines the trend for British Asian footballers to underplay their ethnic identities and adopt certain behavioural strategies in order to try to minimize their 'Otherness' and, consequently, gain inclusion in the dominant player cultures of professional football.

4 Ethnicity, hybridity and cultural capital

Introduction

The paucity of British Asians in professional football first started to receive serious recognition at the beginning of the twenty-first century, as various individuals and groups sought to endorse, extend or contest the findings and recommendations of the seminal *Asians Can't Play Football* report (Bains and Patel 1996). In the years between this publication and its sequel *Asians Can Play Football* (Asians in Football Forum 2005), the topic was analysed by academics (Johal 2001; McGuire *et al.* 2001; Burdsey 2004a; Burdsey 2004b; Magee and Olsson 2005), received attention from governing bodies and the media, and became a primary focus for anti-racist football organizations.

However, despite the detailed and illuminating historical accounts provided, in particular, by Jas Bains and his colleagues (Bains and Patel 1996; Bains and Johal 1998), a significant misconception has remained – the belief that British Asian involvement in the professional game is a very recent occurrence.[1] Consequently, little attention has been given to the select band of British Asians who previously have played at professional level. This failure to highlight their achievements and to allow them to speak about their experiences represents a missed opportunity to establish ways to modify procedures and facilitate greater contemporary inclusion. Furthermore, it has prevented the unearthing of two significant trends regarding their social identities, i.e. that they have tended to be of dual ethnicity and/or that they have experienced an Anglicized process of socialization. This chapter takes the under-representation of British Asians as professional footballers and locates it within wider debates on ethnicity, hybridity, cultural difference, cultural/social capital and 'whiteness'. It examines the significance of these phenomena and their influence on the processes of inclusion and exclusion that dictate the involvement of British Asians in English professional football.

British Asians and the commodification of ethnicity

Concerns about the under-representation of British Asians in professional football are directly related to the increasing emphasis on issues of equity and inclusion in the game. However, the current upsurge in general interest about British Asian footballers – within football, the media and the public – needs to be located firmly within shifting popular cultural politics and patterns of consumption in relation to notions of 'Asianness' in Britain during the early twenty-first century. During this period public perceptions about, and representations of, British Asians were subject to considerable debate and became increasingly contradictory. In 2001, in the aftermath of 9/11 and the urban unrest in northern England, British Asians (particularly young, male Muslims) were considered *persona non grata* and, in sections of the media, they were criticized and admonished to a degree previously only witnessed in the wake of the Rushdie Affair. Conversely, the hypocrisy of the mass media was demonstrated only a year later, as notions of 'Asianness' began to be celebrated and embraced rather than feared and rejected, and the white British 'mainstream' engaged with, and consumed, aspects of South Asian (although usually marketed as Indian) popular culture in a manner unprecedented since the hippy-instigated appropriation of the late 1960s. As Alexander (2000: 230) points out, 'as a mode of consumption, the 'ethnic' has never been so fashionable, nor so profitable'. In 2001 the notion 'British Asian' was anathema; within twelve months it had become a marketing dream.

On the cinema screen aspiring young female (although, significantly, not male) British Asian footballers were encouraged to *Bend It Like Beckham*[2] and this provided the context in which a variety of journalistic pieces about British Asian players were written. Another dominant cultural concept was Bollywood, the Bombay-based centre of the Indian film industry. Channel Four screened a number of Bollywood classics as part of its high profile 'Indian Summer' season, whilst Shekhar Kapur and Andrew Lloyd Webber entertained West End theatre audiences with their production of A. R. Rahman's *Bombay Dreams*. Department store Selfridges and the Victoria and Albert museum both hosted Bollywood exhibitions, and high-street stores Marks and Spencer and Topshop introduced Bollywood-influenced fashion ranges. Bollywood films were screened at Test cricket grounds and at Regent's Park in London and Roundhay Park in Leeds, whilst a bhangra band played a prominent part in the musical displays at the opening ceremony for the 2002 Commonwealth Games in Manchester. Bollywood dancers also achieved an increasing ubiquity on our television screens, in music videos for white musicians ranging from dance duo Basement Jaxx (*Romeo*) to Gareth Gates (*Spirit in the Sky*, the official 2003 Comic Relief charity record), in television advertisements for Halifax bank and Walker's Crisps, and in programme trailers for the BBC.

These contrasting images embody what Hutnyk labels the 'exotica–fanatica' two-step. He argues that British Asians are:

> Characterised in a double strategy, either as demons or as exotica, and neither stereotype comes close to an appreciation of the diversity of those under anthropological examination. The double strategy makes Asians either, and both, a people of curious culture – bhangra, spicy food, Bollywood – and a people of fanaticism – Islam, Hindutva, religious extremism.
>
> (2005: 348)

Whilst many commentators have lauded the appropriation of elements of South Asian cultures and pointed to their wider social significance, these cultural forms are not simply passively transmitted and diffused into British society. In most cases they are purposefully chosen, by a variety of agencies – from television companies to high street retailers – and consciously modified, diluted and marketed to suit a variety of white British audiences. For example, chicken tikka masala, often cited as one of the nation's favourite dishes[3] and evidence of Britons' love of curry, actually bears little resemblance to traditional South Asian food. The profile of British Asian musicians also has begun to register on the mainstream music radar with the dawning of the 'Asian Underground'[4] scene and prime-time shows presented by Bobby Friction, Nihal and Panjabi Hit Squad on BBC Radio. Yet it remains the case that most success has been achieved through traditionally white music genres,[5] such as Indie (Black Star Liner, Cornershop, Echobelly, Whitetown and Babylon Zoo), or by fusing traditional South Asian rhythms with Hip-Hop or House sounds and vocals, e.g. Hard Kaur, Panjabi MC, Ms. Scandalous, MIA and Talvin Singh.[6] Conversely, radical outfits such as Asian Dub Foundation and Fun∧Da∧Mental remain marginal to this scene because the politics of Nation, their record label, are 'a little hot for chart success' (Hutnyk 2000: 8). Furthermore, whilst British Asians have made a small breakthrough in television comedy with shows such as *The Kumars at No. 12*, *Goodness Gracious Me!* and *Meet the Magoons*, they are constructed in the format of traditional 'white' comedy shows, and *The Kumars* tends to involve predominantly white celebrity guests.[7]

The commodification of ethnicity does not *inevitably* result in superficial and banal forms of multiculture (Dwyer and Crang 2002) yet, with the above examples, the transformation and repackaging that occurs as part of their cross-cultural appropriation means that, for the most part, they represent little more than 'spaces which offer a primarily middle-class constituency a sanitized encounter with an imagined Asian "other"' (Banerjea 2000: 65). As Banerjea (ibid.) states, 'they allow for white folk to rub shoulders with a carefully constructed exotica and for the perpetuation of a myth of multiculture'. Similarly, Sharma argues that:

> The celebratory constituents of multiculturalism such as the impact of popular Asian dance music or the declaration that 'Indian curry' is Britain's national dish hardly designate that Asian culture has been finally liberated from its orientalized status. On the contrary, the recognition of multiculture cannot be divorced from the concurrent intensification of the fetishization of ethnic otherness in the West.
>
> (2003: 411)

Whilst for some people this celebration of alterity represents genuine support for multiculturalism, for others it may operate alongside, and assuage their guilt over, criticisms of, for example, arranged marriages or Muslim reactions to newspaper cartoons of the prophet Muhammad. Alexander and Knowles (2005: 3) point out that 'The focus on difference and the celebration of marginality that has accompanied the fragmentation of identity has made the structures that maintain racial violence, exclusion and inequality less visible'. Whilst they may be less visible, they remain enduringly present and it is crucial to recognize that engagements with 'Asianness' continue to exist simultaneously alongside racial and religious discrimination, and violence against British Asians.[8] The trends discussed above provide the context for the issues discussed in this chapter regarding the selective and conditional nature of British Asian inclusion in professional football. The issue of cultural assimilation is explored later, but first the analysis concentrates on the implications of players with dual ethnicities.

From the Cothers to Chopra: Anglo-Asians, identity and English professional football

In recent years, academics have paid increasing attention to the heterogeneity of British Asian communities, and the way that differences and divisions reflect the ethnic, religious, linguistic and caste boundaries of the subcontinent (e.g. R. Ballard 1994a; Ali *et al.* 2006). Furthermore, the birth of subsequent generations in Britain, and the influence of not only subcontinental, but also local and global cultures has led to an acknowledgment of post-modern or fragmented identities which no longer situate young British Asians within the old axiom of being 'caught between cultures'. As Brah (1996: 41–2) highlights, this idea not only propagated an essentialist notion of distinct, monolithic 'British' and 'Asian' cultures, but also it failed to allow for the possibility of cultural interaction and hybridization, and portrayed young British Asians as 'disoriented, confused and atomised individuals'. Instead it has become evident that rather than experiencing these forms of spatial and generational dislocation, there are increasing segments of the British population that are actively creating novel and multiple forms of identity. As Caglar (1997: 170) points out, 'in refocusing on the social formations and "disjunct" subjectivities of persons with multilocale and translocal attachments, a number of concepts have come to be celebrated: "hybrid", "creolized", "hyphenated" and "diasporic" identities are the most prominent among them'.

Nevertheless, considerably less attention has been paid to a specific grouping in the broad British Asian collectivity – Anglo-Asians, i.e. those people with both a white and a South Asian parent. Whilst there has been a recent proliferation in academic studies of people who are 'mixed-race', 'dual ethnicity' or 'multiracial' (Ifekwunigwe 1999; Parker and Song 2001; Tizard and Phoenix 2002; S. Ali 2003; Dalmage 2004; Ifekwunigwe 2004), the lack of qualitative research specifically about Anglo-*Asians* represents a considerable lacuna in this field. This is somewhat surprising, taking into account the marked increase in the number of people to whom this categorization applies (Alibhai-Brown 2001a). In particular, if one looks at those British Asians who have been most successful within 'entertainment' media, it is evident that many of them possess dual

South Asian and white ethnicities, such as the actors Chris Bisson, Raji James and Jimi Mistri,[9] novelist Hanif Kureishi, chat show host Melanie Sykes, and writer/producer Anil Gupta. In sport, some of the most high profile members of the select band of British Asians to participate at elite level are Anglo-Asians,[10] for example, England international cricketers Nasser Hussain and Vikram Solanki, and golfer Sandeep Grewal. Whilst it is beginning to change, this is also the case in football, where the majority of players of South Asian heritage to have played at professional level have been of dual South Asian and white ethnicities (see below).

As these examples demonstrate, it is important to stress that this pattern is not uniform across all ethnic groups. Whilst Indians and East African Asians (predominantly of Indian origin) are relatively likely to marry white partners (19 per cent of British-born men and 10 per cent of British-born women from these groups, respectively), this is not the case for Bangladeshis or Pakistanis who, for a variety of reasons, tend to marry within their specific groupings (Berthoud and Beishon 1997). Consequently, in terms of the overall population, the majority of Anglo-Asians tend to be of Indian origin. However, players are referred to in this chapter who are of heterogeneous Anglo-*Bangladeshi*, Anglo-*Indian* or Anglo-*Pakistani* backgrounds. Where appropriate, these classifications are employed, yet at other times, although it is by no means ideal, it is more logical to use the general category of Anglo-Asians.

The first players of South Asian heritage to play in English professional football were the Anglo-Indian Cother brothers, John 'Jack' William and Edwin 'Eddie', who played for Watford in the late nineteenth century. In the 1950s, Anglo-Pakistani Roy Smith represented West Ham United, whilst the succeeding two decades saw the most significant contribution (in terms of number of appearances) with the Anglo-Indian trio of Brian 'Bud' Houghton (Cambridge United, Oxford United and Southend United), Ricky Heppolette (Preston North End, Leyton Orient, Crystal Palace and Chesterfield) and Kevin Keelan (Norwich City) (Vasili 2000).[11] Heppolette was born in Bhuswal (near Mumbai), but emigrated to Britain with his parents at the age of three. Bains and Patel (1996: 10) state that 'the Heppolette household was English speaking and had little in common with most native Indians...although Ricky Heppolette is of Indian origin, throughout his life he has had little to do with Indian culture or religion'. Two of the most prominent British Asian professional players in the early twenty-first century, Michael Chopra and Anwar Uddin, both have white mothers, and Indian and Bangladeshi fathers, respectively.

Obviously there are a number of exceptions where players whose parents are *both* of a South Asian background have made the grade as professionals. During the 1980s, Naseem Bashir made a brief number of league appearances for Reading, whilst players in the early twenty-first century include Adnan Ahmed, Shahed Ahmed, Zesh Rehman and Harpal Singh. However, it is evident that those players with two British Asian parents who have reached the higher echelons of English football have tended to come from Anglicized backgrounds. A prime example is Chris Dolby, who made sporadic appearances for Bradford City and

Rotherham in the early 1990s. Whilst Dolby's biological mother and father were both South Asian, he was adopted as a baby by white parents and thus his upbringing reflected the culture of his adoptive family. The presence of a small number of British Asians in English professional football suggests that, contrary to popular stereotypes, simply possessing a South Asian background – either partially or fully – cannot completely account for a player's failure to make the grade at professional level. Instead, one needs to unravel a far more complex matrix of factors, processes and power relations in order to understand the nexus between British Asians and participation in professional football. When one examines the personal and career biographies of past and current British Asian players, it is clear that the focus of analysis needs to be directed towards the extent to which they are able to minimize – consciously or unconsciously – their difference and under-emphasize those aspects of their cultural background most antithetical to 'mainstream', i.e. white, professional football cultures.

Assimilated ethnicities and becoming 'one of the lads'

Describing the options facing minority ethnic groups in terms of career progression, Goldberg states that:

> Black people are faced with the dilemma that the principal mode of progress and self-elevation open to them is precisely through self-denial, through the effacement, the obliteration, of their blackness. They are predicated, that is, upon the possibility of rendering a significant feature of their self-definition invisible, if not altogether effaced.
>
> (1996: 185)

The central question for the present analysis is: Do British Asian players acknowledge the cultural parameters that dictate participation, inclusion and a sense of belonging in professional football, and recognize the need to play down their alterity? The following analysis suggests that the answer is yes – like their peers they experience, comprehend and articulate the complexities inherent in notions of 'Asianness' and the fact that it is largely regarded as anathema to the world of English football. Consequently, they believe that deprioritizing aspects of their ethnic and cultural identities is crucial if they are to gain inclusion as 'one of the lads'.

The term 'lad' is subject to contrasting definitions and differs across geographical and temporal contexts. Since the 1960s, in Britain the term has tended to be associated with studies of deviance and white youth subcultures. By the late twentieth century, 'lad' was normally used to refer to a young (usually white) man who indulges in alcohol, football and promiscuous sexual intercourse and 'shuns feminism and homosexuality like the plague' (Redhead 1997: 99). In contrast, notions of 'Asianness' and 'laddishness' traditionally have been viewed as incompatible. However, the involvement of some young, working-class British Asian men in urban unrest, together with an increasing proclivity for designer clothing and, evidence implies, the consumption of recreational drugs, suggests that in some social spheres they are adopting the 'lad' lifestyles associated with some of their white peers.

In professional football, being 'one of the lads' refers to the degree to which players share, and are invited to participate in, the dominant cultural 'habitus' (Bourdieu 1978, 1984, 1988) of their team-mates. One of the most frequently employed definitions of habitus is:

> A system of durable, transposable dispositions, structured structures predisposed to function as structuring structures, that is, as principles which generate and organize practices and representations that can be objectively adapted to their outcomes without presupposing a conscious aiming at ends or an express mastery of the operations necessary in order to attain them.
>
> (Bourdieu 1990: 53)

Fundamentally, habitus refers to the system of dispositions, tastes and preferences that underpin particular lifestyles (Bourdieu 1977). Whilst habituses differ greatly between player cultures at different clubs, there is likely to be a greater degree of commonality amongst *young* players when peer conformity to appearance, clothing, behaviour and recreational activities is arguably greater. Furthermore, unlike some other social spheres, in football being 'one of the lads' still strongly retains its traditional connotations – ones that are inextricably linked to notions of 'whiteness', masculinity and heteronormativity (Parker 2001).

In the 1970s, Rajinder Singh Virdee, a Kenyan-born Indian who had moved to England as a child, signed as a professional for Ipswich Town. After his failure to break into the first team, he embarked on a successful playing career in North America. However, the record books refer to him as Roger Verdi, the pseudonym he adopted to mask his ethnic identity throughout his time in the game (Dasgupta 2005). Whilst such a drastic move has not been repeated, the perceptions and attitudes of a number of former and current British Asian players strongly suggest that they also actively sought, or are seeking, to under-emphasize their 'Asianness'. This is because modifying their demeanour and behaviour in this way is more likely to facilitate their acceptance as 'one of the lads'. For example, the co-ordinator of one British Asian football scheme described the award of a professional contract to a British Asian player. In particular, he explained how the player's ethnicity was not recognized by some of the coaches at the club and how he subsequently 'passed' for white:

> When I first met [my club's] youth team director... and we talked about [that British Asian player], he said, 'He ain't fucking Asian, is he?' I said 'The name's a bit of a clue, isn't it?' and he said, 'Yeah!'.... He hadn't even noticed that [he] was Asian. He'd noticed he was a centre-half and assured me he'd have a career in the game because he's good enough. And they gave him a contract.
>
> (Interview, 20 February 2002)

In describing his transition into the game Anwar Uddin states that 'To be honest, *I wasn't conscious of the fact that I was Asian.* I just wanted to become a football player and I didn't want anything to get in the way of that' (cited in BBC TV 2003a). He adds that 'I don't really think of myself as being an Asian footballer. I'm a footballer, *just one of the lads*' (cited in Herman 2001, emphasis added). Jas Juttla, formerly of Glasgow Rangers and Greenock Morton, recalls that:

> Looking back I am very thankful that no one asked what it was like being an Asian player. That helped me feel as if I was not under the spotlight, and *made me feel very much like one of the lads.*
>
> (Cited in Bains and Johal 1998: 161, emphasis added)

Similarly Harpal Singh remarks that 'I try not to look at the fact that I'm different from everybody else' (cited in Dasgupta 2005: 43).

These sentiments are echoed by a number of other players. For example, one British Pakistani professional player stated that:

> I'm trying to just play my football, not everyone saying, 'Oh, you're Asian, you will be the first Asian player to do this, the first Asian player to do that'. That'd put pressure on me as well. I wouldn't want that pressure. *I just play like any other white kid out there playing, another white person.*
>
> (Interview, 20 March 2002)

Another player added that, 'I didn't say "I'm Asian, I'm different from all the others". I still saw myself as *a normal YTS player like any of the others*, just trying to become professional football players' (interview with British Indian ex-professional player, 11 March 2002). Key to both these testimonies is the notion of 'normality' which, in these instances, tellingly is equated with being white.

Although, in most instances, skin colour and name prevent a fully covert presence within the sport, British Asian professional footballers have sought almost to disguise other aspects of their 'Asianness', such as clothing, argot and religious adherence. This is an interesting development when placed in the context of contemporary trends in the identity politics of young British Asians, as a number of empirical studies have highlighted the tendency for second and third generation British Bangladeshis (e.g. Eade 1994; Gardner and Shukur 1994) and Pakistanis (e.g. Werbner 1996a; Jacobson 1997; Samad 1998; Vertovec 1998; Saaed *et al.* 1999) to promote their ethnic and/or Islamic identities. The re-emergence of Hindu nationalism in India and a desire to distance themselves from Muslims (see Chapter 7) have led many diasporic Hindus to prioritize their 'Hinduness' (Raj 2000), whilst representatives from Britain's Sikh communities have lobbied the government to change their official status from their current designation as British Indians to one that highlights their distinct Sikh identities. However, this chapter only examines British Asian players' identities in the context of their footballing careers. It would be difficult to speculate whether their ethnic or cultural identities are promoted to a greater (or lesser) extent in other private or public spheres, although any differences should not come as a surprise given the dynamic, fluctuating and multiple nature of social identities, and their tendency to change in form and priority depending on the individual, time and context. As Stuart Hall has famously argued:

> The fully unified, completed, secure and coherent identity is a fantasy. Instead, as the systems of meaning and cultural representation multiply, we are confronted by a bewildering, fleeting multiplicity of possible identities, any one of which we could identify with – at least temporarily.
>
> (1992b: 277)

Thus it appears that, within the context of professional football, British Asians are exercising their 'ethnic options' (Song 2003) and exhibiting one of many *situational* identities (Modood 1997a). A pertinent question is therefore: What is it about professional football that means that achieving inclusion as 'one of the lads' requires British Asian players to underplay their 'Otherness'? This is discussed later in the chapter.

'Not just chapattis and stuff': socialization and cultural capital

As well as the degree to which a player under-emphasizes his ethno-cultural difference, equal importance needs to be given to the extent to which the processes of parenting and socialization equipped him with the appropriate cultural capital to play professional football in the first place. For Bourdieu (1984), capital is any resource that is effective in a given social arena, in that it enables a person or group to secure the specific profits arising out of participation in it. For the present analysis, cultural capital refers to the degree to which individuals have absorbed the dominant culture of professional football and are thus able to achieve success in this environment. Professional football therefore represents a 'field' (Bourdieu 1990, 1993), a structured space of positions that imposes specific determinations on those who enter it. A field also represents an arena of contestation where individuals and institutions can maintain – or, indeed, challenge – the existing distribution of power and capital. Involvement and attainment in a field are based on a combination of one's habitus and cultural capital. Those with the most capital can dictate the legitimate means of access to a field (Bourdieu 1986).

To gain inclusion and to succeed in professional football, one has to acquire and abide by the values and regulations, i.e. the dominant habitus, of this field. For young white players, their habituses are more likely to be commensurable with those of professional football. As Bourdieu and Wacquant (2002: 127) state, 'When habitus encounters a social world of which it is the product, it is like a "fish in water". It does not feel the weight of the water, and it takes the world about itself for granted'. Or, put more simply, white players 'merely need to be what they are in order to be what they have to be' (Bourdieu 1990: 11). In contrast, whilst the testimonies cited above highlight that some young British Asians evidently possess the appropriate cultural capital to become professional footballers, many others – particularly those players whose upbringings have not been very 'Westernized' – have not. They *do* feel the weight of the water. They remain marginalized and excluded because the cultural resources that they possess, and the ways in which they are socialized in the family, are not easily converted into the capital – either cultural (the specific patterns of consumption and style) or social (acquaintances and networks) – needed for involvement in professional football.

Traditionally, the scouting procedures by which young players are recruited by professional clubs have revolved around established networks of relations between parents, school teachers, amateur club managers and county selectors, and their inside knowledge of, and contacts within, local professional clubs. Therefore, for those players seeking to enter the professional sphere from amateur youth football, having the appropriate cultural resources and an existing chain of contacts to the professional game is a significant advantage. In the late 1990s the FA sought to standardize and professionalize the way that young players are recruited and developed by introducing a system of Football Academies. These are special development centres, attached to professional clubs and designed to coach talented players aged between seven and nineteen. However, the guidelines published by the Premier League informing prospective players and their parents how they should approach a club for a trial are not widely available and, paradoxically, are usually only obtained when a player has already made contact with a particular club. As a result, those young players who do not possess contacts through which to find out about and access professional football's recruiting system continue to be disadvantaged. This applies to a number of social groups, but particularly is the case for British Asians. Their historical and contemporary exclusion from professional football as players, coaches, managers, administrators and directors[12] means that they do not possess a network of family, friends or professional contacts within the game for current players to utilize, whilst established networks used by white players remain closed and inaccessible. The following players stated that:

> There's loads of [Asian] kids that can play, but they don't know how to get into a team. They need someone to, like, help them get into a team, go for a trial or whatever. But it's hard because the parents don't really understand that much, so they need someone outside the family giving them help and advice.
> (Interview with British Pakistani professional player, 11 February 2002)

> It does depend on how the family is as well, whether they help [the player], because they wouldn't know about it either. No one's experienced it before. And they can't exactly go and ask their cousins or someone they know

because no one else has done it. They don't know someone who's become a footballer.

(Interview with British Indian ex-professional player, 11 March 2002)

Another player compared professional football to other industries:

How are you going to make any contact if you know the contacts are not of your colour? Do you see what I mean, Dan? If you want to go into an Indian industry you don't go to 'John', you go to 'Sanjay' because he's got all the contacts. He knows who to go to and where to go to because it's his industry, he knows all about it.

(Interview with British Pakistani ex-professional player, 20 February 2002)

Jas Juttla is even more succinct, recalling that 'neither my father nor I had any idea of the routine when it came to signing up as a professional' (cited in Bains and Johal 1998: 160). Fundamentally, professional football is a sphere in which British Asians lack the appropriate 'cultural passports' (Bauman 1988) or, to use a more appropriate analogy, it is a game in which they are denied an 'entry ticket' (Back *et al.* 2001b: 141).

In trying to understand the factors that exclude British Asians from professional football, one might draw certain parallels with rugby league, arguably the closest sport to football in terms of its ethos of traditional white, working-class masculinity. Despite the fact that the majority of professional clubs are located within the major conurbations of Lancashire and Yorkshire – thus including towns and cities with significant British Asian populations – rugby league has also failed to facilitate the inclusion of British Asians, both as players and spectators. Long and Spracklen (1996) suggest that this can be attributed to the fact that whilst white players are often inducted into the professional game through a 'traditional' route, such as an introduction by a friend or family member, this route is less accessible to minority ethnic groups. Spracklen (2001) develops this argument through the use of 'imagined communities'. He argues that in rugby league these communities privilege a specific white, masculine, local identity which includes white players, but excludes and discriminates against British Asian and black groups. Taking into account the player testimonies cited above, British Asians' access to professional football appears to be inhibited by similar factors.

Accordingly, there is a belief amongst many British Asian players that those who have been socialized into what can loosely be described as 'Western' as well as 'South Asian' cultures are better equipped to gain access to professional level. It is felt that a more Anglicized upbringing provides a greater degree of the specific cultural capital that young players need to become involved with a professional club. As one British Pakistani professional player recalled:

I had a mixed diet as well and not just Asian food because that's another stereotype. [People] think that the diet is wrong. It is true to a certain extent, but I have a mixed diet because my parents understand that I have to have pasta and potatoes and stuff, not just chapatis and stuff, so I have a mixed diet now.

(Interview, 11 February 2002)

Other players perceive that *Anglo*-Asians are better equipped to become professional footballers than other British Asians because one of their parents is white. One player suggested how this might operate:

The bearing that it could have is possibly that the support has been there for them, you know, from their parents. So, obviously, because their parents are from a mixed marriage, you know, their outlook on life is more Westernized than possibly, you know, if their parents were born back in India or whatever.

(Interview with British Indian amateur player, 5 February 2002)

Interestingly, a further viewpoint proposed that the presence of a white parent could actually result in Anglo-Asians receiving more favourable treatment from professional clubs – albeit often subconsciously – than other British Asians:

I would say the difference is if you've got a lad there who is of mixed-race, if the white side of his parents goes and knocks on that manager's door, he'll probably open that door, sit the person down, give them a nice cup of tea and that, because they'll have the perception that this person knows about football because they've been brought up in this country. But if a parent comes that is Asian, you know, they'll think, 'They don't know anything about football, so we can get away with blagging [lying], you know, we can get away with talking any kind of things because they won't understand it'. Whereas if you've got someone banging the door, [saying] 'What's going on with my son, yeah, he wants to be a footballer', all of a sudden they look up and he's of mixed-race, but the white half of his parents has come in, you know what I mean, it's totally different. I'm not saying they're racist, but it becomes different.

(Interview with British Pakistani ex-professional player, 20 February 2002)

These testimonies represent rather simplistic and essentialist interpretations of what constitute 'Western' and 'South Asian' upbringings, and consequently they reinforce dominant West/non-West binaries. They also, it could be argued, over-simplify both the processes involved in becoming a professional footballer and the complex, multifarious, subtle and nuanced ways that white privilege manifests itself in the game. Notwithstanding this, the broad issues expressed in these statements, and their interpretations of the wider racialized biases inherent to professional football recruitment, clearly possess a degree of accuracy.

'Whiteness' and professional football

Whilst there are evidently a variety of socio-psychological reasons why players wish to modify their behaviour in line with that of the dominant group, in order to understand why British Asians deprioritize their ethnic identities one needs to examine more closely how 'whiteness' operates in the game. Long and Hylton (2002) highlight that 'whiteness' traditionally has undergone little examination within mainstream (sport) sociology, yet as Hemant Shah points out, it has received considerable attention from minority ethnic scholars:

> Whiteness as an unarticulated norm, along with the assumption of its naturalness and correctness, has been under scrutiny from scholars of color for some time. . . . Of course, however, most of this scholarship was relegated to the margins of mainstream academe – in journals with limited or very specialized readership, in the fringes of college curricula, or in programs that are awarded few resources.
>
> (H. Shah 2004: 12)

The testimonies included and the arguments raised in this chapter regarding ethnic assimilation and cultural capital highlight the existence of a normative or hegemonic 'whiteness' that permeates professional football and serves to marginalize and exclude minority ethnic players. As Ismond (2003: 20) points out: 'For British Asians, *whiteness* functions both within recreational sport, and at the level of dissuasion from a professional career'. In this regard, '"whiteness" signals the production and reproduction of dominance rather than subordination, normativity rather than marginality, and privilege rather than disadvantage' (Frankenberg 1993: 237). 'Whiteness' has tended to be seen as amorphous and nebulous, and so '[whites] can't see that we have anything that accounts for our position of privilege and power. This is crucial to the security with which we occupy that position' (Dyer 1997: 9). Yet, as S. Ahmed (2004: para. 1) points out: 'Of course whiteness is only invisible for those who inhabit it. For those who don't, it is hard not to see whiteness; it even seems everywhere'. In football 'whiteness' is seen as normal and unproblematic, and is not racialized in the manner of minority ethnic identities. It empowers and promotes the interests of those in positions of power, whilst its marginalizing and discriminatory effects go ignored and unchallenged.

The implications of 'whiteness' have been examined by King (2004a) in relation to the experiences of African-Caribbean players and coaches. He argues that 'White personnel, through their mundane and everyday actions, develop an institutional culture that manifests the patterns of inclusion and exclusion that are faced by black and Asian men' (ibid.: 96). Puwar analyses the position of racialized bodies in other white spaces, such as the elite institutions of parliament and Whitehall. She argues that:

> Whilst they have to admit that skin colour is a permanent feature of their bodily appearance, they can change or slowly 'whitewash' bodily gestures,

> social interests, value systems and speech patterns. . . . Adherence to the norms and values of this hegemonic culture is almost a condition of entry.
>
> (Puwar 2005: 150)

This 'whitewashing' is also evident in professional football. Long and Hylton (2002: 97) argue that 'The social processes representing whiteness [in football] defend institutions, power relations, the "normal" and the "other". But it is a very particular form of whiteness worked out in a tough, heterosexual, predominantly working/lower middle class domain'. 'Whiteness' dominates player subcultures and permeates the networks by which players are recruited into the game. Thus, as the testimonies in this chapter demonstrate, adherence to a dominant, white cultural code is hugely beneficial for minority ethnic players, resulting in greater achievement and success and facilitating (contingent) inclusion as 'one of the lads'. Put simply, it can be argued that the British Asian players who have been most successful are those that have adopted the 'white mask'. The concept of the 'white mask' was used by Fanon (1986) to analyse the way in which black people in post-colonial societies were forced to adopt the language and culture of whites in order to gain social inclusion and acceptance. This concept has since been employed by King (2004a) in his account of the experiences of African-Caribbean players, coaches and managers in English professional football. He argues that the 'white mask' acts as an internal mechanism whereby black players can manage and adjust their identities to meet the demands placed upon them by the dominant white subcultures of the game. As this chapter has highlighted, a similar process appears to be evident with British Asians.

Ethnicity, hybridity and the politics of identity

Due to the historical absence of British Asians from English professional football, the social significance of the breakthrough made by Michael Chopra and Anwar Uddin (the first British Asian players who have made a significant number of appearances in recent years) is widely acknowledged by other British Asian players and supporters. Nevertheless, it is also the case that the dual ethnicity of these players (Anglo-Indian and Anglo-Bangladeshi, respectively) proves problematic for some British Asians. This is because it is believed that the personal and social backgrounds of Anglo-Asians are significantly different from those of other British Asians to make them unrepresentative of the wider British Asian population. As highlighted earlier in this chapter, many players feel that *Anglo*-Asians are able to overcome some of the factors that inhibit the participation of other British Asian players. Consequently, it is perceived that the attention given to Anglo-Asian players by anti-racist football organizations and the media, and the failure to recognize their dual ethnicity – they are usually perceived in this context solely as 'Asian' – actually masks the fact that few players with two British Asian parents have made the grade. Thus an overly benign picture is painted of the overall inclusion and participation of British Asian players in professional football – one that masks the lack of real progress by governing bodies and professional football clubs. One British Pakistani ex-professional player focused specifically on the implications for anti-racist campaign groups:

> This whole issue of, you know, Kick Out Racism [sic] and all that, they shouldn't use Anwar Uddin, they shouldn't use Michael Chopra as examples. They're not the right examples. If you want to use them as young footballers coming up, then use them for that. Do not use them for the Asian thing because they did not have the same upbringing, right, as an Asian lad who is through-and-through Asian.
>
> (Interview, 20 February 2002)

It is evident that Anglo-Asian players are placed in a particularly difficult and contradictory situation regarding their inclusion in English professional football. On the one hand they are seen by many British Asians as better placed to make it as professionals than players with two British Asian parents, yet on the other hand they are perceived to be unrepresentative of the wider British Asian population. These arguments are right to stress the heterogeneity of the British Asian population and their diverse lived experiences, but some of them tread dangerously close to both giving legitimacy to the notion of 'race' and essentializing notions of 'Asianness'. They demonstrate that Anglo-Asian players (i.e. those of dual heritage) are often perceived not to be 'real' British Asians. In other words, it is perceived that the factors that make an individual more likely to be a professional footballer also make him less Asian. An Anglo-Asian player is not viewed as Asian *enough* to be organically representative of British Asian communities as a whole. As one British Bangladeshi amateur player stated:

> If I'm being honest, if Anwar [Uddin] makes it, you know, I'll be pretty happy. I'll be even happier if somebody makes it who says, 'Before a game I need to pray', you know, or, 'After a game I need to go and see my relatives who are running a tandoori house', you know . . . I don't want to say these guys aren't Asian, because they are Asian, but . . . I would love to see, as I said, somebody who looks Asian, can speak an Asian language, whose parents are Asian, who lives in an Asian community, you know, even after making it.
>
> (Interview, 16 March 2002)

It is clear that players who are categorized as hybrid are often perceived as inauthentic members of both the ethnic and cultural groups that are represented in their identities (S. Ahmed 1997; Anthias 2001; Song 2003). More seriously, this testimony reflects interpretations of 'Asianness' that are not only narrow, fixed and static, but also *biological* and predicated on a notion of racial difference. It is common for 'Asianness' to be related to genetics, skin colour and family history – literally something that you are born with – and subsequently it is perceived that one individual can be markedly and unequivocally 'more Asian' than another. Not only are British Asian identities essentialized but, through implicit references to a dichotomy of purity and hybridity, the fallacious notion that 'race' is a scientific reality is also reinforced. Furthermore the role of agency in ethnic and racial formations is ignored, as 'Asianness' is seen to be something that is externally imposed on individuals.

The final part of this chapter examines the implications of racialized labelling for professional football in general and the wider anti-racist football movement. In order to highlight fully the ways in which certain agencies and organizations attempt to dictate or influence the ethnic affiliations of minority ethnic sports people, it is helpful first to cite a couple of comparative examples – one from golf in the USA and one from English cricket. In May 2000 the National Association for the Advancement of Colored People (NAACP) called for African American athletes to boycott events in South Carolina over the state's refusal to cease flying the Confederate flag on its Capitol building. Whilst a number of sports people supported the action,[13] golfer Tiger Woods, a self-styled 'Cablinasian'[14] of multiple ethnicities, refused to do so. He stated that, 'I'm a golfer. That's their deal, not mine' (cited in Donegan 2002: 20). Woods's decision not only surprised the American public, but also ostensibly problematized his relationship with his sponsor, the sportswear company Nike who, in a measure clearly contrary to the personal aspirations and ethnic identifications of the player himself, have openly marketed him as a 'black', i.e. African American, sportsman (Cole and Andrews 2001).

A year later, in May 2001, Anglo-Asian England cricket captain Nasser Hussain expressed his disappointment that, at a Test Match between England and Pakistan, most of the British Asians in the crowd were supporting Pakistan. Hussain explained that, 'It was disappointing to see a sea of green shirts with the names of Pakistani players instead of ours. It reminded me of when we played India at Edgbaston in 1999. It was like an away game because so many people supported their side' (cited in Chaudhary 2001). He added that, 'I cannot really understand why those born here, or who came here at a very early age like me, cannot support or follow England' (cited in Campbell 2001b). He was subsequently criticized for failing to pay sufficient attention to the South Asian component of his heritage. For example, *Guardian* journalist Vivek Chaudhary declared that, 'My message to Hussain is this. You need to get in touch with your brown side' (Chaudhary 2001). Whether these reactions accurately interpret his comments is a moot point, but Hussain's statements do suggest a lack of appreciation of how his sport reproduces ethnically exclusive notions of 'Englishness' (see Chapter 5). Another critic was Piara Powar, co-ordinator of the anti-racist football organization Kick It Out, who stated that:

> I think with Nasser Hussain the issue is the way he puts his identity out to the wider world, if you like. He very rarely talks about being of mixed Asian parentage, he very rarely talks about the way he is perceived by the majority of the population, which is as an Asian player. Now, I think if he was stronger in those terms, if he nailed his colours to the mast, so to speak,

I think we'd have more people in the Asian community who say, 'Yes, he's one of us, we respect him, we want to do what he's done'.

(BBC Radio 2002)

Not only is it debatable whether Hussain is generally seen primarily as an 'Asian' player – his name may be associated with the Middle East and he has a very light skin tone – but these comments also reproduce the 'one drop' rule of ethnic and racial identity in that Hussain is expected to identify as 'Asian' because of his Indian father. Whether he should do so any more than promote his white identity is a matter of significant contention. Attempts to establish some form of affiliation between Nasser Hussain and British Asian cricket fans also represent an essentialist interpretation of 'Asianness' through the assumption that simply sharing a South Asian name or heritage is sufficient for mutual identification with all British Asians. Hussain was born in Madras and is from a middle-class background, and thus his identity and lived experiences are hugely different from those of most young British Asians. Nevertheless, agencies involved in highlighting the absence of British Asians from professional sport and trying to facilitate their inclusion are inevitably promoting the South Asian heritage of these players. Similarly, these agencies rely to a great extent on the players themselves publicly emphasizing their 'Asianness'. However, as this chapter has shown, British Asian professional players frequently seek to underplay their ethnic identities (see also Chapter 7), which often presents distinct problems for organizations working towards British Asian inclusion. For example, Chopra acknowledged his hybridity when he said that 'I don't see myself as a role model just for the Asian community because that would mean me thinking of only half of my family' (cited in Harrison 2003). In response, a member of one anti-racist football organization stated that:

My fear about someone like Michael Chopra is that because he's mixed-race and because he will have been in a very closed environment for a long time, he may not even see himself as Asian. That is a problem and that's why you're kind of hoping [the next Asian player] is a Harpal Singh or Amrit Sidhu [both of whom have two British Asian parents] who know where they're coming from.

(Interview, 28 June 2002)

The cases of Chopra, Tiger Woods and Nasser Hussain, demonstrate how sports-people of multiple ethnicities are popularly perceived as being disorientated by their diverse heritage and unable to engage in coherent self-identification. They also show how a variety of agencies impose upon multi-ethnic people those identities that they believe to be the most relevant for their own agendas (Ifekwunigwe 1999; Tizard and Phoenix 2002). Representations of ethnic identity in football are often based on simplistic and essentialist models and an inadequate understanding of the processes by which role models are selected and admired.

The next chapter continues the focus on hybridity and multiple identities. It widens the lens of investigation to a global setting, examining the manner in which football is used as a means of articulating diasporic British Asian identities, and the way that allegiances and affiliations within the realm of international sport reflect notions of citizenship and belonging in early twenty-first-century Britain.

5　Identity, diaspora and citizenship

Introduction

In 1990, Conservative MP Norman Tebbit made his now infamous speech regarding citizenship, belonging, and the ethnic and national identities of migrant groups in Britain. He proposed that being a British citizen and taking up residence in England should preclude any continuing connection and affiliation with the nation(s) of one's ancestry. Speaking before a Test match between England and India, he stated that:

> If you come to live in a country and take up the passport of that country, and you see your future and your family's future in that country, it seems to me that is your country. You can't just keep harking back.

> (Cited in Werbner 2002: 226)

Exemplifying the racist political rhetoric of the New Right (perhaps most famously espoused in Margaret Thatcher's 'swamping' speech[1]), according to the 'rules' of the 'Tebbit test', possession of multiple, globally situated forms of identification and allegiance were not conducive to the stability of the modern British state. The argument purported that retaining cultural attachments to their 'homeland(s)' prevented the assimilation of minority ethnic groups into the national polity and thus was likely to result in social conflict rather than cohesion.

Nearly two decades later, Tebbit's comments remain insidiously audible. The nomenclature may have changed – 'integration' has replaced 'assimilation' as the new political buzzword of 'race relations' – but debates surrounding 'race', multiculturalism, identity and citizenship continue to permeate political agendas and media discourses. This is particularly the case in the post-9/11 climate in which 'Britishness' and 'Asianness', according to certain dominant discourses, have become oppositional and conflicting identities (Sayyid 2006). Evidence comes from media allegations about British Muslims from Crawley and Luton fighting in Afghanistan for the Taliban against British and American armed forces, and the fact that the 7/7 London suicide-bombers were 'home-grown' British-born young men. The hugely unrepresentative nature of these examples and the role of British foreign policy in fuelling Muslim resentment are ignored. However, critical voices have challenged the illogical and racist nature of Tebbit's statement and his supporters. For example, Lady Amos, Leader (yet one of very few minority ethnic members) of the House of Lords was recorded as saying that 'it depresses me that people still give credit to the Tebbit test, not least because it's an incredibly un-British test to make. Un-British because it can't get past the colour of someone's skin' (cited in White 2004: 10). Instead, she proposed what she called 'Amir's boxing test', which rather than arguing about the antithetical nature of 'Britishness' and minority ethnic identities, sought to endorse and celebrate their mutuality. Invoking notions of hybridity and diasporic identifications, the 'test' was based on the statement of British Asian boxer, Amir Khan: 'I'm Asian, but I'm British – I was born here, I went to school here, all my mates are British, and I'm proud to represent my country' (cited in ibid.).

Both 'tests' reinforce dominant contemporaneous discourses surrounding ethnic and national identity and citizenship. In particular, they reflect the continuing centrality, and contested position, of British Asians in public, political and media debates about belonging and social inclusion. Of further significance, yet widely ignored, is the fact that, in both instances, it was sport that was selected to articulate wider political rhetoric. This demonstrates that sport is not simply a marginal, trivial form of popular culture that exists outside and uninfluenced by wider socio-political structures and patterns of stratification, as is often purported in both popular and academic discourses. Rather, sport is indisputably a primary arena in which issues of identity are constructed, contested and modified. For example, as Carrington and McDonald (2001a: 2) claim, 'sport is a particularly useful sociological site for examining the changing context and content of contemporary British racisms, as it articulates the complex interplay of "race", nation, culture and identity in very public and direct ways'. Similarly, Carrington (2004b: 2) points out that, 'As a form of physical culture, sport has a particular corporeal resonance in making visible those aspects of social life that often remain hidden and submerged in other domains'.

The above examples do not refer simply to sport, but to the role of teams or individuals themselves as symbols of 'the nation' and thus, by implication, 'the people'. Put simply, Gilchrist (2005: 119) suggests that sport stars act as 'corporeal representatives of broader collectivities' and thus their representation elucidates wider concerns regarding nationality, citizenship and belonging. As the focus of this book is on football, it is the role of sport *teams* that is of particular relevance here. It is often remarked that the symbolism that sport teams possess, and the feelings and emotions that they generate amongst their supporters, are so immense that they represent one of the most prominent outlets for popular articulations of nationalist sentiment. For example, as Hobsbawm (1990: 43) observes, the identity of a nation of millions 'seems more real as a team of eleven named people'. However, in seeking to understand this phenomenon and to analyse its social repercussions, one has to begin by identifying who exactly are 'the people' that these teams are perceived to represent? Despite its vernacular of inclusion, such rhetoric can be partial, contingent and ephemeral, and evidently is not endorsed by all social or ethnic groups. Similarly, the processes of selection, affiliation fandom that operate in relation to national teams, in particular, can sustai well as challenge structures and patterns of inclusion/exclusion, discriminat and prejudice in the wider society (Carrington 1998a; Back *et al.* 2001a).

This chapter examines contemporary discourses surrounding issues of 'race', nation, culture and citizenship, and the manner in which they are constructed, articulated and contested within the frame of international sporting competition. It analyses how these trends influence and reflect the racial, generational and spatial subjectivities of young British Asians, and demonstrates how patterns of sporting affiliation reflect the nuanced and complex nature of twenty-first-century diasporic lifestyles and identities. The first part of the chapter traces the origins of 'cultural racism' (Fanon 1967) in post-war Western Europe and examines its manifestations and effects in late twentieth-century Britain, particularly in relation to the migration and settlement of South Asians. It highlights how entrenched racism and xenophobia, and socio-economic transitions, have contributed to increasingly ethnically exclusive notions of 'Englishness' and 'Britishness'. It is important to point out that these two notions are sometimes covered collectively because in dominant discourses they are often (incorrectly) seen to be synonymous. The second part of the chapter illustrates how the nexus between 'race' and nation is enacted within English sport. It argues that national identities remain complex and contentious within this sphere. Through an examination of the contrasting (yet not necessarily conflicting) affiliations of young British Asians in football and cricket, it indicates how sport embodies the fragmented and seemingly contradictory nature of identity in late modern society. The final section of this chapter attempts to theorize these trends by locating them within the actualities and potentialities of diasporic lifestyles, especially the ways in which young British Asians (re)create syncretic forms of identity. It argues that the diverse sporting allegiances of young British Asians enable them on the one hand to preserve or engage with the cultures and traditions of the subcontinent, and on the other to emphasize the permanency of South Asian settlement in Britain and the status of South Asians as British citizens.

(Re)imaginations of 'home' and empire: 'race', nation and culture in post-war Britain

From the era of British colonialism in the Indian subcontinent to the period succeeding their mass migration to Britain, South Asians have been regarded as the 'Other' within Western racial discourses (Said 1985). Within this constant, however, one can trace an ideological shift in the hegemonic imagination whereby South Asians (or, more accurately, certain groups within this collectivity) have been transposed from being located *outside* the national imagination to becoming enemies or threats *within* it. The main contributing factor to this transition has been the settlement in Britain of substantial South Asian populations. The South Asian presence in Britain can be traced back to previous centuries (Ramdin 1999; Visram 2002; Ali *et al.* 2006) yet, during the first half of the twentieth century

South Asians – or Indians as they were, officially, until the bifurcation of the subcontinent into India and Pakistan in 1947 – were still perceived within the British imagination with quasi-anthropological curiosity, i.e. literally as an exotic, yet primitive, people, living in an inconceivably distant and different continent. However, from the middle of the twentieth century, rapid and sizeable migrations of South Asians to Britain began to take place. These migrations were prompted by a variety of factors, often over-simplistically labelled 'push and pull' factors, including a demand for labour within Britain's manual industries and public services, combined with a striving amongst migrants to improve their standard of living. This transition was clearly a further stage in the systematic deskilling of indigenous labour and restricting of subaltern economies that had begun under colonialism. Britain's metropolises soon experienced major demographic changes: residents of previously white, working-class districts soon found themselves living and working alongside South Asian neighbours and colleagues, whilst religious and cultural institutions, restaurants and clothing emporia began to alter the sights, sounds and smells of local urban landscapes (Shukla 2003). In certain locations, the muezzin's call to prayer became as aurally ubiquitous as the clamour of heavy industry, whilst outlets selling beautifully coloured materials for *saris* and *shalwar kameez* became as common as pie 'n' mash shops.

These processes of migration and settlement had considerable implications for ideas of 'race' and nationhood, the repercussions of which continue to reverberate throughout contemporary Britain. Balibar (1991b: 43) argues that the arrival of migrants from former colonial territories represented an 'interiorization of the exterior' and identifies this process as the key context for the significant and widespread (re)construction and (re)contestation of notions of 'race', nation and culture across late twentieth-century Western Europe. He states that, in essence, what was taking place was a progression from the *external* racism that characterized perceptions of colonized populations during the era of empire to a notion of *internal* racism which, in contrast, involved prejudice against a recently constituted minority within one's own national collectivity. Whilst Balibar's exemplar is France, his observations apply equally to other contexts, perhaps most notably Britain and, for the purposes of this book, the place of South Asians within it.

This change was fundamental in providing the antecedents for the emergence of 'cultural' (Fanon 1967) or 'new' racism (Barker 1981) in Western societies. As the term suggests, in contrast to cruder biological racisms, which revolve explicitly around phenotypical characteristics and racial hierarchies, the key tenet of cultural racism is the idea of cultural difference and the degree to which minority ethnic groups are believed to conform to, and assimilate into, the norms and values of 'traditional' domestic life. Thus it has been argued that it is, indeed, 'racism without races' (Balibar 1991a: 21).[2] However, in such discourses, culture becomes a euphemism for 'race' as, despite the changing nomenclature, cultures are also interpreted as being fixed, discrete and impermeable. Different cultures are viewed as being inherently incompatible and those minorities that do not share the dominant values of Western societies are believed to represent a threat to their cohesion and, therefore, their social stability. During the early phases of migration, South Asians were seen to be bestowing unabated threats to the social composition of Britain and thus also the existing racial status quo. In particular, anxieties emanated from the belief that South Asians provided competition for scarce jobs (in fact they accepted shifts and areas of employment widely rejected by white workers) and housing (as in other areas of social life they were actually subjected to racial discrimination in the housing market) and allegations that adult males sexually harassed white women (Pearson 1976). It was also perceived that their different religious and social practices, together with a lack of identification with certain elements of the host culture, were not conducive to a modern, Western, Christian nation. In the current context, discourses of threat and fear within white communities remain strongly gendered, but are now articulated in conjunction with images of hyper-masculine 'rioters', 'home-grown suicide bombers' and 'honour killings'.

The central constant within these shifting images is the existence of a siege mentality, i.e. a belief amongst certain white populations that their community is being ignored, under-resourced or discriminated against and, as a result, that their way of life is under threat (Dench *et al.* 2006). According to Hewitt (2005) the belief that it is *white* communities that are being treated unfairly in areas such as politics, education and housing is part of a wider backlash against multiculturalism in Western Europe, North America and Australia in late modernity. An understanding of this siege mentality is crucial in mapping and challenging contemporary racisms. As Anthias and Lloyd argue:

> In order to understand and fight racism (as opposed to sorting out empirically who are its targets at any particular point of time), it is important to focus on processes, structures and outcomes, through looking both at changing configurations of ideas about fear, threat, otherness, undesirability, *and* at how groups who are targeted may be responding to these challenges.
>
> (2002: 8)

Furthermore, what is also significant about these siege mentalities and the racialization of social relations between majority and minority populations is the link between local communities and national collectivities. In other words, what happens at a local level is seen to be symptomatic of wider threats to England/Britain and 'Englishness'/'Britishness'. As Solomos and Back (1996: 18) point out, the focus of cultural racism is on 'the defence of the mythic "British/English way of life" in the face of attack from enemies *outside* ("Argies", "Frogs", "Krauts", "Iraqis") and *within* ("black communities", "Muslim fundamentalists")'. The modern metropolis increasingly has become the setting where the 'multicultural question' (S. Hall 2001) is enacted (Keith 2005) and, on a local level, siege mentalities often manifest themselves not only in further racial discrimination and violence towards minority ethnic groups, but also in what Cohen terms a 'racialization of space'. He argues that this:

Involves the colour-coding of particular residential areas, housing estates, or public amenities as 'white' or 'black' in a way which often homogenizes ethnically diverse neighbourhoods and turns relative population densities into absolute markers of racial division. This process is usually articulated through images of confrontation – 'front lines', 'no-go areas', and the like – that serve to orchestrate moral panics about 'invasion' and 'blacks [or Asians] taking over'.

(P. Cohen 1996: 71)

Fundamentally, the presence of large numbers of British Asians in adjacent neighbourhoods is interpreted irrationally, fuelling the belief amongst certain white groups that they are becoming minorities within their own towns and, by implication, that their country and way-of-life is under threat. McLoughlin (2005: 1047–8) states that 'some members of the ethnic majority tend to read the re-inscription of "old" spaces with "new" cultural meanings in terms of an ever-expanding (Islamic) "threat" to "the English way of life"'. For example, in 2005, the Stoke-on-Trent BNP campaigned against the building of a new mosque in the town, arguing that it would lead to the creation of a 'Muslim ghetto'[3] (Lowles 2005b). The inherent contradiction in such scenarios is poignantly proposed by Alibhai-Brown (2001b: 4) who states that 'they hate it that their Brontë-land has become a balti land, even though most of them have never watched a television version of *Jane Eyre* and could not survive a week without a curry'.

Cultural racism operates around the nexus between notions of 'race', culture, nationalism and patriotism, and facilitates dominant redefinitions of what it means to be English and British (Kundnani 2000; Parekh 2000). Perceptions of a threat to England and 'Englishness' have resulted in the emergence of a defensive 'Little Englander' mentality. This worldview is constructed around the celebration of a quasi-mythical English history and utopian images of suburban/rural life, free from the alleged problems of inner city (and, by association, minority ethnic) communities. It stresses a perceived common ancestry and homogeneity of English culture and, in the process, constructs a notion of 'Englishness' that is palpably monocultural. As Gilroy argues, the significance of cultural racism is that:

The emphasis on culture allows nation and race to fuse. Nationalism and racism become so closely identified that to speak of the nation is to speak automatically in racially exclusive terms. Blackness and Englishness are constructed as incompatible, mutually exclusive identities. To speak of the British or English people is to speak of the *white* people.

(1993: 27–8)

He adds that 'Brit nationalism cannot be purged of its racialized contents any more easily than a body can be purged of the skeleton that supports it' (Gilroy 2004: 121). Whilst such discourses are reproduced within all social milieux, they often find their most public expression within the dictums of the political

Right. For example, in 2001, echoing Margaret Thatcher's 'swamping' rhetoric, Conservative MP John Townend argued that 'our *homogenous Anglo-Saxon society* has been seriously undermined by the massive immigration ... that has taken place since the war' (cited in White 2001: 10, emphasis added). Similarly, speaking after the urban unrest in Oldham during April 2001, BNP activist Michael Treacy stated that 'I have no qualms against Asians or people of any colour. *It's a matter of the country losing its identity and culture*' (cited in Vasagar *et al.* 2001: 7, emphasis added).

Stuart Hall (1992b: 293) highlights how popular images of 'Englishness' have invoked notions of empire, militarism, ritual and commemoration, through their associations with public ceremonials, such as Trooping the Colour and Remembrance Sunday. In reality, these specific connotations register more among older generations. For example, former Home Secretary, David Blunkett – in a speech ironically entitled *A New England: an English Identity within Britain* – proposed a series of signifiers that represented his interpretation of 'Englishness'. These included the National Trust; poets such as Chaucer, Shakespeare and Keats; classical composers including Elgar, Britten and Williams; and comedy shows like Round the Horne and Monty Python. Not only does his selection betray the dynamic and valuable cultural industries of *modern* Britain, but also, more perturbingly, its components are strikingly and almost universally white. The only minority ethnic figure to warrant a mention is the eighteenth-century slave-turned-abolitionist Olaudah Equiano (Blunkett 2005). Blunkett's racialized (and gendered) portrayal is conservative, backward-looking and does little to contribute to a more inclusive notion of national identity. In this sense it serves to reproduce the 'white-washed', ethnocentric nature of hegemonic accounts of British history. In 2006, *Icons: a Portrait of England*, a government-funded project to discover England's most popular icons, listed the SS Empire Windrush as one of its original twelve icons – an encouraging selection, but the only one to refer explicitly to the nation's multi-ethnic composition.

Similarly, young white people are inclined to define themselves as an English ethnic collective (Anthias and Lloyd 2002), yet their notions of 'Englishness' are more likely to be constructed in relation to style and consumption than to history. Nonetheless, the sense of cultural separation between whites and minority ethnic groups can be reproduced through the alienation of the latter from these contemporary white, youth-orientated forms of 'Englishness' as well. For example, an exercise I carried out with (predominantly white) undergraduate students found that their images of England and 'Englishness' rarely acknowledged minority ethnic figures and cultures, a trend often replicated by school pupils (Ofsted 2005).

Nation, identity and sporting affiliation

Sport is not only one of the most significant means through which notions of 'Englishness' and 'Britishness' are constructed, contested and resisted, but it also elucidates the subtleties and complexities inherent to their manifestations.

Studies of the nexus between ethnic, racial and national identities traditionally have tended to focus on black Britons and have identified that popular manifestations of 'Englishness' are often exclusionary, alienating or irrelevant (e.g. Gilroy 1987; Gilroy 1993; Back 1996). Far less attention has been paid to British Asians, yet many are also antipathetic to dominant images of English national culture and demotic manifestations of nationalism. For example, the National Centre for Social Research annual survey of 2000 found that the notion of 'Englishness' proves particularly problematic for British Asians. Whilst more than a third classified themselves as British (not English), only 7 per cent classified themselves as English (not British) (Carvel 2000). Similarly, according to the Office for National Statistics (2004), whilst 67 per cent of Bangladeshis see themselves as British, only 6 per cent identify as English.

Reasons for affiliations with 'Britishness' rather than 'Englishness' are multiple and complex. Like all forms of identity they shift across time and place, and are often referenced to issues of 'race', citizenship and the cultural politics of post-colonialism. For example, in Eade's (1994: 389) east London-based study, one young Bangladeshi Muslim explained that 'I don't know why, I just feel to be British, you don't actually have to be white. But to be English I always have this feeling you have to be white'. 'Englishness' appears to be perceived as an ethnically exclusive identity, yet young British Asians and black Britons are challenging the racialized nature, and seeking to create pluralistic notions of 'Britishness' (although this continues to be resisted in some quarters). Another participant argued that '[I am] British because I am a British citizen. No matter what the white [sic] say, I am British. Not English, but British' (ibid.). Young British Asians are thus articulating a sense of 'Britishness' that is based on *citizenship* rather than on national identity *per se*. As Hussain and Bagguley argue:

> For the younger generation, their British citizenship is *central to their self-understandings and assertion of who they are*, and for them the threat of the BNP is just as much a threat to their Britishness as *citizens* as it is to their ethnic identities. However, their accounts of this threat are not in terms of a British or English national identity, but in terms of their rights as British-born *citizens*. They are expressing and defending a British multicultural, multi-ethnic citizenship identity.
>
> (2005: 411)

However, whilst the prefix 'British' is preferred to 'English' as a means of self-identification, there is a contradiction evident in the symbol used to reflect this. Whilst the (British) Union flag is perceived by many young British Asians to symbolize colonialism, racism and the politics of the Far Right, the (English) St George flag is regarded as a symbol of multi-ethnic Britain[4] (Kumar 2003: 262–3; Bagguley and Hussain 2005). A further irony here is the association of the latter with the Crusades and conflict between Christianity and Islam (ibid.: 213).

This rejection of 'Englishness' by British Asians manifests itself in a variety of contemporary social and cultural spheres. One of the most significant and powerful forms of identity contestation is cricket. In recent decades increasing recognition has been given to the fact that large numbers of British Asians choose to support their country of ancestry – Pakistan, India, Bangladesh or Sri Lanka – especially when they are competing against England (Werbner 1996b; Crabbe and Wagg 2000; Williams 2000; BBC Radio 2006). This trend has infuriated various individuals, ranging from Norman Tebbit to Nasser Hussain (see Chapter 4), who have failed to appreciate the function that such teams perform for diasporic populations. Fundamentally, supporting the national team of an ancestral 'homeland' is a prominent means of constructing and maintaining an 'imagined community' (Anderson 1991), enabling the celebration of histories and traditions, sustaining familial and kinship ties, and creating symbolic links for British-born generations. Furthermore, affiliations with subcontinental teams are also a means by which British Asians are able to articulate an 'oppositional postcolonial sensibility' (Werbner 2004: 468), circumventing and symbolically rejecting aspects of 'Englishness' that they find exclusionary, alienating or oppressive. This dual process is identified by Werbner (1996b: 101) who argues that 'it is in the field of sport, through support of the [Pakistan] national team, that young British Pakistanis express their love of both cricket and the home country, along with their sense of alienation and disaffection from British society'. Similarly, Wazir proposes that:

> These days with increasing numbers of religious leaders, community elders and even family members unable to articulate, or even understand, the contradictions that an East–West upbringing plant in the minds of [young British Asians], a generation of twenty-somethings . . . has turned back to its oldest and most popular form of cultural heritage: cricket.
>
> (2001: 16)

However, traditionally very little attention – either in academe or in the media – has been given to the role that football plays in the articulation of ethnic and national identities for British Asians. Due to the widespread, yet erroneous belief that football is an insignificant leisure and social activity for young British Asians, the game's role as an arena for the construction and expression of social identities rarely has been considered.

Nevertheless, research has highlighted the ways that the ethnically exclusive and marginalizing aspects of 'Englishness' are reproduced in football. For example, focusing on the 1996 European Football Championships – held in England and widely labelled as 'football coming home' – Carrington (1998a) demonstrates that the manner in which notions of 'Englishness' were portrayed by the media, by politicians and within the game itself, together with the forms of popular culture that were celebrated (e.g. 'Britpop' music and comedians David Baddiel and Frank Skinner[5]), reproduced 'Englishness' as the preserve of young, white males, and thus further contributed to increasingly narrow, exclusive and culturally racist representations of the nation. He argues that:

> The fact that the majority of the black population living in England had either a large degree of ambivalence towards England or openly supported 'anyone but England' underscores the points being made that the form of national identity produced failed to be inclusive and actually alienated large sections of the nation from view.
>
> (Carrington 1998a: 118)

Repercussions were evident six years later by the time of the 2002 World Cup finals. In a poll conducted by the black British newspaper *New Nation* on the subject of national identity and footballing allegiance, readers were asked the following question: If it came down to a direct choice between England and Nigeria – as it very nearly did due to them playing in the same first round group – who would they prefer to be knocked out of the World Cup? The results showed that 67 per cent of readers favoured an English exit ahead of a Nigerian one. With regard to the team that readers wanted to win the trophy outright, 34 per cent wanted England to be victorious, 33 per cent chose Nigeria and 20 per cent opted for Brazil (Kelso 2002).

It might be argued that British Asians would have replicated this trend as their sense of exclusion has been compounded by their absence as elite players. Whilst significant numbers of African-Caribbeans have played for the England national football team, British Asians have not yet progressed beyond under-20 (Zesh Rehman) and under-21 (Michael Chopra) levels to win full caps (although it is encouraging that in the women's game Aman Dosanj has played for the full side). The relationship between 'Englishness' and British Asian identities often continues to be seen as antithetical in dominant discourses, as reflected in the actions of some white football fans at a match between Brentford and the Indian national team:

> On 24 July 2001, as part of their tour of England, the Indian national football team played Brentford FC at Griffin Park. Before the match (an evening fixture) commenced, a group of approximately eight white, male teenagers were sitting in the Ealing Road end of the main stand. One was sporting a replica England shirt and the youths were proudly and provocatively displaying both St George and Union flags. These flags were new, but of cheap quality and in contrast to the flags normally displayed by supporters at professional matches, which include some form of affiliation such as a club name, nickname or town, they had no identifications. It was evident that the youths had bought the flags especially for the occasion, and as a means of celebrating their English/British identities rather than their allegiance to Brentford *per se*. A number of other supporters wore items of England replica team strip or leisurewear such as t-shirts, shorts and baseball caps. One man notably sported an ostentatious polo shirt – an *ersatz* version of the design

produced by the Hackett brand that is favoured by many hooligans – with the word 'England' embossed in large letters on the front and a George Cross covering the whole of the back. As the team line-ups were announced, the name of each Indian player was greeted with loud booing from the youths described above and disparaging comments were made about the referee – a turban-wearing Sikh. After the match, a significant proportion of the crowd moved towards Brentford railway station. The crowd slowed down as it reached the main road. A large number of young white men were present, including those identified above. As a car of Indian supporters reached the junction, loud cries of '3–0!' [the match result] and 'England! England!' went up. The youths surrounded the car, placing their flags over the windows, thus preventing the vehicle from moving. Various threats were made, such as 'Don't let him [the driver] through, he's Indian!' and 'Smash the windows!' The atmosphere was aggressive, but the youths soon moved on. At Brentford railway station, approximately thirty young men – including a couple who were of dual white and African-Caribbean heritage – and five young women entered the westbound platform. On the eastbound platform (across the tracks) approximately ten Indian supporters were gathered. The white youths stood in a confrontational stance, displaying their flags and chanting 'England! England!' Sporadic abuse was aimed at the Indians, together with deliberately confrontational questions and threatening stares. The white group decided to walk rather than wait for the train and, as they made their way up the steps, a number chanted 'We're coming to get you' and shouted 'Fucking Pakis'. Two glass beer bottles were thrown by the white youths, which smashed, but missed their intended targets.

(Fieldnotes, 24 July 2001)

This chapter has demonstrated that affiliation with a sports team from an ancestral country is based on a variety of factors, relating both to one's life in Britain and one's feelings about, and connections with the 'homeland'. As described above, a significant factor is a sense of social exclusion and alienation within Britain, and marginalization from player and supporter collectivities. One might predict, therefore, that incidents such as those at Brentford would increase the emotional distance between British Asians and the England football team.

However, whilst this seems to be the case with cricket, certain contradictory trends appear to be evident in English football. Sarita Malik points out that:

When television brought us scenes of British-Asians watching the 1996 cricket Test Match between England and India at Lords and simultaneously cheering when news broke that the England football team had just qualified for the Euro '96 semi-finals, it was clear that whilst they may have failed Norman Tebbit's 'cricket test', they would have passed a comparative 'football test' with flying colours.

(2002: 124)

For example, referring to the country that he would wish to represent should the chance materialize, one British Pakistani professional player stated that, 'I was born here, brought up here and lived and raised here so I see myself as British Asian. I want to play for England. I'd love to play for England' (interview, 11 February 2002). Another player stated that:

> Obviously [players] will have sentiments attached to [the subcontinent], but, you know, if you ask a lot of the Asian community, they would like to play for England. . . . A lot of Asian players don't even see themselves as, you know, Indian or Bangladeshi, etc. because they see themselves as *British Asian* individuals.
>
> (Interview with British Bangladeshi amateur player/member of British Asian sports organization, 14 May 2002)

Another player recalled a conversation he had had with his son, a talented young player:

> I know my son [who is affiliated to a professional academy] certainly says to me at times, 'Dad, what am I?' And I say to him, 'Obviously by parents you're Indian – because we're both Indian – but by your right of birth, you know, you're English'. So he's already said to me, 'If I ever play football Dad, can I play for England or India?' And I said 'Who do you want to play for?'. He said 'England', so I thought then, there you are, you know, it's your choice.
>
> (Interview with British Indian amateur player, 5 February 2002)

Other professional players unequivocally express their desire to play for England. Anwar Uddin, who has a Bangladeshi father and an English mother, states that:

> My mum's English and I was brought up in the East End [of London]. I think of myself as English and would be so proud to represent my country. I was asked to captain Bangladesh recently, but I turned it down, because if I played for them, I won't be eligible to play for England.
>
> (Cited in Hawkey 2002)

Harpal Singh is particularly succinct on this issue: 'England – no question' (cited in Bhatia 2003b). Zesh Rehman states that his 'perfect day would be to score a goal for [his] country in an important game. Would that be England or Pakistan? Huh, England!' (cited in Donovan 2003). However, as is discussed below, his desire to do this at full international level will now never come true.

Such testimonies offer a powerful riposte to those who claim that there is 'no black in the Union Jack' and to the likes of Robert Henderson who infamously questioned the loyalty of England's minority ethnic cricket players. Writing in *Wisden Cricket Monthly*, Henderson argued that:

Norman Tebbit's cricket test is as pertinent for players as it is for spectators. It is even possible that part of a coloured England-qualified player feels satisfaction (perhaps subconsciously) at seeing England humiliated, because of post-imperial myths of oppression and exploitation.

(1995: 9)

The player statements cited above are important as they highlight the shifting identity politics among younger generations of British Asians, and offer a challenge to discourses that equate the nation with 'whiteness'. It should also be recognized that affiliations between minority ethnic sportspeople and English national sport teams are of considerable significance, and possess substantial ideological capital, for a range of groups (Burdsey 2005a; Fortier 2005). For the political right, they are used (erroneously) to suggest that racism is on the decline and that Britain is no longer a hostile place to live, whilst for New Labour these proclamations underpin and reinforce contemporary rhetoric around integration and community cohesion, which posits that proclamations of national pride and loyalty to the nation state are intrinsic components of British citizenship (Werbner 2004; McGhee 2005).

Football's role in the articulation of hybrid identities is further demonstrated by the affiliations of British Asian supporters (see also Bagguley and Hussain 2005), illustrated in the following two quotations:

> I think that it is a misconception [that British Asians do not support England] because there's loads of Asians that support England. If you go to local cafes, [British Asians] are England supporters. It's natural because they're living in this country and they're supporting the country, you know. There's nothing wrong with that.
> (Interview with British Bangladeshi semi-professional player, 11 May 2002)

> I've spoken to a few people I know about this and all of us were actually up for England in this [2002] World Cup. And that's a first because in the past we've not really felt affiliated to England, or whatever. But for some reason we felt more English on this occasion. . . . I think people are realizing that they're English or British or British Asians, or whatever, and want to fit in. . . . I think more and more sort of British-born Asian people are thinking that they are, or looking at themselves as, English and if they were given a choice in playing sport, they'd play for England.
> (Interview with British Indian football supporter, 27 June 2002)

In contrast, whilst the matches played by India and Pakistan in England have certainly attracted some British Asians as spectators, the numbers in attendance have been very low – with the exception of the match at West Bromwich Albion – considering the fact that the majority of games were staged at clubs based in areas with significant British Asian populations.[6] Although subcontinental teams generate mild interest and curiosity amongst British Asians, there is very little evidence of fully fledged support or affiliation.

It is clear that patterns of national identification and support in football and cricket differ considerably amongst British Asians. What, therefore, are the factors that account for the different affiliations of these players and supporters? One should point out that their patterns of allegiance are no more or less multifarious, complex and contradictory than those of other ethnic groups. They simply reflect the fragmentation of identities that influence attitudes, behaviours and choices across different social spheres in late modernity. As Stuart Hall argues: 'National identities do not subsume all other forms of difference into themselves and are not free of the play of power, internal divisions and contradictions, cross-cutting allegiances and difference' (Hall 1992b: 299).

Furthermore, contrary to what is often suggested in dominant discourses, these identifications do not represent a threat to integration or community cohesion for, as Parekh (2000: 205) rightly points out, 'a multicultural society requires that the prevailing view of national identity should allow its members to entertain dual and even multiple identities without arising fears of divided loyalties'.

Before the analysis moves to a theoretical framework by which to try to understand this phenomenon, a number of specific reasons, related to the respective sports themselves, can be proposed. The first two relate primarily to players and the latter two to supporters. The first reason that might contribute to these diverse affiliations is the status and success of subcontinental teams in their respective sports. According to the FIFA rankings of May 2006, although they are showing a gradual improvement, South Asian teams were ranked poorly in the global 'league table'. India were placed 117th, Bangladesh were 140th and Pakistan were 153rd (out of 205). Whilst the desire to play international football evidently is not simply based on the possibility of playing success, and issues of national pride and family ties are often equally important, playing in major global competitions is widely regarded as the pinnacle of a professional player's career. However, since the turn of the century, the India and Pakistan national teams have been convincingly beaten by English *club* sides.[7] These nations will not qualify for the finals of a major regional or global championship in the foreseeable future, and so representing them will not result in significant international success or the enhancement of global reputation. It is also the case that until a standardized global football calendar is implemented, England-based players representing non-European countries still have to miss substantial sections of their club seasons in order to fulfil their international commitments. Many players are becoming increasingly reluctant to jeopardize their place in their club teams in order to play for their countries, particularly if those nations have little or no chance of qualifying for a major championship. There have been a number of confrontations between English professional clubs and non-European national associations regarding the scheduling of games. In contrast, India, Pakistan and Sri Lanka (and, to a far lesser extent, Bangladesh) are world forces in cricket and consequently their successes are likely to engender greater interest, support and allegiances from those in the diaspora.

It is important, however, to recognize that football identities, like other identities, can be fluid and changeable. For example, two players talked about playing for other countries if they were not selected to play for England:

> I'd like to play for England, but it would be hard because there's loads of young kids and they're quality players as well. So if I didn't have a chance to play for England I would probably go for, like, Pakistan. At the end of the day, it's all like international play, isn't it? I wouldn't mind. My dad wouldn't say nothing, my mum wouldn't say nothing. I've got a cousin in Pakistan and that, and he'd probably say 'Yeah, play for Pakistan', but my dad would say 'Look, play for who you want to play for'.
>
> (Interview with British Pakistani professional player, 20 March 2002)

> What I would say to anybody is, if you make it as a sportsperson and you don't get selected for England, then always look at the option of playing for the country of your parents' origin or whatever, and if it's India or Pakistan, then fine. And if people start knocking it then we'll say hold on a minute, look at the Republic of Ireland, look at Wales, look at Scotland. They've been doing it since time began so what's the difference in this. Then you look at the Reggae Boyz, Jamaica in 1998. Robbie Earle and them guys. Never in their wildest dreams would they have thought they'd play in a World Cup, yet they went back to their roots, played for Jamaica and *voilà*! And that, to me, you can look at as an advantage, that you've got a choice of playing for either.
>
> (Interview with British Indian amateur player, 27 June 2002)

As these testimonies make clear, for the majority of players the option of playing for a subcontinental nation would only become an issue if the opportunity to represent England did not exist. This has occurred, however, with Zesh Rehman. Despite his stated desire to represent England, his frustration that he had not been selected for the under-21 team led to him accepting the offer to play for his parents' place of birth, Pakistan, in 2005. He states that 'I'll be just as proud to represent Pakistan as England', yet his decision appears to be based as much on the opportunity for competitive international football as on issues of national identity (Football Association 2005). This has led to condemnation from key figures in the British Asian football scene, such as Nadeem Nabi, chairman of the Asian Football League, who states that 'his decision sends out the wrong message' (Sky Sports 2006).

Second, the English tours undertaken in recent years by the India and Pakistan national teams do not appear to have forged significant sporting links between subcontinental and diasporic South Asian players (for an in-depth critique of these tours see Chapter 7). A distinct demarcation between subcontinental and diasporic populations remains evident in terms of player selection for Bangladesh, India and Pakistan (Dimeo 2002b). This is in contrast to nations such as Jamaica, Nigeria and the Republic of Ireland who have taken advantage of changes in FIFA regulations that state that a player is eligible to play for a country if one of his grandparents was born there. They have subsequently selected large numbers of English-born players, yet Bangladesh, India and Pakistan (with the exception of Rehman) have failed to recruit players from their respective diasporas. This is most significantly the case with India where the All India Football Federation's (AIFF) negative attitude towards NRIs (non-resident Indians; see Walton-Roberts 2004) has historically resulted in their decision not to allow non-nationals to represent the country. Thus, whilst players of Indian origin (PIOs), such as Harpal Singh and those plying their trade elsewhere in Europe, including Vikash Dhorasoo (Paris St Germain, France), Kiran Bechan (FC Groningen, the Netherlands), Thomas Pereira (Viking FK Stavanger, Norway) and Vicky Chand (Ängby Stockholm, Sweden), theoretically would qualify to play for India under FIFA regulations, their inability to acquire an Indian passport (should they so desire) until dual citizenship was introduced in 2004 means they have not met AIFF rules (Indianfootball.com 2006).[8] This decision to exclude diasporic Indians reflects wider socio-political developments that have sought to restrict the boundaries of 'Indianness'. As Dimeo (2002b: 87n) suggests, 'It is interesting that the AIFF and the Indian Government have tried to maintain a stricter sense of national identity, as if the question of being Indian is more important than building a successful sports team'. A member of a British Asian football federation raised his concerns about how this reduces the positive and sustainable repercussions that such tours can have for *British* Asian football:

> I wouldn't put too much emphasis on representation at national level for any Indian side to be perfectly honest because unfortunately our perception of how one gets selected into a national team over here [in Britain] is not necessarily [based on] the same criteria that would be applied back home. And that worries us as well because we feel – and certainly we felt this last year when the Indian national football team was over – that there is very little representation from the UK or anybody outside India representing India at football. But I think a lot of that is down to the way the team is selected and what their policies are for that selection.
>
> (Interview, 19 March 2002)

Furthermore, whilst one of the stated objectives of the Indian tours to Britain was to encourage links between subcontinental and diasporic footballers, whether it was achieved is a moot point. Although British Indians Harpal Singh and Nevin Saroya (a former professional with Brentford now playing non-league football with Yeading) trained with the Indian national team during their visits to England, the real intentions of the organizers, Sapphire Enterprises, perhaps can be gauged by the fact that they chose to prioritize high-profile dinner engagements ahead of allowing the Indian players to visit British Asian football clubs or school pupils (Dimeo 2002b).

Third, the standard of subcontinental teams in international cricket and the global competitive structure of the game mean that India, Pakistan and Sri Lanka all regularly play against – and frequently defeat – England.[9] Despite, or perhaps because of the fact that cricket was a key instrument in the British imperial domination of India, this process has undergone a direct reversal whereby, for the duration of a match or series, former colonial peoples are afforded the opportunity to compete on equal terms with, and even defeat, England. In football, on the other hand, the likelihood of such matches, let alone such a result, taking place is almost non-existent. Consequently the inherent ideological capacities of sport are accentuated in cricket, which continues to operate as an arena where significant political and post-colonial symbolism can be achieved through 'beating the masters at their own game'.

Finally, in contrast to football, international cricket matches enable British Asian supporters to enjoy their sport in a manner that is not only more closely associated with how it is experienced in the subcontinent, but is also often excluded from lower levels of the English game (McDonald and Ugra 1998; Carrington and McDonald 2001c). In amateur and, to some extent, professional county cricket, British Asians can be alienated by a hegemonic 'traditional Englishness' and notions of rural idyllism that equate a cricket match with village greens, church spires, polite applause and the quaffing of real ale. Conversely, spectatorship of the international game appears to facilitate greater opportunities for recreating 'traditional' South Asian forms of cricket fandom. Although increasingly stringent and restrictive stewarding practices mean that this is becoming less feasible, international Test cricket has allowed British Asians to celebrate the game on their own terms, through the use of chants, flags and musical instruments. Werbner (2005) identifies the importance of cricket in the articulation of South Asian masculinities and, as Crabbe and Wagg (2000) suggest, the cricket ground is more conducive to such behaviour as it is not dominated by the white, working-class masculinity that characterizes English football stadia.

Home teams and homelands: sport and cartographies of diasporic British Asian identities

Sport is evidently an extremely important social arena for the articulation and contestation of identity. The differing allegiances of British Asian sportsmen/women and supporters not only challenge essentialist interpretations of ethnic and national identity, but also dichotomous models that purport such young people to be 'caught between two cultures' (Anwar 1998). Contrasting sporting affiliations elucidate the complex, multifaceted nature of social identities, demonstrating the way in which they are created in specific contexts and fluctuate across time and space. In seeking to analyse the dynamic, fragmented nature of young British Asian identities, and the role of sport in their expression, it is useful to revisit the concept of 'diaspora'. Anthias (1998: 559–60) suggests that the term primarily 'references a connection between groups across different nation states whose commonality derives from an original but maybe removed homeland'. She adds that 'a new identity becomes constructed on a world scale which crosses national borders and boundaries'. However, it must be acknowledged that diasporas are not homogenous, monolithic entities and South Asian communities in, for example, Britain, Canada or Singapore possess not only similarities and connections, but also significant differences that emanate from the ways that their identities and habituses have been modified within their specific states. As Brah (1996: 183) argues, 'Diasporas, in the sense of distinctive historical experiences, are often composite formations made up of many journeys to different parts of the globe, each with its own history, its own particularities'. It is also important to point out that, analogous to social identities, boundary maintenance of diasporas is predicated on a range of different criteria related to, for example, nationality, ethnicity, religion and caste. In this analysis one needs to be aware of the existence of, for example, South Asian, Indian, Bengali, Sikh or Jat diasporas, and to appreciate that the importance attached to membership of each one fluctuates spatially and temporally. Following Stuart Hall (1990) and Gilroy (1993) who use the concept of diaspora as a means of progressing beyond representations of the essentialist black subject, it is used here to theorize the myriad identities that comprise British 'Asianness'. Thus it should be seen not as a descriptive term, but more as a social condition (Anthias 1998) or as a practice, project or stance (Brubaker 2005).

The concept of diaspora is crucial in subverting the belief that there is a primordial connection between 'race' and place. As Alexander and Knowles (2005: 8) point out, 'It disrupts modernist racialized associations between peoples and nation states as roots, tackling the idea of fixed origins'. Diaspora challenges dominant discourses about authenticity, belonging and citizenship, and illustrates how the formation of 'new ethnicities' (S. Hall 2000b) often renders national borders insignificant. In particular, it enables us to disentangle the relationship between place(s) of 'origin' and place(s) of 'settlement', and the respective significance attached to them. Put simply, by examining diasporas we can attempt to comprehend how the identities of second- and third-generation British Asians are subject to both global and local, or, as Robertson (1995) puts it, 'glocal', influences. Cohen argues that:

> All diasporic communities settled outside their natal (or imagined natal) territories acknowledge that 'the old country' – a notion often buried deep in language, religion, custom or folklore – always has some claim on their loyalty and emotions. That claim may be strong or weak, or boldly or meekly articulated in a given circumstance or historical period, but a member's

adherence to a diasporic community is demonstrated by an acceptance of an inescapable link with their past migration history and a sense of co-ethnicity with others of a similar background.

(R. Cohen 1999: ix)

For large numbers of British Asians, cricket is commonly, at least in part, associated with their own or their parents and grandparents' pre-migration lives. Supporting India, Pakistan, Bangladesh or Sri Lanka in international cricket thus generates substantial symbolic capital by forging ties – real or imagined – with 'the old country'.

However, Clifford (1994: 305–6) critiques models of diaspora that are 'oriented by continuous cultural connections to a [single] source and by a teleology of "return"'. He suggests that South Asians, for example, are 'not so much oriented to roots in a specific place and a desire for return as around an ability to recreate a culture in diverse locations'. Similarly Anthias (2001: 632) points out that diaspora tends to be used in a manner that privileges the point(s) of 'origin' in constructing identities and solidarities, and does not sufficiently acknowledge transethnic, as opposed to transnational, processes. Brah (1996: 180) makes the broad point that 'not all diasporas sustain an ideology of "return"'. By way of a specific example, Falzon (2003) describes the situation of Sindhi (Pakistani) migrants in Mumbai. He questions the central significance of a primordial homeland in the diasporic imagination and argues that these migrants do not wish to return to Sindh. Instead they see Mumbai as their new 'cultural heart'. Furthermore, with the Sikh diaspora, for many the desired 'homeland' – an independent Sikh state of Khalistan – is a figurative rather than literal entity. Unlike the original (and, in some cases, continuing) aspirations of some of their parents and grandparents, most young British Asians have no desire to permanently 'return' to the Indian subcontinent. In contrast to cricket, football is equated with their own residence in England and, in this regard, supporting the national team acts as an arena where the permanency of settlement, and the associated implications for citizenship and the construction of identity can be emphasized. Sport is thus a means by which diaspora is *performed* in the public sphere by young British Asians. In other words, their involvement in football may be conceived of as a situating strategy, literally a means of signalling their attachment to what is regarded as 'home' as well as what might be perceived to be the 'homeland(s)'. The irony here is that, like the use of the St George flag (discussed above), it is an English symbol that is being used to represent a British identity. A British team does not compete in football (although it has been mooted for participation in the Olympic Games), yet if it did, it would be very interesting to observe how its presence alongside or instead of an England team might influence patterns of support and affiliation.

The lives of young British Asians are grounded not only in the cultures and traditions of their parents and the Indian subcontinent, but also in the social practices of Britain and beyond. As Clifford (1994) succinctly enunciates, diasporas think globally, but live locally. Whilst the post-modern axiom of 'it's not where you're from, it's where you're at' is not wholly accurate, one should consider how identities are forged through *routes* as well as *roots* (ibid.). As Stuart Hall (1990: 235) has famously argued, the 'diaspora experience . . . is defined, not by essence or purity, but by the recognition of a necessary heterogeneity and diversity; by a conception of "identity" which lives with and through, not despite, difference; by *hybridity*'. Diasporic identities thus do not simply entail reproducing existing cultures or appropriating new ones; they inextricably revolve around notions of fluidity, creolization and syncretism.

The arguments raised here do not, therefore, symbolize an equation of cricket equals 'Asianness' and football equals 'Englishness/Britishness'. Diasporic identities are intrinsically comprised of a panoply of diverse cultures, ethnicities, histories, genealogies, migrations and settlements. These are inherently imbricating and cannot be disengaged from each other. Instead, the construction of young diasporic British Asian identities emerges at the intersection of local and global dynamics – an imagined spatial arena that has been dubbed 'Transl-Asia' (Kaur and Kalra 1996) – and these 'new' identities are underpinned by a plethora of factors that transcend ethnic, cultural, generational and national boundaries: increasing commonalities with multi-ethnic peers and decreasing continuities with previous familial generations; a growing 'imagined' distance between their lives in Britain and their relationship to the subcontinent; the influence of Western commodities and new patterns of consumption; and a desire to construct a multilateral social identity that simultaneously emphasizes their British citizenship, ethnicities and multiple identities as 'Asian', 'Bangladeshi', 'Punjabi' or 'Hindu'. Crucially, the formation of and relative importance attached to these identities are influenced not only by processes within the diaspora itself, but also the socio-political transformations and fluctuating boundaries of belonging in the original point of migration.

In conclusion, it is important to acknowledge the caveat proposed by Song (2005) who argues that in much sociological and cultural studies literature, 'the postmodern emphasis on fluid identities and positionings is far too celebratory' (ibid.: 63). She adds that:

> The politics and dynamics of diasporic peoples' ethnic affiliations and identifications are far more constrained and subject to negotiation than suggested by the rather breezy and celebratory writings about diaspora and hybridity. Not all diasporic people may be equally successful in their efforts to assert hybridized identities or occupy and enunciate a 'third space'.

> (Song 2005: 63)

Such a position is espoused by Hanif Kureishi, the British-born Anglo-Pakistani author, in his essay 'The Rainbow Sign', where he states that, as a young man, his outsider status in both England and Pakistan meant that he 'couldn't rightfully lay claim to either place' (Kureishi 2005: 24). He recalls that 'when I was growing up, they'd say: "You're a Pakistani, you're not British". Then when I went to Pakistan they'd say: "You're a 'Paki', you're not one of us, you're not Pakistani"' (Kureishi

2006: 21). Therefore it must be recognized that the trends outlined in this chapter do not signify either a universal, unconditional embracing of 'Englishness' by young British Asians or a substantial shift towards multiculturalism in the English game. As Brah (1996: 193) argues, 'It is quite possible to feel at home in a place and, yet, the experience of social exclusions may inhibit public proclamations of the place as home'. In other words, the fact that increasing numbers of British Asians are affirming their support for the England football team does not mean that notions of 'Englishness' are no longer problematic or offensive, or that, despite their gradually increasing presence as 'live' supporters (Laville 2004; Perryman 2006), they are necessarily granted inclusion in 'mainstream' (predominantly white) player and fan collectivities. By way of a reminder of the ephemeral and restricted effect that selections and representations of national sport teams have on wider racial relations, one should note with caution the situation in France. The success of the multi-ethnic *black-beur-bleu* team in the 1998 World Cup was widely heralded as a positive endorsement of the nation's republican ideology and as challenging the rise of Jean-Marie Le Pen's *Front National* (Hare 2003). As Fortier argues, with such cases:

> In a mimetic relationship between representation and identity, the assumption is that if the visual referent changes, 'we' change, consequently satisfying the disenfranchised communities who will feel greater pride in being part of the national community by virtue of seeing 'fellow members' of 'their' communities within the representational field.
>
> (2005: 573)

Yet the urban uprisings by African and Arab youths in the Parisian *banlieux* (low-income apartments and social housing estates on the outskirts of the city) and throughout the rest of France in October 2005 highlighted the continuing presence of racism, poor educational and employment prospects, and police harassment in the lives of minority ethnic communities (Esbé 2005).

This chapter has shown how British Asians are articulating a sense of identity based on their status as British citizens and the importance of the England football team in its expression, but one must remain cautious about the extent to which it signifies either a tangible improvement in racial equality in football or society, or a dramatic shift in British Asians' wider social location. The arguments raised here, together with the issues discussed in the previous chapter, represent a detailed exposition of young, male British Asian lifestyles and identities, and the ways that these influence the involvement of British Asians in, and their exclusion from, professional football. The focus of the book now turns to the strategies that have been employed to try to increase the inclusion of British Asians in this sphere, assessing their rationales and effectiveness, and the degree to which they reflect the aspirations, attitudes and opinions of British Asian footballers themselves.

6 British Asians and anti-racism in English football I

Strategies and symbolism

Introduction

The recent history of English football's dominant social policy agendas is characterized by two main themes. The mid-1980s to the mid-1990s is primarily associated with the problem of hooliganism, issues surrounding spectator safety (in the wake of a series of stadium tragedies), and increasingly draconian legislation regarding permissible forms of fandom and behaviour inside the stadium. The prevailing theme of the following decade – which indeed stemmed from many of the changes taking place in the game in the preceding years – is without doubt anti-racism.

Despite a long history of associations between racism and English football, which can be traced back to the 1930s and Oswald Mosley's attempts to recruit supporters to join his British Union of Fascists (Garland and Rowe 1996), organized campaigns to eradicate racism from professional football and to increase equality of opportunity for all ethnic groups are a relatively recent phenomenon. Whilst small, spontaneous anti-racist fan groups (primarily mobilized against organized fascism) existed in the late 1970s (Renton 2006: 87–9), it was not until the 1990s that they began to achieve a significant presence. More specifically, within the years in which anti-racism has become increasingly institutionalized within English football, one can trace a rapidly growing prominence attached to British Asian footballers and their continuing exclusion from the professional sphere. Following Bains and Patel's seminal *Asians Can't Play Football* report (1996) and the establishment of overcoming British Asian exclusion as one of Kick It Out's six original (and continuing) primary objectives (see e.g. Kick It Out 1998a), a variety of organizations, schemes, projects and initiatives – comprising what can be loosely termed the anti-racist football movement – have invested considerable time, money and resources in both raising awareness of the lack of British Asian professional footballers and seeking to ameliorate the problem. Indeed, the topic has gone from being a fairly minor concern on the game's anti-racist agendas to one of the most important and contentious issues.

In its capacity as the national co-ordinating anti-racist body, Kick It Out has published a number of pamphlets and newsletters specifically relating to British Asian footballers (e.g. Kick It Out 1998b, 2000a). Furthermore, after years of inaction, the football authorities have also begun to recognize the problem of this exclusion and are acknowledging their own responsibility in working to overcome it (see e.g. Football Association 1999, no date), although the FA's original Asians in Football working group was extremely limited in scope and the progressive rhetoric was not reflected in practice. In 2005, the National Asians in Football Forum also came to prominence, primarily through the publication of *Asians Can Play Football* (Asians in Football Forum 2005) and the staging of a conference entitled *The Future for Asians in British Football* at Leicester City FC in November 2005. Encouragingly, this was the first major event to bring together a variety of representatives from professional and British Asian amateur football clubs, coaches, governing bodies, anti-racist organizations and academics, and to provide an opportunity for the sharing of best practice. The status of this heavily publicized event was confirmed by the presence of high-profile figures, such as Sir Trevor Brooking, the FA's Director of Football Development, and Richard Caborn, the Sports Minister, although the contribution that they were able to offer to the debate is a moot point. Whilst all the keynote speakers were men – an unfortunate, if not surprising, state of affairs – a major positive point was that the conference was chaired by a British Asian woman, Aasmah Mir of BBC Radio Five Live. These developments demonstrate the progress that anti-racism has made in football and the changing approaches to trying to overcome the exclusion of British Asians from the professional game. In this regard, they represent a prime example of what Carrington and McDonald (2003: 138) label a 'bureaucratic managerialist' approach to anti-racism. However, as the following two chapters demonstrate, whilst this helps to ensure that relevant issues remain in the public eye, it can also be problematic in terms of the manner in which anti-racism is implemented.

In a broad sense, this chapter and the following one examine institutional approaches to anti-racism and the issue of British Asians in English professional football. Chapter 7 concentrates on specific empirical examples, whilst the analysis here is more theoretical. This chapter examines some of the wider issues related to the role of the anti-racist football movement in trying to increase the representation of British Asians in professional football. It does not seek to provide a generic history of anti-racism in football or the development of the various constituent organizations (see Garland and Rowe 2001 for a detailed account), but instead to examine how wider ideological debates and shifting approaches to anti-racism are encompassed and articulated in professional football and, in particular, how they affect British Asians. This chapter traces the rise and fall of the notion of 'political blackness', and the respective prominence of multiculturalism and anti-racism as hegemonic anti-discrimination discourses and practices. The implications of these developments are considered in the context of football, together with a discussion of appropriate anti-racist frameworks needed for increasing the participation of British Asians. The chapter also discusses the wider socio-political influences that have contributed to placing British Asian footballers so prominently on football's equity agenda.

British Asians and the trajectories of 'race relations' discourses

Following their arrival in Britain, migrants from the Caribbean and the Indian subcontinent immediately experienced animosity, hostility and violence from sections of the white population. For example, in 1958, African-Caribbeans were attacked by Teddy Boys in the St Ann's district of Nottingham and in Notting Hill, west London, which culminated in the murder of the black Antiguan Kelso Cochrane. Violent opposition to minority ethnic groups continued throughout the following decade and reached unprecedented levels during the 1970s. As Chapter 5 demonstrated, the flames of racist violence were fuelled by politicians such as Enoch Powell and an associated increasing prominence of fascist groups such as the National Front and the British Movement. A phenomenon that was to become known as 'Paki-bashing'[1] also began to manifest itself in a number of towns and cities (see e.g. Pearson 1976), and the latter part of the decade witnessed the racist murders of Gurdip Singh Chaggar in Southall, Altab Ali in Whitechapel and Akhtar Ali Baig in Newham. By the end of the 1970s, it had become apparent that, despite their diverse backgrounds and histories, Britain's minority ethnic communities were experiencing a broadly similar fate: they were all victims of racism, whether it be violence, or discrimination in employment, in housing, from the police and in other social spheres. Recognition of their common experiences as migrants in 'multi-racist' Britain (Cohen and Bains 1988) and the relative powerlessness of individual groups in challenging the systems and apparatuses of their oppression led to the belief that the most productive way of challenging racism was by forming a coalition of racialized groups. Consequently, in many areas, a sense of unity and solidarity developed between South Asian and African-Caribbean communities (Campaign Against Racism and Fascism/Southall Rights 1981; Sivanandan 1981/2).

Throughout the 1970s, multiculturalism was the dominant anti-discrimination paradigm. Originally it was promoted by those possessing a liberal approach to 'race relations' because it represented a movement away from the assimilationist models of the 1960s, and positioned ethnic and cultural difference as something that should be celebrated and embraced rather than feared and resisted. Focusing on the clothing, music, artefacts and cuisines of minority ethnic groups, multi-culturalism was perceived to be an appropriate method for familiarizing the white 'mainstream' with their identities and lifestyles. It was widely criticized by the political right who argued that it encouraged minority ethnic groups to retain the cultural elements of their ancestral countries rather than those of Britain, and to eschew assimilation with the majority population. The main argument from the radical left against multiculturalism was that it essentialized ethnic groups and their cultural traits, ignored the structural and economic facets of racism, and was tainted with traditional connotations of the 'exotica of difference' (S. Hall 1991; Hutnyk 2000). More recently, certain left-wing critiques have begun to mirror the underlying arguments of the right, with the likes of the Commission for Racial Equality (CRE) chairperson, Trevor Phillips, and cultural critic Kenan Malik arguing that the primacy attached to multiculturalism by metropolitan councils, such as Bradford, during the 1980s facilitated unabated ethnic segregation. This lack of integration and a related absence of 'shared values' are widely regarded as contributing to the poverty and social exclusion experienced by many minority ethnic groups today (K. Malik 2005b). Fundamentally, during its heyday, multi-culturalism was a non-subversive celebration of diversity and rarely represented a radical challenge to the social and racial status quo (Bonnett 2000).

Multiculturalism was succeeded in the late 1970s to early 1980s by anti-racism, which represented a more critical and radical approach to 'race relations'. In contrast to its predecessor, anti-racism was characterized by a focus on the (perceived) *commonalities* experienced by minority ethnic groups. As Anthias and Lloyd state, anti-racism:

> Stressed structural racism rather than the targeting of individual prejudice, and was contrasted to different types of multiculturalism which promoted cultural tolerance and the celebration of cultural difference as modes of struggling against racism. To this end anti-racists stressed 'race' difference and awareness and a critique was launched against the colour blindness of liberalism as well as the culturalism of the emphasis on ethnicity found within multiculturalism.
>
> (2002: 6)

Consequently, drawing inspiration from the Black Consciousness and Black Power movements in the USA during the 1960s (Carmichael and Hamilton 1967), the term 'black' became the main operating concept of anti-racism in Britain. Reclaimed from a term of abuse to become a signifier of 'race' pride 'black', in this context, was used in a symbolic, political sense to refer to *all* non-white groups (and sometimes also white minorities, such as Irish migrants). The term was conceived to facilitate a unity between diverse, relatively powerless minorities, for it was perceived that such collective identification was necessary to form an effective anti-racist movement. As Stuart Hall states:

> The term 'black' was coined as a way of referencing the common experience of racism and marginalization in Britain and came to provide the organizing category of a new politics of resistance, among groups and communities with, in fact, very different histories, traditions and ethnic identities.
>
> (1996: 441)

Accordingly, throughout the late 1970s to early 1980s, 'political blackness' became the dominant strategy in anti-racist discourse and practice.

However, during the 1990s, the 'cultural turn' (S. Hall 1997) in 'race relations' thinking and the emergence of ethnicity as the hegemonic concept in this field of social sciences meant that the framework of 'political blackness' began to lose status and support in academe. According to Pilkington (2003: 1–2), the cultural turn 'entailed deconstruction of the central categories, White and Black, sensitized us to diversity among members of both the majority group and minority groups, and highlighted how all human beings have multiple and shifting identities'. This theoretical shift was also influenced by wider social events, such as the Rushdie Affair of 1989 (see Chapter 3) which challenged the prevailing emphasis on the commonalities shared by racialized groups and brought to public attention the different experiences and social positions of minority ethnic communities in Britain. It demonstrated an increasing diversity in the manner in which minority ethnic groups construct and articulate their identities, together with the different ways that they make sense of the prejudices that they encounter. Fundamentally, it showed that the existence of pan-British Asian solidarities, let alone pan-minority ethnic ones, were contingent, potentially problematic and, at times, unachievable. As Alexander (2002: 553) points out, with the benefit of hindsight, 'that inclusive version of black Britain seems a distant mirage of unfulfilled and unfulfillable idealism and optimism, inevitably lost in the grim reality of real lives, incompatible needs and the competition for too-limited opportunities'.

Critiques of the way that 'political blackness' silenced the interests and identities of British Asians have come from prominent scholars, such as Stuart Hall (2000a) and Modood (see below), although they differ significantly in their beliefs regarding the degree to which the concept should be retained. Stuart Hall argues that a rejection of the essentialist 'black' subject represents:

> The recognition of the extraordinary diversity of subjective positions, social experiences and cultural identities which compose the category 'black'; that is, the recognition that 'black' is essentially a politically and culturally *constructed* category, which cannot be grounded in a set of fixed trans-cultural or transcendental racial categories and which therefore has no guarantees in nature. What this brings into play is the recognition of the immense diversity and differentiation of the historical and cultural experience of black subjects.
>
> (1996: 443)

He does, however, believe that there is still a potential role for a political 'black' identity, yet one which is cross-referenced to other issues, such as ethnicity, class, gender and sexuality. Modood (1994) has arguably been the most vehement and subsequently most controversial critic of the category 'black'. Whilst he recognizes that use of the term 'black' essentializes minority ethnicities *per se*, he argues that British Asians particularly are marginalized for a number of reasons: the term is often linked to Afrocentrism, slavery and the social histories of migrants from the Caribbean and sub-Saharan Africa, and so cannot have a neutral political capacity; it is used ambiguously within the same context, with reference to all minority ethnic populations in one instance and then purely to African-Caribbeans in another; and British Asians are increasingly unlikely to use 'black' as a self-descriptor. He states that 'the choice, then, is not between a separatist Asian ethnicity and unity of the racially oppressed; the choice is between a political realism which accords dignity to ethnic groups on their own terms and a coercive ideological fantasy' (Modood 1988: 403).

Modood (1997b) argues that any form of anti-racism that emphasizes skin colour above other aspects of identity, such as ethnicity, culture or religion, is likely to exclude and alienate British Asians and will be insensitive to their concerns and vulnerabilities. He claims that this approach ignores the specificities of anti-Asian racism and, particularly, the significance of a *cultural* component in the construction and manifestations of anti-Asian prejudices (Modood 1994). Instead he proposes a model of 'race relations' which appreciates that any oppressed group experiences its subjugation in relation to the identities that *it* and not the oppressor values the most. He posits that 'antiracism begins (i.e. ought to begin) by accepting oppressed groups on their own terms (knowing full well that these will change and evolve) not by imposing a spurious identity and asking them to fight in the name of that' (ibid. 1992a: 272; see also Modood 2005 for a collection of his work in this area).

Modood, in turn, has been subject to stringent criticism. For example, Solomos and Back (1996: 135) argue that in attempting to differentiate British Asians from other minority ethnic groups, he actually essentializes and reifies British Asian ethnicities and identities. They argue that different groups are subsumed within the category 'Asian' and, in this respect, Modood is equally as guilty as those who propose a spurious 'black' identity (see also Bhatt 1997). The authors also challenge Modood's assumption that being both British and of South Asian heritage – i.e. British Asian – makes 'Asianness' the more important component of identity. Others have pointed out that although anti-Muslim prejudice is undoubtedly particularly prevalent at the moment, this does not mean that racism towards other groups has decreased (see Kim 2004 and Song 2004 for debates around racial hierarchy/positionality). Furthermore, it has been argued that privileging the oppression of one group can be interpreted as disregarding the existence of shared problems or racial solidarities.

British Asians, collective identities and anti-racism in football

The issues discussed above have a plethora of implications for the politics of identity and strategies to combat racial discrimination. The aim of the following analysis is to consider their consequences for anti-racist strategies in football and, in particular, how they affect approaches to increasing the participation of British Asian players.

Anti-racism in English football has tended to be influenced by, and to follow, those debates occurring in other social institutions and organizations, albeit with an inevitable time delay as changes to dominant beliefs and practices filter into the game. When issues of 'race' first began to permeate football's policy agenda, racism was interpreted simply as a black/white issue. In part, the discourses and practices of the anti-racist football movement were simply mirroring the adherence to 'racial dualism' found in other spheres. There are, however, a number of more specific reasons why this position remained dominant and unchallenged in English football for longer than in other institutions. First, socio-political transformations in professional football tend to be reactionary rather than agenda-setting. Second, and relatedly, many organizations and bodies within the game have historically been resistant to change. In terms of anti-racist strategies, this intransigence has been compounded by a long and stubborn history of denial regarding the presence of racism and thus the need to challenge it (see Chapter 3). Third, anti-racism in football traditionally has tended to concentrate on challenging discrimination towards participating groups, rather than seeking to overcome the exclusion of under-represented ones and, until the 1990s, the only minority ethnic group represented as professional footballers in any substantial capacity was that of African-Caribbeans. Migrant Irish players, of course, have played professional football in Britain since the end of the nineteenth century, yet their 'whiteness' means that prejudice against them has not been recognized as racism. This state of affairs is further sustained by a historical and contemporary emphasis on racism in the *professional* game, which has meant that much less attention has been given to the diverse ethnic groups that have participated in amateur, recreational football in Britain. As this book has detailed, popular recognition that British Asians play football *at all* is only a recent development, so it comes as no surprise that their specific issues and problems were ignored or marginalized for so long.

Alexander (2002) identifies that whilst use of the notion 'black' as a political identity has become rare in academe, it has been retained to a greater degree in activist and campaign circles. A pertinent example is Southall Black Sisters (SBS). SBS was formed in 1979 as a feminist and anti-racist organization which aimed to protect the human rights of, and offer support to, minority ethnic women in the Southall part of London (Gupta 2003). For SBS, the term 'black' 'served as a useful mobilising term, potentially expansive when underpinned by progressive socialist principles, by including the various black and minority communities' (Patel 2002: 130). Whilst the term continues to be contested by some black and British Asian women, it is retained by the group in order to promote a socialist and secular anti-racist ethos in the face of the fragmentation of identity along religious lines in British Asian communities (ibid.). A similar approach can also be detected in the early work of Kick It Out, which often made reference to working with 'local black community groups' (e.g. Kick It Out 1998a). However, in recent years, increasing recognition has been given to the different forms of racism that exist in the game and anti-racist football organizations are now making reference to the issues experienced by a variety of minority ethnic groups, for example, Irish people (Kick It Out 2000b) and refugees/asylum seekers (Show Racism The Red Card 2002; Football Unites Racism Divides 2004).

What are the implications of the arguments raised above for anti-racism in football? In many ways it can be argued that British Asians experience different forms of racial prejudice and discrimination from those experienced by other minority ethnic groups, particularly African-Caribbeans. The way that the respective groups' physicalities are racialized and the stereotypes that are constructed in relation to them differ considerably. Physical stereotypes strongly influence beliefs about footballing competences and, consequently, impact on issues of inclusion/exclusion. It is also apparent that racial abuse in stadia often includes specific cultural referents, as demonstrated by the increasing incidence of Islamophobic discourses (see Chapter 3). Furthermore, in terms of the use of 'black' as a signifier of identity, British Asian footballers are extremely unlikely to describe themselves in this way. If the participants in this book had been pressed on the point – and, as has been highlighted, in practice the majority actually de-emphasize their ethnic signifiers – they would have been far more likely to describe themselves as, for example, Bengali, Muslim or British Asian.

However, there is also a degree to which the experiences of black and British Asian players at all levels of the game are commensurable. Whilst it is important not to essentialize the notion of a minority ethnic playing experience in the singular, there are many issues and problems that these groups *in general* undergo in English football. For example, they are similarly marginalized and excluded by the hegemonic 'whiteness' that permeates the game's structures and constructs professional clubs as 'white' institutions. Relatedly, they are heavily underrepresented in non-playing roles, as coaches, managers and directors, and in administrative roles in the club shop or ticket office. There are also instances where they are commonly 'Othered' in racist fan discourses at matches. Despite the evidence of specific prejudice outlined above, players from a variety of minority ethnic groups are also routinely labelled 'Pakis' or 'black bastards'.[2] For the racist, it is the 'non-whiteness' of the recipient that is significant in these discourses, rather than the specific ethnic referent. Experiences are perhaps even more common at amateur level where on-pitch racism and discrimination by local leagues and county associations are similarly endured by all minority ethnic groups (Long *et al.* 2000).

In order to increase the participation of British Asians in English professional football, one needs to acknowledge two key issues. On one hand there must be an appreciation of the specific issues and problems faced by British Asian players, both in general and by the heterogeneous groups that comprise this category. It is clear that discrimination and exclusion are based on, and experienced in relation to, not only skin colour, but also with regard to ethnic and religious identities, and an acknowledgement of this must be intrinsic to any anti-racist strategy. On the other hand, it is important to locate the discrimination against, and exclusion of, British Asians within the broader racial dynamics of British football, sport and society (both historically and contemporarily) and to not lose sight of the experiential commonalities of British Asian and African-Caribbean players in the game. As Song (2004: 185) points out, 'In our explorations of groups' racialized experiences, we . . . need to achieve a balance between the recognition of differential group trajectories and histories, and the fact that various processes of racialization are often mutually constitutive of one another'.

A further reason why it is important not to polarize the experiences of different minority ethnic groups and consider British Asians in isolation is because it ignores the role and importance of multi-ethnic solidarities in fighting racism. Werbner (1997: 247), for example, points out that 'effective anti-racist struggles depend on the evolution of common, unitary narratives and the *suppression* of cultural differences between victims of racism'. In football, mobilizing around a broad, symbolic 'black' identity has been a significant facet of anti-racism campaigns – the most recent example being the 'Stand Up, Speak Up' initiative, pioneered by Arsenal and France star Thierry Henry, and based around a wristband of intertwined white and black loops. Due to the vast number of ethnic groups now represented in the game – both as professionals and in an amateur capacity – it may be the case that for these groups to resist racism and to have their voices heard, Spivak's (1990) notion of 'strategic essentialism' – a deliberate, tactical move by oppressed groups to essentialize their identities as a way of resisting subjugation – has particular resonance in football. As Thierry Henry states 'racism is a problem for everyone, a collective ailment. . . . It shows that people of all colors [sic], even adversaries on the pitch, are banding together in this, because we're all suffering from it' (cited in Crumley 2005). It is important to point out that such a political strategy must come from the racialized groups themselves – any external imposition from other agencies simply reproduces the homogenizing, reifying tendencies of existing dominant discourses (Spivak 1990). To summarize this position, it is helpful to return to Alexander who argues that:

> Perhaps what we need is a third space, but one that is more than notional. This is one that holds on to the recognition of diversity within Britain's black communities but does not lose sight of the commonalities of experience, socio-economic, spatial, cultural, even emotional, which exist.
>
> (2002: 567)

While her proposal refers to social theory, it is also extremely relevant for practical attempts to eradicate racism from, and increase the participation of British Asians in, professional football.

A question of multiculturalism or anti-racism?

The other main issue discussed above that has implications for British Asians in football relates to the relative emphases placed on multiculturalism and anti-racism. Anthias and Lloyd (2002: 2) correctly point out that the two ideologies should neither be dichotomized nor regarded as identical, but positioned along a continuum. However, in football, anti-racism and multiculturalism are often conflated, and the nuances and differences between them are not appreciated. Whilst policies directed at British Asian players are usually labelled 'anti-racism', they often represent no more than a rather soft, banal, 'official' form of multiculturalism. Although this approach does possess benefits, there are some inherent problems: a tendency to essentialize ethnic identities and to reproduce stereotypes, and a failure to challenge entrenched, structural forms of racism.

Echoing wider social trends, popular images of British Asians in professional football continue to link their lifestyles and identities predominantly to the subcontinent and fail to appreciate the influences of living in Britain. Consequently, policies that aim to facilitate their inclusion in the professional game tend to adopt an outdated, stereotypical interpretation of young, male British Asian lifestyles and identities. For example, the following description by the Community Affairs manager at a Premier League club of some of the work they are doing to try to promote the inclusion of British Asians coaches illustrates this orientation:

> What we're doing at the moment is looking at ways that we can further attract Asian people onto our coaching programmes, by producing our literature in a range of languages, by delivering the coaching more local to where they live so they don't have travelling obstacles to overcome and by using key people in the communities who are already established there and working with them. . . . If they have an individual need, we will work with that. For example, if there's a dinner going on or if there's an awards ceremony and there's food we'll make sure that the food will be suitable for all tastes and maybe a vegetarian menu as opposed to a meat menu. If you're looking at language barriers then again we will try and work around that in the best way we can. If you're looking at uniform or suitable attire for people to play in, we will obviously operate with whatever religious constraints we have to work with.
>
> (Interview, 21 June 2002)

These concessions represent an important step in seeking to destabilize the hegemonic 'whiteness' that permeates the structures of professional football clubs. However, it can be argued that at one level these interventions do not reflect the sensibilities of the specific groups they are aimed at. As Burnett (2004: 5) points out, 'the promotion, through stereotyping, of the belief that there is a cultural 'otherness' intrinsic to Asians is in itself a means of marginalising, isolating and segregating them'. With regards to language, for instance, it is very unlikely that young British Asians would find this problematic. As Modood (1997c: 60–1) points out, with 16–24-year-olds, 99 per cent of Indians, 99 per cent of African Asians, 97 per cent of Bangladeshis and 96 per cent of Pakistanis speak English fluently. Furthermore, the commonsense idea that traditional South Asian clothing might inhibit participation in football shows little appreciation of the style and consumption patterns of young, British Asian footballers. A cursory glance around the pitches and playgrounds of Britain's inner cities reveals that young British Asian players are just as likely to be dressed in the replica jerseys and branded sportswear as their contemporaries from other ethnic backgrounds. Despite their anti-racist intentions, discourses of cultural difference are actually very similar to the racial stereotypes discovered by Long *et al.* (1997a) in their study of rugby league, where they encountered the claim that British Asians are under-represented in this sport because they 'cannot wear turbans in the scrum'. Such perceptions are symptomatic of a failure to engage and consult with British Asian players or to value their ideas in decision-making processes (see Chapter 7). Instead, the players are seen simply as objects or a 'problem' for institutional discussion.

Cultural stereotypes are also prevalent in attempts to increase the number of British Asians as supporters at live matches, revolving around the idea that professional clubs can make themselves more welcoming environments simply by celebrating ethnic diversity and offering incentives that are perceived to make British Asians feel more comfortable, such as subcontinental cuisine and musicians. However, there is a fine line between meeting the desires and requirements of different groups, and being seen as patronizing and tokenistic. As the following players make clear, experiences of racism, feelings of discomfort or fear experienced in stadia, plus other factors that contribute to the paucity of *all* minority ethnic groups as 'live' spectators, are too deeply entrenched to be overcome simply through selling onion bhajis and hot balti pies, or inviting a bhangra band to perform at half-time:

> I don't want to go to a football match for an onion bhaji! I want to go to a football match to see good football! I've been to games, but I like to, you know, go for the atmosphere and the football, not [laughing] for an onion bhaji!
>
> (Interview with member of a British Asian football federation, 25 April 2002)

> For the white community it is quite nice, you know, to hear a bhangra band or have a bhaji, you know, it saves them from going to the curry house after the game really! But to me a lot of it is tokenistic and, you know, they want to say, 'Well, we've done that, isn't that great and, you know, that's fantastic'. If the desire's there and if the will's there and they really want to make a difference and reach out to the Asians they've got to go the *whole way*.
>
> (Interview with British Asian amateur player, 16 March 2002)

> It's very sad. I don't know where they're getting the advice from, but certainly people like myself – I'm not saying I'm that educated or anything – my views are such that I've actually experienced things and know where I want to go and that's a huge difference to what these clubs believe. . . . To say well we need to introduce onion bhajis or we need to have this, by all means if they're having a cultural awareness [day] and there is a particular theme behind it, fair enough, but if they think that by doing that they're going to bring more Asians into football, I don't think that's the case.
>
> (Interview with British Asian ex-semi-professional player, 19 March 2002)

The second major problem with the dominance of multiculturalism over anti-racism in English football is that whilst it may enable the celebration of ethnic and cultural diversity, the power of racism and the entrenched, yet often subtle, ways that minority ethnic communities are discriminated against and excluded from clubs and their stadia tend to go ignored. King (2004a: 113), for example, argues that professional football clubs have sought to embody a multicultural ethos so as to avoid accusations of institutional racism, yet in doing so they have failed to address the structural barriers that prevent the progress of black players into positions of coaching and management or British Asians into the game at any level. Such an approach tends to present a primordialist, reified interpretation of British Asian 'culture', which 'is taken to mean values, beliefs, knowledge, and customs that exist in a timeless and unchangeable vacuum outside of . . . racism' (Razack cited in Karis 2004: 167). Racism is marginalized from the analysis of exclusion, thus ostensibly purporting the belief that discrimination and oppression can be eradicated simply by generating knowledge about other cultures.

Jazeel (2005: 236) points out that 'British multiculturalism, many would argue, is a tool that simultaneously reifies the boundaries that demarcate ethnicized communities as it cultivates the privileges of whiteness' (see also Kim 2004 on the situation in the USA). In this regard, multiculturalism in football has tended to ignore the fact that differences have been constructed through white supremacy. Consequently, multicultural policies reinforce existing power relations and ethnic hierarchies, offering a contrived and sanitized environment – ignoring the racism taking place in the stadium, surrounding streets and other local institutions – for an ephemeral engagement by white groups with the ethnic/exotic 'Other' in their midst. Such policies – alongside other forms of contemporary popular culture that seek to appropriate and commodify alterity (Banerjea 2000; Hutnyk 2000) – tend to 'museumize' cultures (Friedman 1997), further perpetuating the white, Western gaze and a neo-Orientalist desire to 'know about' and consequently control British Asians (Kaur and Hutnyk 1999). As Alexander (2002: 560) states regarding the current transient, contingent public engagement with 'Asianness': 'multicultural, multiracial "cool Britannia"; individualistic, inclusive, meritocratic, marketable, with just a hint of colour for emblematic danger. Same difference, safe difference'.

Conflict and internal segmentation in British Asian communities

Kim (2004: 989) argues that 'today's official multiculturalism is a discourse that formally and abstractly acknowledges racial and ethnic differences while suppressing the tensions and antagonisms that arise when different groups' struggles collide. It cannot help to resolve a problem whose existence it denies'. However, for anti-racist strategies focusing on British Asian footballers, recognition of the internal segmentation of, and tensions between, British Asian communities must be intrinsic to any framework. Whilst the fallacious existence of a unified British Asian community and a pan-British Asian consciousness is increasingly clear, it is also the case that British Asian communities are often characterized by intra-group antagonisms and tensions. As Lewis (1997: 126) argues, 'Britain is not immune to the impact of inter-religious tensions in South Asia or the Middle East, and this renders any homogenising discourse about black and Asian identity increasingly problematic'. He adds that '[British Asians] see each other in some British contexts as rivals, rehearsing ancient antagonisms, fuelled by the recrudescence of what has been called "religious fundamentalism"' (ibid.). Traditionally there has been a reluctance to discuss ethnic conflict or communalism within, or between, British Asian communities (Kundnani 2002a). This is partly due to the fact that British Asians traditionally have been perceived as a singular, homogenous community, and thus the existence of ethnic, religious and caste conflicts has tended to go unrecognized or has been ignored. It is also the case that attaching significance to such antagonisms has been seen as threatening the multi-ethnic political solidarities that have represented such an important component of anti-racism.

The inter-Asian conflicts that have arisen are part of the global repercussions of events in the Indian subcontinent, including territorial disputes over Kashmir, and debates between Hindus and Muslims over the religious denomination of the Babri Masjid in Ayodhya, northern India[3] (Kundu 1994; Burlet and Reid 1995). Tensions have become particularly pronounced in the wake of 9/11. A poll carried out shortly after the disaster revealed that 44 per cent of British Asians believed that it had accentuated divisions between their various communities (Neiyyar 2001), and evidence suggests that some Hindus and Sikhs are seeking to distinguish and distance themselves from Muslims (Kundnani 2001; BBC Radio 2005a).

Sport is not insulated from manifestations of these hostilities. For example, in 1992, a cricket match between Indian and Pakistani teams at Crystal Palace to raise funds for Imran Khan's cancer hospital was abandoned after fighting broke out between rival supporters. In 1996, fans fought on the pitch at Lord's after India beat Pakistan in the under-15 Cricket World Cup. In 1999, police were called to a cricket match in Leicester between Hindu and Muslim sides after a player assaulted an opponent with a cricket bat (Williams 2001: 177). The degree to which similar occurrences are present in football is unclear, with many players playing down their likelihood:

> Certain clubs don't like certain other teams. Like within these [British Asian football] tournaments you will find there are always individuals who, you know, don't like one team or another team, or don't like individuals. But it's not racial, if you see what I'm saying. Whereas in society there are racial issues within Asian communities, you know, like Pakistanis and Sikhs, and they do have problems like that. . . . But I don't think there's racial tension in sport in Asian games, there can only be tension between individuals.
> (Interview with British Asian amateur player, 5 February 2002)

> [Intra-Asian tension] certainly is evident at the moment. I must be frank, purely on the basis of the Muslim activity both following September 11 and very recently the Hindu and Muslim [conflict] in terms of the temple and the mosque issue [in Ayodhya] in India. But beyond that, within our organization, in terms of [our] football federation, it's been predominantly footballing banter – if I may call it that – where, you know, one would swear at somebody and you'd possibly use a particular phrase which, if you were standing in the pub, or whatever, you wouldn't necessarily use, but that's just

in the heat of the moment. But beyond that there certainly isn't anything evident.

(Interview with member of a British Asian football federation,
19 March 2002)

One (Muslim) British Asian amateur player spoke of his involvement in tournaments run by the Khalsa Football Federation (KFF), a Sikh-based organization:

> The Khalsa Federation is a Sikh organization, so they are Sikhs and those tournaments that do happen are, I guess, primarily meant to be for Sikhs. But there is such a good mix of Asians it's not necessarily just for the Sikhs. Although there are supposed to be huge sort of, like, conflicts between the Sikhs and the Muslims, in the events that the Khalsa Federation have organized – I've played in some of the tournaments – I've not seen any tensions whatsoever. Actually they organize it really well, I must say, and they treat you like you're one of their own really.

(Interview, 16 March 2002)

Whilst there is little recorded evidence of intra-Asian tensions in amateur football, their likelihood should not be dismissed, especially since antagonisms exist in other social and leisure spheres where young, male British Asian identities and masculinities are being articulated and contested (Bennett 2000). One pertinent example demonstrates how tensions can be articulated through the vernacular of terrace 'banter'. During the match between Bangladesh and India, at Leicester City's Filbert Street stadium in July 2000, Indian supporters openly celebrated not only the ethnic differences, but also the increasing socio-economic divide, between the two populations in Britain. Referring to the large number of Bangladeshi men that are employed in the restaurant trade – one third of all British Bangladeshi men work as cooks or waiters (D. Walker 2002) – some Indian supporters mocked their opponents with chants of, 'Waiter, waiter, what's the score?' and 'Curry and chips'.[4]

British Asians, football and social inclusion

In examining why the absence of British Asians as professional players has become such an important issue on football's anti-racist agenda, a number of contributing factors can be identified. First, and most importantly, it is a significant, inveterate problem that has shown little sign of abating. In spite of the committed and assiduous lobbying by various organizations, the exclusion of a large population of potential British Asian players continues and can no longer be ignored. Second, for some organizations, initiatives and fan groups, the original problem or issue that they were established to deal with (for example, opposition to a board of directors or proposed stadium relocation) no longer exists and so they have broadened their remit to cover other areas, such as anti-racism and, in particular, the exclusion of British Asians (Bradbury 2001a). This re-orientation has taken place in a socio-political climate in which issues surrounding 'race' and racism have permeated both political discourses and the public consciousness. More specifically, this is a result of the Macpherson Report (Macpherson 1999) and the introduction of new legislation, primarily the Race Relations (Amendment) Act 2000 (which states that public authorities have a statutory duty to promote racial equality). Subsequently, in the realm of sport, partnerships have been forged between agencies such as the CRE and Sport England to promote racial equality within national governing bodies and key sports organizations (Long *et al.* 2005). These developments have led to what King (2004a: 113) describes as 'an institutional obsession, almost compulsion, to implement anti-racism and social inclusion' in English football.

A concomitant trend has been the shift by New Labour towards the reciprocal tactic of prioritizing social inclusion in sports policy and using sport to combat wider social problems (Spracklen 2003). As part of this transition football, in particular, has been increasingly cited as a means of promoting social inclusion, especially through its role in integrating minority ethnic and migrant groups. As Armstrong (2002: 479) points out, 'the topic of football and reconciliation is relevant and even fashionable, and the influences that the game can have on people are thus recognized by a whole host of organizations'. A widespread consensus regarding football's role as an educational tool and, indeed, as a social panacea, has meant that, at the beginning of the twenty-first century, it is a prominent item on political agendas and its conciliatory capacities have been strongly championed by the government and other agencies.

In its early manifestation as a tool for promoting social inclusion, football was seen as a medium for challenging dysfunctional behaviour and rehabilitating persistent criminals. However, with increasing political attention being paid to racial tensions and urban unrest between British Asian, black and white youths in many areas of the country, together with debates over refugees and asylum seekers, the game's social role has been extended to cover these areas as well. The government has proposed that local authorities should organize sport competitions in order to diffuse racial tensions, particularly those involving asylum seekers (Travis 2002). Other projects are undertaken and funded through Positive Futures, a national social inclusion programme aimed at marginalized youngsters in deprived neighbourhoods and managed by the Home Office's Drug Strategy Directorate. One example is *Kickstart*, a football project based in Southwark, south London. The original aim of the project was to use football to rehabilitate young offenders, but it now uses the game to promote understanding and co-existence amongst different ethnic groups on adjacent housing estates. Specifically, the scheme has initiated a football league for teams representing local Bengali, Irish, Somali and Traveller communities (Stear 2002). Football has also been used within educational initiatives, such as the *We All Stand Together* project at West Bromwich Albion FC and the Arc Theatre Group's trilogy of anti-racist plays for schoolchildren: *Kicking Out* premiered in 1994, *Ooh Aah Showab Khan* – which focused specifically on British Asian footballers – in 1997, and *My England* in 2000. The activities of the Charlton Athletic Race Equality (CARE) partnership 'involve the use of arts and sports to break down different forms of barriers faced by many people living in the Borough, particularly members of ethnic minority communities' (Charlton Athletic Race Equality 2000: 1), whilst the Sports Participation and Cultural Equality (SPACE) project in Huddersfield states that, 'our main objective is to use sport as a social tool and use this approach to breakdown social barriers' (Kick It Out 2001: 7).

Many of the players interviewed for this book argued that the current tendency for anti-racist football projects to focus on British Asian players needs to be placed firmly within these wider socio-political developments. As a result of the involvement of young, British Asian men in the urban unrest of 2001 and the London bombings of 2005, there has been a notable emphasis on this section of the population in contemporary political discourses of social inclusion. Whilst the exclusion of British Asians as professional footballers is, in day-to-day practice, an internal issue for the game itself, it is apparent that projects that attempt to overcome this problem have been influenced by contemporary governmental policies that aim to address the issues and problems facing young British Asian males in general. This was highlighted by a member of an anti-racist football organization:

> The fact is that maybe some Asian lads are dealing in drugs, or whatever, but it's like they [politicians] can't say there are *some* Asian lads without saying they're *all* at it, know what I mean? So now it will just be like, 'Oh, we'll divert them, we'll get them to play football', you know, 'If they're playing football then they won't be selling drugs or something'.
>
> (Interview, 16 July 2002)

There are a range of potential problems that arise through conflating schemes that seek to increase the participation of British Asians as professional footballers and those that use football as a medium to improve the social inclusion of young British Asian men. One British Asian amateur player argued that:

> I think obviously social inclusion has, politically, risen to a high priority as far as this government is concerned and I suspect that in some parts of the country, Asians in football is being seen as a vehicle to promote social inclusion. . . . At the moment I think Asian footballers are being used as sort of tokens by some organizations to promote, if you like, much wider sociological and political agendas. But they're not agendas that are focused and centred on sport and the development of footballers.
>
> (Interview, 23 April 2002)

As this testimony elucidates, the aims of the two types of project ostensibly are very different. One is about elite sport and talent development, the other is about a socio-political process and sport for all. It is important that this is recognized and the two types of project are not homogenized into a single strategy that seeks to achieve a multitude of outcomes. However, despite their divergent rationales, aims and philosophies, and the fact that social inclusion projects can only, at most, partially assist the drive to increase the participation of British Asians in the professional game, they do arguably have a role to play. For example, the Positive Futures project in Coventry works with increasing numbers of young British Asians and has links with Coventry City FC. At present this gives project participants the opportunity to attend matches through the provision of free tickets (Asians in Football Forum 2005), thus partially challenging the exclusion of British Asians from the professional game. Such partnerships need to be extended though, so that talented players can be identified and given the opportunity to progress into excellence programmes, rather than simply receive free tickets to help fill up half-empty stadia. Involvement in social inclusion projects is currently the primary link between many young, urban British Asians and the professional game, and so this is a connection that must be explored to its full potential.

By way of conclusion to this chapter, it is important to highlight that support for current manifestations of anti-racism in football has been neither unconditional nor universal. In particular, criticism has come from British Asian footballers themselves. Whilst they generally welcome developments aimed at overcoming their exclusion as professional players, many are critical of aspects of current projects. Their concerns focus primarily on the rationales that they perceive to be behind these schemes, the manner in which they have been implemented, and the extent to which they have achieved their objectives. Furthermore, a corollary of the perception that British Asian football projects are heavily influenced by a contemporary fascination with football, 'race' and social inclusion is that a number of players are worried that the current anti-racist focus on British Asian footballers is simply an ephemeral – politically astute, but superficial – development and subject to the whims of politicians, football clubs and the game's governing bodies. They are apprehensive that the attention given to British Asian footballers might evanesce if success is not achieved or if another 'ism' becomes politically fashionable. The thoughts of one British Asian ex-professional/semi-professional player are worth quoting at length:

> I sat in on a couple of meetings with [an anti-racist football organization]. There's one or two people involved with this set-up and I sat back and looked over the last few years. They're local people and I think, what are they trying to achieve? Right, obviously they care about Asians in football. [Yet] two years have gone by and they're still doing the same job. I'm thinking is there something in it for them? I've seen these people walking round [this city] eating in restaurants and doing whatever. I'm thinking, right, so they're getting funded for doing this, what do they want to get out of it? Or are they just jumping on the bandwagon, doing things for the sake of doing them and not really achieving anything? . . . People see it as Asian football's a problem, I'm going to jump on the bandwagon and have a piece of this pie. . . . I just think people are in it for themselves. They see it, you know, I'll jump on this because it can help me gain publicity and keep me in a job for a few years.

I think people do that and I think it's wrong because it happens all over the country, you know. It's just a craze at the moment, isn't it? Oh, *Asian* football, *Asian* this, *Asian* that.

(Interview, 5 March 2002)

Another player added that:

From my point of view it's got to be something that lasts and something that's sustainable and at the moment I fear that we're just in the middle of a sort of a fad – Asians in football. But I wonder how long before the headlines change to something else.

(Interview with British Asian amateur player, 23 April 2002)

To suggest that *all* people involved with this issue are 'in it for themselves', as purported in the first example, is clearly both unfair and erroneous. Furthermore, whether the above testimonies represent an accurate long-term prediction obviously is impossible to predict, although the topic's continued prevalence suggests that it has greater longevity than was felt at the time of the interviews. Nonetheless, one can empathize with the concerns of players, clubs and communities that have sought to overcome the exclusion of British Asians from professional football clubs for almost a third of a century, for the most part without the interest, support or intervention of any other institution or organization, either within or outside of the game. As one member of a British Asian football federation stated:

[Asian] people have been playing football and organizing football for a number of years, well before, you know, this media interest came through or the clubs' interest came through. So [if the focus changes] we'll still be here and hopefully far better positioned than we are at the moment and hopefully achieve our vision of getting a player from this local area, not just nationally, an Asian or a Bangladeshi, who's come through our ranks, our system, getting into professional football.

(Interview, 25 April 2002)

This critique of current policies and strategies aimed at increasing the participation of British Asians in professional football continues in the follow chapter, which focuses on some of the schemes and initiatives that have been implemented in recent years.

7 British Asians and anti-racism in English football II
Case studies and critique

Introduction

This chapter offers an in-depth critique of some of the contemporary policies and activities implemented by professional clubs and anti-racist football organizations with regard to increasing the participation of British Asians in professional football. Some of the issues discussed emanate from personal observations, but the majority are those raised by British Asian players themselves. It should be noted that the topics covered are intended to be illustrative, rather than exhaustive, of the issues facing British Asian footballers and the problems that they perceive to exist with aspects of anti-racism in football. This chapter examines the following areas: the manner in which professional football clubs and anti-racist football organizations attempt to engage in community consultation; the significance of ethnicity in coach–player relations; the implications of collaboration with the police in anti-racist projects; the use of matches between British clubs and teams from the Indian subcontinent as participation-raising initiatives; and the effects of media publicity on young British Asian professional players.

The position taken here is one that is unequivocally supportive of anti-racism and the need to continually and actively challenge racism in English professional football, yet is critical of the manner in which certain aspects of anti-racism are implemented in the game, particularly in relation to British Asians. In this regard, theoretical influence is taken from the work of radical 'race' thinkers, such as Paul Gilroy, particularly the trenchant and polemical critique of anti-racism espoused in his essay, 'The End of Antiracism' (Gilroy 1992). Bell points out that:

> One of the main problems of writing 'The End of Antiracism' was of course that Gilroy ran the risk of his critique being cast back into the lines of the debate itself: how could he take a stand that was both sympathetic to the intent of the anti-racist campaigns and be critical of them?
>
> (2002: 511)

However, as Gilroy and others have argued, anti-racism needs to undergo continual critical evaluation if it is to be successful. For example, P. Cohen argues that:

It is often said that one of the problems with antiracism is that it knows what it is against, but not what it is for. But do we really know enough about the whys and wherefores of racism? If not, then perhaps the models of racism which are implicitly present in anti-racist policies and practices may be inhibiting the development of more positive and effective strategies?

(1992: 62–3)

Similarly Rattansi (1992: 11) argues that to increase the efficacy of anti-racism it is 'necessary to take a hard and perhaps painful look at the terms under which [it has] operated so far'. This rallying call remains equally pertinent today. Engaging in critical reflection on current anti-racist strategies is a crucial component in striving – as scholars, activists and/or supporters – to map and challenge contemporary racisms, and seeking to overcome the exclusion of British Asians from professional football.

Community service? Representation, dialogue and club-community relations

One of the most widely raised and enduring criticisms of professional football clubs, in terms of their relationships with local British Asian communities, has been their failure to initiate substantial dialogue with them. This lack of engagement was also reflected in the work of the pioneering anti-racist football schemes and organizations. Dominated by well-meaning, yet generally ill-informed, white, middle-class activists, these groups failed to engage sufficiently with minority ethnic communities and thus often misunderstood or ignored the issues and problems facing, among others, British Asian players. As Lentin (2004: 250) points out, 'Often in anti-racism, representation has been constructed on the basis of assumptions by white anti-racists, made without consulting the populations whose interests they feel themselves to be representing'. The membership of anti-racist football organizations now reflects more closely the diverse ethnic groups they work with, although a white male hegemony still exists in the majority of co-ordinating committees and steering groups. Furthermore, it is now generally recognized that projects aimed at increasing the representation of British Asians in professional football are unlikely to achieve credibility unless consultation with the local British Asian communities is nurtured. It has become apparent that British Asians are being given a voice, albeit gradually, selectively and contingently, through which they can contribute to initiatives.

In the vast majority of cases, consultation with British Asian communities is undertaken through dominant religio-cultural institutions, such as mosques, temples and community centres, and with the spokespeople (usually middle-aged men) who claim, and are perceived, to represent them. In one sense, this is because in many towns and cities they are the most well-established and publicly prominent British Asian organizations. It is also because in the popular imagination, the lives of *all* British Asians are still perceived to be strongly linked to religious practices, and subcontinental cultures and traditions. As a result, institutions and individuals that invoke such connotations are seen to be the most representative of British Asian communities and the most organically authentic. In this regard, they represent the most obvious and applicable source of collaboration for anti-racist football organizations. The following statements are representative of this:

> One thing that we have done, and pioneered in [this town] in my time, is outreach work with the Bangladeshi community. . . . I think one of the problems faced there was, initially, that if we'd just gone in and said we are [a professional] football club, we'd have had a very poor response. What we actually did was we advertised this [project] through the local mosque and community centre, on their letter-headed paper, making it clear to that community that the scheme had the full approval of their elders and the people to whom they looked up to for advice and guidance.
>
> (Interview with former chairperson of a club-based anti-racist scheme,
> 13 June 2002)

> Specifically, in the community department, we work at the moment with [the] City Council Equal Opportunities [department], we work with the Race Equality Advisory Board, we work with lots and lots of local schools, we work with the Hindu Charitable Trust, the Sikh Temple, the Pakistani Centre, as well as lots and lots of other different ethnic minority groups.
>
> (Interview with Community Affairs manager, Premier League club,
> 21 June 2002)

This inchoate consultation represents a tangible improvement in club–community relations, taking into account the almost total absence of dialogue of around ten years ago. However, it has significant repercussions for the ways that clubs and anti-racist football organizations interpret and represent British Asian identities.

Baumann (1999) argues that not only are community leaders often self-appointed, but also that they frequently claim to speak on behalf of, for example, 'the Muslim community' as a singular entity or, indeed, *for* Islam. This has significant implications for hegemonic representations of Muslims in Britain, in that 'whatever a spokesperson may say about the views or attitudes of the Muslims he [sic] claims to represent is stylized into "*the* attitude of *the* Muslim community"' (ibid.: 70). By controlling the images and discourses that are articulated to outside groups, community leaders are able to influence the way in which their communities are perceived in the wider society, including professional football clubs and anti-racist football organizations. However, it has become apparent that community leaders (and the institutions within which they operate) are increasingly unable to represent the heterogeneity of the communities that they claim to speak for (Bunting 2005). Issues of representation are particularly salient in the aftermath of 7/7, with community leaders and their institutions widely, and contradictorily, charged with either engendering or failing to subdue religious extremism in Britain's Muslim communities (Abbas 2006). It is important to stress, though, that issues regarding community representation and inter-generational conflict are certainly not exclusive to Muslim or other British Asian communities, as is often purported in dominant media and political discourses. Problems regarding community leadership and representation are arguably occurring in all communities.

In particular, the (in)ability of community leaders to represent the needs and interests of *young* people has undergone substantial scrutiny. With reference to the public inquiries that were undertaken into the involvement of young British Asian men in urban unrest in northern England in 2001:

> All [reports] draw attention to the extent [to] which young people's voices have been largely ignored by decision-makers in the areas where there were disturbances. Some young people complained that the older community and religious leaders who claimed to represent them failed to articulate the experiences of the young.
>
> (Home Office 2001a: 14)

With British Muslims this situation has been accentuated by a tendency for British mosques to recruit *imams* (leaders of Islamic congregations) from nations such as Pakistan and Bangladesh. Whilst their habituses may be commensurable with older British Asians, a frequent failure to speak English and their inexperience of life in Britain mean that they are often unable to connect with, and earn the respect of the younger members of their communities (Lewis 2002; McLoughlin 2005).

The tendency for clubs and anti-racist football organizations to adhere to a 'hierarchy of credibility' (Becker 1970) and collaborate primarily, and often exclusively, with dominant community leaders and institutions means that young voices are marginalized from vital discussions and decision-making processes. This represents a problem as it is the younger sections of the British Asian population that are most likely to have an appreciation of the issues facing British Asian footballers. Conversely, many within the older generations have no interest in, or knowledge of, football and may even possess a negative opinion of the game. Thus the absence of young people in prominent positions within their communities means that many British Asian players are prevented from establishing contact and channels of dialogue with professional clubs and anti-racist football organizations. These agencies might therefore be provided with an inaccurate portrait of the issues facing British Asian football players, and also risk alienating the specific people with whom they need to be working.

Colouring over the (touch) lines? British Asian coaches as cultural intermediaries

The under-representation of British Asians as professional footballers is mirrored by their near absence in non-playing roles, as managers, coaches and talent scouts, as well as in administrative positions within clubs, leagues and governing bodies (Commission for Racial Equality 2004; Independent Football Commission 2004). For example, a survey carried out during the 1999/2000 season found that only twenty-five British Asian coaches and nineteen scouts were working in professional football, with fourteen of the coaches based at just two clubs (Bradbury 2001b). Furthermore, at the present time it remains the case that not a single British Asian is employed in 'front-line' management, i.e. as team manager, assistant manager or first-team coach, which suggests that those who are employed are likely to be on only part-time or temporary contracts. This exclusion of British Asians is a consequence of the stereotypes, patterns of racial exclusion and the system of contacts and networks described throughout this book, which promote the interests and career progressions of whites, yet marginalize and discriminate against those of minority ethnic groups. It still remains the case that a former professional player is far more likely to be employed as a manager or a coach than somebody who has not played at this level, even if the latter's qualifications are superior.[1] The absence of British Asians as players thus severely limits their opportunities to reach the higher levels of management.

Instead, those British Asians who are employed as coaches or scouts at professional clubs work exclusively within the youth academies or are involved in specific outreach projects with minority ethnic, particularly British Asian, communities. This is a result of wider barriers restricting the progression of minority ethnic coaches (King 2004a) – often known as the 'glass ceiling' syndrome – yet this situation also occurs because establishing a system of British Asian youth coaches and scouts is believed by many in the game to be one of the most effective methods of increasing the inclusion of British Asians as professional players. There is an assumption that British Asian coaches and scouts have the appropriate contacts within British Asian communities and a suitable knowledge of local British Asian clubs and leagues (Football Association 1999). It is also perceived that the presence of British Asian coaches and scouts would act as a point of contact – literally a 'friendly face' – to assist the inclusion of young British Asians into the ostensibly alien environment of a professional football club. For example, the Director of the Youth Academy at one Premier League club suggested that:

> An Asian scout might be able to tap into the Asian community and get you decent players. I think it would be a good idea, yeah. . . . An Asian person is going to have more success in recruiting Asian kids than a white person, generally speaking, I would say.
>
> (Interview, 16 January 2002)

British Asian coaches have been used in this way by anti-racist football organizations including Football Unites Racism Divides (FURD), the Leicester Asian Sports Initiative (LASI) and Respect All Fans Football Initiative (RAFFI), as well as by schemes based at professional clubs in areas of significant British Asian populations, such as Leeds United, Northampton Town and West Ham United (Kick It Out 1998a; Football Unites Racism Divides 2001; Frampton *et al.*

2001). Confirming the implementation of this philosophy, the former chairperson of one club-based anti-racist scheme reported that:

> We got funding from [our] Borough Council – which was from the SRB [Single Regeneration Budget] funding – for a fifteen-month project, the objective of which was to train or get three adult [British Asian] coaches to get their FA coaching badges, so that they could legitimately help to train young Bangladeshi kids.
>
> (Interview, 13 June 2002)

The presence of British Asian coaches at professional clubs certainly has a number of benefits. Primarily, it helps to destabilize the hegemonic 'whiteness' that permeates the professional game, it provides a visible presence in the occupational culture, and it slowly opens up contact networks to British Asian players. Coaches may also be able to access certain untapped sections of British Asian communities. Furthermore, an increase in the number of British Asians with coaching qualifications is crucial to the holistic progress of British Asian football and the long-term development of players from recreational participation upwards.

However, despite these advantages, the contention that employing British Asian professional coaches is an effective – or, indeed, the best – means of recruiting British Asians into professional football as players overlooks some potentially problematic repercussions. Basically, it implies that a coach's ethnicity is more important than his qualifications. The theory underpinning this strategy is that British Asian players are most likely – or, indeed, only able – to relate to, and work with, coaches from a similar ethnic background. Yet until sufficient numbers of British Asians achieve high-level coaching qualifications (which is increasing, albeit gradually), those organizations and club-based schemes that choose to provide only British Asian coaches to British Asian clubs and coaching schemes will, in most cases, be offering only a basic level and quality of coaching. Thus whilst it may play an important role in talent identification and early years' coaching, ethnic-matching may restrict development at higher levels. Many British Asian players are critical of this trend and argue that, by promoting it, many professional clubs and anti-racist football organizations are actually failing to meet their needs and desires. For example, one player reported his personal experiences of this phenomenon:

> My nephew would come home [from school] and say, 'Oh, we had this coach come and [teach] football'. [One day] I went down there to pick him up and I saw my goalkeeper from my Sunday league side. I said to him, 'What are you doing here?' I know he does coaching for [a professional club] but [he only holds] the prelim [FA preliminary] badge. What is that, yeah?! The credentials on that, anyone can do that! . . . He goes, 'I coach here' and I thought to myself, hang on a minute, [this professional club] is offering these inner city kids the lowest end of their coaches and they call this an

improvement, or trying to develop these kids into playing football! Why didn't they send their best lot? Why are they giving a coach who plays in a Sunday league youth side, a goalkeeper, who's only learnt the basics and he's come out and he's teaching them? Because they're Asian kids – the majority in that school – are they supposed to, all of a sudden, look up and relate to him because he's Asian also? Do they not think they'll relate to a white coach in the same way?

(Interview with British Pakistani ex-professional player, 20 February 2002)

The 'British Asian coaches for British Asian players' approach is therefore inherently contradictory. On one hand it indulges in the 'ethnic absolutism' – the belief that cultures exist and develop in homogenous, hermetically sealed units that are isolated from, and share little in common with, other ethnic groups – that Gilroy (1992) rightly criticizes. On the other, it essentializes British Asians as a social group and fails to recognize the ethnic, religious, cultural and socio-economic divisions that exist between them. As one British Indian amateur player suggested, if an organization offered his club a Bengali coach, his players would be no more likely to identify with him than with a white or African-Caribbean coach. Put simply, the approach seeks to distinguish British Asians from other ethnic groups, yet simultaneously homogenizes them in the process. Accordingly, there is an assumption that a vague, shared general sense of 'Asianness' (whatever that may be) is the most important factor in establishing a working relationship between a coach and his players.

In order to ensure that British Asian players reach the standards achieved by players of other backgrounds, it is crucial that they are given opportunities to access the best coaching possible, irrespective of the ethnicity of the person(s) providing it. For example, one British Indian amateur player argued that:

There is a belief amongst some football authorities that actually Asians are only understood by Asians or that Asians want to see more Asians in football coaching and that, culturally, it is only Asian coaches that can understand them. . . . I think what people want is the very best for their personal development, regardless of whether that individual's from the same race as them or from the same culture or even from the same caste. I think, you know, it simply is sort of a misconception to think that actually only Asians can coach Asians and therefore what you need to do is bring more Asian coaches in. What you need is the *very best* coaches, coaching all the players and then identify Asians as a group that might need additional help to get them up to the same level as everybody else.

(Interview, 23 April 2002)

Another player echoed these sentiments:

When [my British Asian club] were first formed, in the first year or two, our coach was a white chap. He'd been involved with our local football for a number of years, so we knew him prior to him being the coach. I think it is a sort of narrow-minded view to think that Asians can only relate to Asians because in some ways I've felt, and I've seen, that actually Asian kids probably relate or have more respect for *non-Asian* coaches. For example, in our area, on a lot of occasions you tend to get [British Asian] coaches who try to coach, but they're not getting the respect because [players] feel that it's just one of us, nothing special. . . . I think it doesn't really matter what colour a coach is. It's got to be the best coaches available.

(Interview with British Bangladeshi amateur player/member of a British
Asian football federation, 25 April 2002)

A failure to receive the best coaching possible regardless of ethnic background is accordingly perceived to inhibit the development of football within British Asian communities and their passage into the professional game. This parallels the concerns raised by British Asian players in Chapter 3 regarding the restrictions that prevent many British Asians playing with or against players of other ethnicities. Participating in coaching and training sessions that only involve other members of their communities does little to overcome this situation. At present, British Asian coaches possess neither the status nor contacts within the professional game that white (and to a far lesser extent African-Caribbean) coaches do and so it is crucial that British Asian players access contact networks outside their own communities (see Chapter 4).

A related problem with this approach is that it can give the impression that clubs and organizations do not take British Asian players seriously enough to justify providing 'mainstream' coaches, and do not rate British Asian coaches sufficiently to employ them higher up the coaching pyramid. Thus an unintended consequence of channelling the involvement of British Asian coaches is that it reinforces ethnic hierarchies and power relations within the game by implying that they are merely assisting the more serious work undertaken by white coaches with white and African-Caribbean players, both at first team level and in other projects.

More generally, this trend demonstrates the widespread hypocrisy inherent in debates about ethnic and racial integration. This issue has become particularly prominent in 'race relations' rhetoric, with segregated communities – in particular the notion of 'parallel lives' – cited in the official investigations as the 'problem' which 'caused' the urban unrest in northern England in 2001 (Burnley Task Force 2001; Home Office 2001b; Oldham Independent Review 2001; Ouseley 2001). More recently, in 2005, CRE chairperson Trevor Phillips argued that Britain was 'sleepwalking into segregation' and would soon possess racial ghettos like the USA (Gillan 2005: 7). In dominant discourses, these patterns of segregation are usually blamed on the perceived social preferences of minority ethnic groups and rarely on the material deprivation, social exclusion and institutional racism that contribute to them. British Muslims, for example, are often castigated for what is perceived to be their self-imposed cultural and geographical isolation, and campaigns to establish state-funded Islamic schools are widely opposed outside Muslim communities for contributing to 'educational apartheid'.[2] Yet in such instances, little acknowledgement is given to the racist and Islamophobic social practices that contribute to such trends. Furthermore, not only does research suggest that ethnic integration in Britain is actually increasing (Dodd 2005b), but also that *white* communities are more likely to state a desire to live alongside people of the same ethnic background (Dodd 2004). However, changing demographics do not apply to all cultural spheres and British Asian footballers being coached exclusively by other British Asians only accentuates the distance that exists between British Asians and professional football. On one hand, British Asians are admonished for the fact that many players and teams compete in all-Asian leagues but, on the other hand, they are often denied the opportunity to engage in coaching projects with coaches and players of other ethnicities.

Footing the bill: the role of the police in anti-racist football projects

Most anti-racist football initiatives and organizations now recognize that the issues and problems they encounter are connected to wider social phenomena and that adopting a multi-agency/partnership approach with other groups is crucial. External agencies also play a fundamental role in providing financial assistance to many anti-racist football organizations, particularly those that are independent or autonomous, i.e. not linked to specific clubs. The steering groups and funding committees for many initiatives consist of, or involve collaboration with, a number of disparate agencies, within both the public and private sectors. For example, as well as its own personnel, a club-based initiative might include members of the local council, teachers and academics, representatives from minority ethnic community groups and football clubs, and local businesses. A further prominent source of funding and partnership has been the police. Both Kick It Out and Show Racism the Red Card have received funding and/or sponsorship from their local forces (Kick It Out 1998a; Show Racism the Red Card 2000), whilst Football Unites Racism Divides receives financial support from the South Yorkshire Police Community Initiatives Programme. The Metropolitan Police have been involved in auxiliary projects, such as distributing free match tickets to Kosovan refugees on behalf of Millwall FC (Back *et al.* 2001b) and sponsoring (through its Positive Action Team) the Asian Champions Cup, a British Asian 5-a-side football tournament (Eastern Eye 2002a). A similar tournament has taken place in Bolton under the auspices of GEMS (Getting Ethnic Minorities into Sport) and the Greater Manchester Police Authority.

What might be the possible motives behind collaborations between clubs, anti-racist football organizations and the police? Certainly the police are aware of their continuingly problematic presence and status within minority ethnic communities, especially in the wake of the evidence of institutional racism that was uncovered by the Macpherson Report (Macpherson 1999) and, more recently, a BBC television exposé of racist officers (BBC TV 2003b). The popularity of football, especially with young people, and the existence of a well-established and high-profile anti-racist football movement on which they can 'piggyback' means that the game provides an ideal medium for the police to attempt to improve their community profile. Furthermore, by continuing to fund the anti-racist football movement, the police are able to reaffirm their public commitment to fighting discrimination and to shift attention from problems of racism within their own institution to issues of racism in football. The relationship is symbiotic, however, and funding from the police is very attractive to anti-racist football organizations. Not only are the police able to provide much-needed financial input, but also they represent a *reliable* source of funding as, in the current political climate, it is extremely difficult for the police to reject requests to fund anti-racism. It is also the case that a shift within the anti-racist football movement towards a bureaucratic managerialist approach means that anti-racist football organizations are increasingly likely to undertake collaboration and consultation with dominant social institutions, such as the police. Ironically, the funding provided by the police to anti-racist organizations is still minimal compared to the compensation they have paid out in cases of racial discrimination or improper conduct against members of the public and their own officers.[3]

The police clearly have an important part to play in eradicating racism from football. They are able to prosecute supporters who are found guilty of racist abuse at professional grounds or recreational pitches, and players who have committed racially aggravated assaults in amateur football. However, in recent years, the police have broadened their involvement and have started to collaborate with anti-racist football organizations and club-based schemes on their outreach project work with young British Asians. For example, the Community Affairs manager at one club stated that:

> We've got a project at the moment whereby we're linking up with the police community workers who work out in these local Asian communities. . . . For example, we will give out x number of free tickets to the police and they will use them to break down their barriers in their local community.
>
> (Interview, 21 June 2002)

This chapter has stressed that schemes seeking to forge links between professional clubs and their local British Asian communities – especially younger members – are crucial in providing a channel for recruiting players and supporters. Yet one might question what role the police have in this capacity. As the previous chapter highlighted, in the current political climate, such projects often possess wider socio-political connotations. It is these additional purposes, rather than the footballing content *per se*, that makes these projects attractive to the police. In particular, it may be the case that the police are seeking to use their involvement in football as a means of increasing their knowledge and surveillance of young British Asian men. This has already been instigated in other areas, such as the Metropolitan Police's Operation Quadrant, which aims to promote the social inclusion of young British Asian men and divert them from anti-social behaviour and/or criminal activities (Cowan and Hyder 2005). Furthermore, in the wake of the 7 July London transport bombings, the Met. also declared its intention to 'get inside' and improve its intelligence of Britain's Muslim communities. Under the ostensibly benign message of 'community relations', football offers a less politically contentious or racially sensitive hook for the police to extend their work in this area. It enables them to increase their contact with young British Asian men and to gain the foothold in these communities, which they believe to be crucial in combating religious extremism and terrorism.

However, by aligning themselves with the police, anti-racist football organizations might be inhibiting the extent to which they are able to forge positive relations with young British Asian men. An inquiry in 1995 into the urban unrest by British Asians in Manningham, Bradford stated that, 'It is impossible to overstate the mistrust with which younger members of the community viewed the police' (cited in Macey 2002: 36). Six years later, the urban unrest of 2001 demonstrated how badly the relationship had deteriorated, as young British Asian men fought violent street battles with police officers in Bradford, Burnley, Leeds, Oldham, Southampton and Stoke-on-Trent. In Leeds, the arrest of a British Asian man, Hossein Miah, is believed to have instigated the violence against the police in the Harehills district (*Guardian* 2002), whilst allegations of police inaction over racial harassment and assaults were cited as a major factor behind the urban unrest in Oldham (Jenkins and Kennedy 2001). The failure of the police to sufficiently curtail the activities of Far Right parties was also a factor in many towns. Yet the problematic role of the police was barely acknowledged in the official inquires into this disorder. As Kalra (2003: 149) argues, 'What is missing from the equation . . . is a clearer picture of the role of the police in creating and managing the conditions for civil unrest'.

The severity of the sentences given to many of the men convicted for involvement in the urban unrest of 2001 (see Alexander 2005) led to widespread criticism by British Asians of the Crown Prosecution Service (CPS).[4] Furthermore, increased stop-and-searches by the police on British Asians, a manifestation of increasingly draconian anti-terror legislation, have also had a detrimental effect on community relations. In the year following 9/11, the number of British Asians stopped and searched by the police increased by 16 per cent, with the figures for the Metropolitan police revealing a 40 per cent increase (Dodd 2003b). After 7/7 British Asians were five times more likely to be stopped and searched than beforehand (Dodd 2005a). Indeed, the police were accused of 'racial profiling' following the statement from Ian Johnston, Chief Constable of the British Transport Police, that his officers would not be searching 'little old white ladies' (Observer 2005: 23). Fears amongst British Muslims that they are being singled out for surveillance and control have been accentuated by the comments of Hazel Blears who, during her period as Minister of State for Policing, Security and Community Safety, stated that Muslims will have to accept as a 'reality' the fact that they are more likely than other ethnic groups to be stopped and searched (Dodd and Travis 2005).

Relations between the police and British Asian communities (particularly young, working-class men) can clearly be problematic. It is necessary, therefore, to recognize that anti-racist football schemes that collaborate with the police might be sending out ambiguous signals to minority ethnic communities. These schemes may be met with negativity and suspicion, if not outright resistance, from young British Asian footballers. In locations where there have been tensions between young men and police officers, the presence of an agency that is seen to undertake oppressive surveillance, leading to marginalization and disaffection, is likely to cause offence, fear and/or resistance. Football initiatives that involve the police may be viewed as guilty by association.

(Im)perfect match? South Asian football tours to Britain

Since 2000, a number of English professional clubs have played friendly matches against international teams representing countries with significant diasporic populations in Britain. On some occasions, English clubs have simply taken on the role of hosts and allowed their stadia to be used for matches between international teams. One of the primary sources of competition has been teams from the Indian subcontinent: Brentford, Fulham, Leyton Orient, Nottingham Forest, Walsall and West Bromwich Albion have played matches against India, whilst Bury and Coventry City have entertained Pakistan. Leicester City, Watford and Wolverhampton Wanderers have hosted matches featuring India and either Bangladesh or Jamaica. Bangladeshi clubs, including Abahani and Mohammedan, have also played matches against British Asian amateur sides. These matches are usually organized and funded by commercial companies and anti-racist football organizations, in collaboration with professional clubs. The stated rationales for these matches encompass a number of factors. Taking the Indian team as an example, the official reason given by the All India Football Federation (AIFF) for the tour of England in 2000 was that it would help players prepare for their forthcoming World Cup qualifying matches (Kapadia 2001). However, according to Dimeo (2002b), if one considers the objectives of the organizers and promoters of the tour, three further reasons are apparent. First, to give Indian players experience of playing against European teams. Second, to establish meaningful links between the subcontinent and the South Asian diaspora that might result in coaching exchanges and, eventually – Indian politics permitting – the selection of diasporic players for the national side. Third, to promote anti-racism and increase the representation of British Asians in professional football. It is this final reason that is of most significance here.

The hosts, organizers and funders of these events have received considerable commendation, both within the game and in the media, for their perceived role in promoting anti-racism and extending links with British Asian communities. However, this positive feedback is not universally endorsed and British Asian players have raised three main criticisms regarding their effectiveness. First, these matches do little to overcome the exclusion of *British* Asian footballers from the professional game. Second, they have no significant long-term benefits for the development of British Asian football. Third, the tendency to focus on adult players limits the capacity of these games to act as a 'shop window' for professional clubs to identify and recruit talented young players.

Friendly matches against subcontinental teams represent an opportunity for English professional clubs to make an overt, public declaration of support for anti-racism and for increasing the inclusion of British Asians in professional football. They also generate significant publicity for clubs and images of British Asian supporters watching a game in their stadia are of considerable marketing value in trying to access under-represented minorities. Indeed, these matches serve the needs and fulfil the agendas of a variety of other agencies with an interest in this area, namely anti-racist football organizations, funders/sponsors and tour organizers. However, whilst these events give the *impression* that these agencies are actively and successfully working towards overcoming the barriers faced by British Asians in professional football, they actually provide an inaccurate portrayal of the extent to which meaningful measures are being implemented. Although there are a few exceptions, clubs that have hosted subcontinental teams have not implemented changes that challenge institutional barriers, such as establishing grassroots coaching projects with British Asian children or forging links between their academies/centres of excellence and British Asian clubs. With regard to their public stances against racism and towards overcoming the exclusion of British Asians, clubs are aware that such projects do not generate the immediate impact and publicity of international friendlies. On the other hand, grassroots initiatives are of little interest to funders and organizers, who stand to make minimal financial gain in comparison to the commercial advantages that can be generated from a tour match. Consequently, many British Asian footballers believe that publicity and profit, rather than increasing their representation as professional players, are actually the most important criteria for the organizers of these friendly matches. For example, one British Bangladeshi amateur player stated that:

> People say, 'We'll bring a team over, you know, for a couple of weeks'. It's all about PR. You are getting organizations and initiatives just going after the PR job really, which is a bit of a shame for me.
>
> (Interview, 16 March 2002)

Another player focused specifically on the benefits for commercial companies:

> The people who are really behind it are just there for the quick buck and they just use 'Kick Out Racism' [sic]. . . . And they know that West Brom[wich Albion] would give them the backing of the ground to use because if they don't people will say, 'Why not?'. The real problem lies with the people organizing it. They're really behind it. Not the clubs, not 'Kick Out Racism'. Are they in it for the football or for the money?
>
> (Interview with British Pakistani amateur club manager, 16 April 2002)

Dimeo (2002b) claims that, taking into account the excessive match admission prices,[5] financial gain was clearly a significant criterion for Sapphire Enterprises, the company that organized the Indian tours. Furthermore, whilst the number of British Asians who begin regularly watching their local team after attending an international friendly is negligible, professional clubs are aware that British Asian supporters represent a large, untapped market and a potential source of considerable financial income.

Irrespective of the minutiae of club marketing and economics, the under-representation of British Asians as players and as supporters are clearly different issues. Whilst events that encourage British Asians to attend matches as supporters are important in terms of their wider inclusion, they have very little effect in increasing the participation of British Asian *players* in the game. Furthermore, the desire and capacity for these matches to include British Asian players is cast in doubt by the fact that Raj Prohit of Sapphire Enterprises is also the agent of Baichung Bhutia, an Indian international who joined Bury in 1999. Indeed, Prohit was negotiating Bhutia's transfer at the same time that Sapphire were organizing the Indian tours to Britain (Dimeo 2001a). This suggests that one of the more likely objectives of the tour was to provide a showcase of Indian players to generate other sales to British clubs, rather than the publicized aim of increasing the inclusion of *British* Asians as professional footballers.

A second criticism of matches between professional/British Asian clubs and subcontinental teams is their lack of sustainability. As one-off events they have no long-term benefits for the development of British Asian football and its links with the professional game. As one British Indian amateur player stated:

> I think all these events like, you know, these sort of celebrity matches or show matches against national teams from India and Pakistan, they're great as one off events. But they are essentially, if you like, tokenism in that they are just a publicity issue. What grows from those matches is not sustainable. It doesn't result in any long-lasting benefit to Asians in football. It's just a great event, a circus almost, around publicity. That will not do. They do nothing to build a foundation for promoting Asians into football in this country.
>
> (Interview, 23 April 2002)

Another player recalled his own personal experiences:

> Against [the club visiting from Bangladesh] I was actually playing, I was in the team that night. It was a very good occasion. I mean, again, I look at it from a selfish point of view as a player and it was brilliant, tremendous. But even then I thought – and I think it even more now in my role as chairman of [a British Asian football federation] – there's no real long-term benefit from these friendlies. I mean, the guys from Bangladesh enjoyed themselves – they got a free ticket to the UK. We enjoyed it because that's probably the highest level we've played and we measured ourselves against

the top players in Bangladesh. It was a good occasion, but there's no long-term benefit.

(Interview with British Bangladeshi amateur player/member of a British Asian football federation, 25 April 2002)

Some players argued that the matches between British Asian amateur clubs and teams from the subcontinent further inhibit the long-term development of British Asian football because they involve only South Asian – subcontinental and diasporic – players. Consequently, such events contradict the importance that many players attach to playing in integrated competitions and coaching projects. These games possess the potential to demonstrate the standard of British Asian football, but they arguably represent missed opportunities in terms of forging links with the professional game as very few, if any, non-British Asian people are present to witness them. As one British Bangladeshi semi-pro player argued:

Most of the games [involve] just Asian communities. Where's the mixture in that? It's Asian teams coming from Bangladesh and playing a [British] Asian team. Who else knows about it? What about the [talent] scouts? What about the professional clubs? Do they know this game's going on? It's just a one-off game amongst your community, nothing else. It's not a development – it's just publicity stuff.

(Interview, 11 May 2002)

Whilst such matches serve important community functions, in terms of developing links with the professional game it is arguably more productive for British Asian clubs to play matches against *English* professional opposition. In recent years, a UK Asian XI has played against Bradford City, Sporting Bengal United has played Leyton Orient and a representative team from the Sikh-based Khalsa Football Federation (KFF) has competed against Millwall. Evidence suggests that the sustainability of these games is still limited, but in theory – and if organized appropriately – they have the potential to give the best British Asian players the opportunity to perform in an environment where professional clubs, and not just other members of their communities, are able to observe their talents.[6]

One way in which the sustainability of these matches could be improved is through greater involvement of young players. Although matches between Millwall and the KFF, for example, have involved their respective youth teams, a third area of criticism is that the majority of matches against sub-continental teams – plus other competitions, such as the UK Asian Football Championships – only involve adult players. This reduces their capacity to operate as a 'shop window' of British Asian talent for professional clubs. With professional clubs now scouting players at increasingly younger ages and coaches suggesting that it is highly advantageous for a player to be registered with a professional club before his teenage years, it is unlikely that professional scouts would see much benefit in watching an adult amateur/semi-professional match. Thus, as long as the majority of matches between British Asian teams and professional clubs – either from England or from the subcontinent – and prominent tournaments involve purely adults, the opportunities for players to be recruited as professionals are almost non-existent. For example, one British Bangladeshi semi-professional player stated that:

> Here in east London, there's Bengali teams coming from Bangladesh. I mean that's just one day, two hours, when everyone's going to watch this game. But what about the development of the young kids, you know? Most of them playing [in these matches] are [aged] twenty-five/thirty anyway, so what's the benefit in that? I don't know.
>
> (Interview, 11 May 2002)

Another player remarked that:

> I have invitations – because I'm on the [club's] management committee now – come in to me saying, 'We're organizing this big tournament for Asians. Oh, we're going to have a couple of the Asian digital channels [filming it], you know, and we'll have some scouts from the professional clubs as well'. And I'm saying, 'Hold on, what's the point in bringing scouts to this tournament when most people – 99 per cent of the players – would actually be at an age where scouts just aren't interested?'
>
> (Interview with British Bangladeshi amateur player, 16 March 2002)

Whilst British Asian men's football has burgeoned in recent years, the youth game remains significantly under-developed in comparison. Although some clubs have teams representing a range of age groups (including Albion Sports, Guru Nanak [Gravesend], London APSA, Luton United and Sporting Bengal United), the majority revolve around adult sides, and many leagues and tournaments have a specific focus on adult football.

Nevertheless, matches against subcontinental teams remain popular events for clubs, anti-racist organizations and commercial companies. Whilst many British Asian players believe that establishing 'grassroots' coaching programmes, improving facilities, or initiating partnerships with professional clubs would be more productive in terms of the long-term development of British Asian football, high profile, one-off fixtures enable certain groups to achieve their short-term agendas. One British Indian amateur player summed up the dialectic between the short-term and long-term development of British Asian football, as follows:

> I think this is where really, Dan, we get down to what is the most effective way of promoting Asians into football. I think you have a choice. You either go for the high profile, one-off events which attract a great deal of publicity in the media, even coverage on TV, but do nothing in the long-term in

terms of helping grassroots football. Or you go for the other alternative which is to say, actually, the national bodies like the Football Association, the Premier League, the Football League and even lottery giving bodies, have to start putting more money into saying, 'How do we support better coaching facilities at grassroots level?', 'How do we provide better facilities so that *all* footballers, *all* young people can participate in football?' and within that, 'How can we target Asians because they are a group that is under-represented?'

(Interview, 23 April 2002)

At the current time, the former approach is often adopted. One of the reasons for this is the influence of funders in the organization of tour matches. In a highly competitive financial environment, in order to meet the criteria laid down by funders, applicants/recipients are under considerable pressure to demonstrate their achievements. Under such demands, a one-off friendly match featuring British Asian or subcontinental teams represents an immediate, visible and quantifiable achievement. It is far more difficult to measure the success of a long-term player development programme and so, whilst it would be more beneficial in challenging institutional barriers and overcoming the exclusion of British Asian football, it does not offer the financial and publicity-oriented benefits of one-off events.

A related development is the belief that forging links with football clubs in India can help English professional teams improve relations with their local British Asian communities. Aston Villa, for example, plan to repeat *Villawannabee* – a 'reality' television series that awarded the winner, a young British Asian player, a trial at the club (see Burdsey, forthcoming) – in India. Furthermore, in 2004, Leicester City formed a partnership with East Bengal FC (from Calcutta) and the All India Football Federation (AIFF), the aim of which is to exchange players, coaches and marketing and commercial staff. The choice of East Bengal is itself interesting as one might have expected the club to make links in Gujarat, the area from where most of Leicester's Indian population originate. Steve White of *Foxes Against Racism*, the club's anti-racist initiative, states that, 'I hope this initiative will animate clubs and players in our community to become involved with Leicester City. I know it will help nurture and identify talent right on our doorstep. This is a creative and imaginative way of linking the club and the local community' (cited in Leicester City FC 2004). Similarly, Roger Blackmore, leader of Leicester City Council, argues that, 'By signing these agreements, Leicester City has shown that it's keen to forge closer links with the Indian community in Leicester' (ibid.). Whilst Leicester City's recognition of the city's large Indian community and its inveterate exclusion as players and supporters is undoubtedly a positive development, it is difficult to see how a partnership involving a club situated thousands of miles away will significantly benefit young British Asian footballers in inner-city Leicester.

Don't believe the hype? The effects of media publicity on young British Asian professional players

During the late-1990s, the under-representation of British Asians in professional football first began to receive public recognition, resulting from the coverage provided by both Kick It Out (e.g. Kick It Out 1998b, 2000a) and the quality press (e.g. Chaudhary 1996; Freeman 1996). At this stage, media features and articles tended to focus on the statistical under-representation of British Asians at professional level and often included testimonies from players who felt that racism had restricted them from pursuing a career in the game. Since then, coverage – which now also extends to television, radio and the internet – has typically provided more detailed biographical profiles of the small number of British Asian professional (or academy-registered) players, e.g. Michael Chopra (Campbell 2001a; Hussain 2001b; Harrison 2003), Harpal Singh (Lindsey 1999; Bhatia 2003b; Bhatia 2003c), Anwar Uddin (Herman 2001), Zesh Rehman (Hussain 2001a), Bobby Singh (Licudi 2003), and Nevin Saroya and Neerav Patel (*Brentford, Chiswick and Isleworth Times* 1995). These profiles offer an important opportunity to gather information about British Asians currently attached to professional clubs and they enable young players to identify role models. However, the manner in which this coverage is undertaken raises a number of problems.

Publicity and intrusive media attention are inevitable aspects of being a professional footballer, even for those players who have just started their careers, yet British Asian footballers express three specific concerns regarding the way in which they are represented when they reach professional level. First, descriptions and assessments misrepresent their actual stages of development. This misleads the public and paints an overly benign picture of the inclusion of British Asians in the game. Second, comparisons with established international players are unjustified and subject them to an unfair level of expectation. Third, singling players out for attention because of their ethnicities contravenes their wishes and is not beneficial to their long-term development.

In the vast majority of cases, the British Asian players that have been profiled by anti-racist organizations and the media have been aged in their mid-to-late teens and have made few, if any, first-team appearances. Nevertheless, rather than being described in terms of their modest, yet significant, achievements, these players have received a series of glowing accolades that considerably exaggerate their actual stage of development. In the late 1990s, most attention featured on Amrit Sidhu at Derby County and Nevin Saroya at Brentford. For example, in one of their promotional pamphlets, Kick It Out (1999: 8) claimed that 'Amrit Sidhu's goals have attracted the attention of Jim Smith the Derby manager', and that 'Nevin's progress has been such that [Brentford] manager Ron Noades is almost certain to throw him into first team action later this season'. However, Amrit Sidhu never played for the Derby County first-team and subsequently left the professional game. Nevin Saroya made one first-team appearance for Brentford and is now playing semi-professionally for Yeading in the Ryman League.

A number of British Asian players believe that such profiles inflate the standard of the players, often falsely implying that they are on the verge of playing first-team football. For example, one British Bangladeshi amateur player stated that:

> I hear about these players and you tend to look at the teamsheets, but you never see their names. So if they're doing *that* well, why aren't they on the teamsheet, you know, not even amongst the subs? I've never seen Harpal [Singh] turn out for the first-team at Leeds, I've never seen Anwar Uddin. I don't know why Sheffield Wednesday bought him, but I've never seen him, and I do try to look out for him.
>
> (Interview, 25 April 2002)

Another player argued that the situation is further misrepresented by the failure of anti-racist organizations and the media to report those British Asian players who have been unsuccessful:

> By the time they've released those [publicity brochures], [the players] have probably been released. But that doesn't get followed up, that they've been released. They don't say, 'Oh, he's actually been released now and he's training with [a] non-league [team]'. It's just, 'Right, forget about him, who's the next one coming through? Find him, get a photo of him and stick him in'.
>
> (Interview with British Indian ex-professional player, 11 March 2002)

This tendency to over-build players' reputations takes place at the higher end of the scale as well, with other young British Asian players compared to established international stars. For example, when he was just fifteen, Kick It Out (1999: 8) labelled Newcastle United's Michael Chopra a 'wonderkid'. A couple of years later another profile cited the claims of his club coach, Peter Beardsley, that he was potentially a better player than his team-mate Alan Shearer (Campbell 2001a). Les Reed, FA Director of Technical Development, was also quoted as stating that, 'The way he [Chopra] dribbles the ball and gets behind defenders reminds me of Michael Owen' (ibid.). Kick It Out (1998b: 4) also widely published the claim made by former Leeds United manager George Graham that 'Liverpool may have Michael Owen but we have Harpal Singh' (cited in ibid.: 4). Similarly, Alan Hill, United's Academy Director boldly stated that Singh would be 'the first Asian to play for England' (ibid.). Michael Chopra made his first Premier League appearance for Newcastle United at the beginning of the 2003–04 season, having been loaned to Watford during the previous campaign. He was subsequently loaned to Nottingham Forest and Barnsley before leaving Newcastle for Cardiff in 2006. Harpal Singh never played for the Leeds United first-team. He played on loan at Bradford City, Bristol City and Bury, and permanently for Stockport County before being released in 2006.

The perception amongst British Asian players is that it is unfair to compare a young player of any ethnicity to an established international player. With regard to the current crop of British Asian professional players, it is felt that these comparisons are completely unjustified, as Chopra and Singh had not even played first-team football when they were made. Indeed, some players are somewhat suspicious of the rationale behind these comparisons. For example, one British Indian amateur player felt that not only has Harpal Singh been over-hyped, but that there is a 'hidden agenda' behind this state of affairs. He argues that:

> These guys that are saying that he's the next best thing to Michael Owen – on what basis have they compared that? If you look on ability, you know, Harpal Singh hasn't even played for Leeds yet, Michael Owen is European Player of the Year! How can you compare the two, right, unless there's something else behind it? Obviously, you know, it's agents and managers and businesses. I think there is a hidden agenda. I can't compare the two. I can't compare Harpal Singh with Michael Owen.
>
> (Interview, 5 February 2002)

Another player suggests that Singh was used by Leeds United as part of a public relations exercise, in light of the problems they experienced with Lee Bowyer and Jonathan Woodgate (see Chapter 3):

> I think there are agendas being pursued which have got nothing to do with Harpal Singh as a footballer. . . . I think Leeds United have got problems of their own in terms of the way that their public image is portrayed and so on, and I think it's really, really regrettable that Harpal Singh is being hyped up to such an extent that I wonder if he will ever deliver what people's expectations of him are. But if he was left alone, as Harpal Singh playing for Leeds United, he may well be the first *Harpal Singh* to play for England. And then we might say, 'By the way, he's of Asian origin as well'. That's the way round it ought to be.
>
> (Interview with British Indian amateur player, 23 April 2002)

This testimony demonstrates how British Asian players are forced to carry the 'burden of representation' in that they 'are seen to represent the capacities of groups for which they are marked and visible *per se*' (Puwar 2005: 62). The resultant pressure placed on a small number of players is immense as they are seen to be representatives, role models and spokesmen for all other British Asian players, whilst they are simultaneously subjected to the 'terrorizing white gaze' (hooks 1992) or 'look' (Fanon 1986) which inscribes their position as objects of fascination within the world of football and beyond.

The *Asians Can Play Football* report states that 'the proliferation of clumsy promotional events and of occasional claims that we have unearthed the next Asian 'superstar', a role model for others to follow, is merely a distraction from the much more pressing need for structural change' (Asians in Football Forum 2005: 7). Over-building players' reputations gives the impression that they have been more successful than they actually have and thus mistakenly suggests that institutional barriers and structures of exclusion are being broken down. This echoes the issues raised in the previous section regarding how publicity-generating developments are often prioritized ahead of making more substantial changes to the cultures of professional football. However, it is evident that (over-)hyping the reputation of British Asian players not only makes them more attractive to the media, but also provides a more positive reflection of the work being undertaken by professional clubs and anti-racist football organizations. They need to provide evidence that they are achieving their objectives – both to justify their existence and to continue receiving funding – and so they need to give the impression that, as a result of their activities, British Asians have started to progress into professional football. Comparing a player to an established international clearly has more benefits than stating that he has made one reserve team appearance for a League Two club. As one British Indian amateur player explained:

> Let's face it, if those stories were portrayed [as an accurate reflection of players' development], who would give the funding to a national organization to continue with their work? And this is where, you know, my point about well, what agendas are we following comes in, because if the agenda was really about saying, you know, 'We're all in this business to promote footballers at a young age and Asians in particular, to try and get them more into the game', then we wouldn't be hyping them up. They [organizations] are desperate for role models. Anything will do. And I think they're doing an injustice and a disservice to Asian footballers because no sooner than a kid's able to kick the ball ten yards straight, then he's hyped up and then, you know, a big fall comes.
>
> (Interview, 23 April 2002)

Similarly, another British Indian amateur player stated that:

> I can see the [view of] 'Kick Racism Out' [sic] and all these other media-related organizations who have obviously been pursuing this issue. They need to see the first Asian make it to meet their goals, to say that since we've been fighting this campaign, you know, now we've suddenly got an Asian who's on the scene. Whereas from the individual's point of view, you don't want any limelight do you? It's hard enough as it is without someone saying, 'Well, you've only fucking made it because you're Asian'.
>
> (Interview, 5 February 2002)

This player highlights the fact that most British Asian professional players consciously under-emphasize their ethnic identities and often resent the way their ethnicities are highlighted simply to serve the needs of various agencies and organizations (see Chapter 4). Unlike young white and African-Caribbean players, British Asians are singled out for attention primarily because of their 'Asianness', despite the fact that they prefer to be judged on their footballing abilities. As one British Pakistani ex-professional player stated:

I've spoken to you before and I said to myself, if I ever made it into football, if a reporter came to me and said, 'What's it like being the first Asian player?', I would have really ripped into that person. I would have said, 'I don't know. I know what it's like it being a *player*. I know what it's like being like Steve, who's also made it. I don't really know. You tell me, what is it like?...I can tell you what it's like being an Asian at home, but I don't know what it's like [to be an Asian footballer] because I see myself as a *footballer*'. That's the question the media doesn't ask. It always asks, 'What's it like being an *Asian*'.

(Interview, 20 February 2002)

As Puwar (2005: 64–5) points out, because racialized bodies are seen as visible carriers of their ethnicities, unlike white bodies, they are perceived to be marked and bounded by their ethnic identities. Thus minority ethnic players are prevented from speaking for or representing the universal, i.e. footballers in general, and are only considered and permitted to speak on behalf of *British Asian* footballers.

However, by focusing on the ethnicities of British Asian players, Kick It Out, for example, are not only contravening the wishes of these players, but they have also contradicted their earlier approach to anti-racism. In the mid-1990s, the Let's Kick Racism Out of Football campaign appropriated a Nike television advertisement for use in its publicity material (see e.g. Commission for Racial Equality 1995). The advertisement – which originally took the form of a duologue involving Les Ferdinand and Eric Cantona – stated, 'What do you see? A black man, a Frenchman or a footballer? Why argue about differences? I'd rather play football'. The underlying sentiments were ability first, ethnicity second. However, in 2003, Kick It Out co-ordinator, Piara Powar, argued that players' ethnicities remain extremely salient. In response to Michael Chopra's statement that he does not wish to be held up as a figurehead purely for British Asian communities, Powar stated that:

Maybe he [Chopra] doesn't want that pressure of being a standard-bearer but, nevertheless, the cultural politics of football and race in this country are quite rich. In that context alone people will attribute a status to him, whether he likes it or not. Michael's known as somebody who has a dual heritage, and people look at that as a signifier of diversity.

(Cited in Turnbull 2003: 5)

British Asian footballers therefore represent an exception to Kick It Out's earlier mantra. In the eyes of this organization, these players are clearly British Asian first, footballers second.

The issues highlighted in this chapter demonstrate the complex and contradictory nature of the politics of anti-racism in English football. It is evident that, despite their good intentions, a number of professional club initiatives and anti-racist football organizations are failing to meet the needs and requirements of young British Asian footballers. The start of this chapter referred to P. Cohen's

(1992: 62–3) avowal that, 'Perhaps the models of racism which are implicitly present in anti-racist policies and practices may be inhibiting the development of more positive and effective strategies'. It appears that a number of the policies, strategies and activities aimed at increasing the representation of British Asians in professional football, are incongruent – if not conflicting – with the identities, lifestyles and aspirations of young British Asians and consequently are restricted in their effectiveness.

It may seem churlish to criticize club-based schemes and anti-racist football organizations for misinterpreting the lifestyles of young British Asians. Most of them are in the relatively early stages of initiating policies and strategies specifically aimed at British Asians, and their intentions are, for the most part, altruistic. However, some individuals within the anti-racist movement are unhesitatingly confident about their supposed understanding of the issues and are openly resistant to critical and sensitive investigation, using phrases such as 'You don't necessarily need a lot of detailed research to know what your issues are' (co-ordinator of anti-racist football organization, 28 June 2002); 'We don't have to *research* them [local British Asian communities] because we *work* with them' (Community Affairs manager, Premier League club, 21 June 2002); and 'We haven't done any specific research to find out what people think of the project' (co-ordinator of anti-racist football organization, 19 June 2002). With such a state of affairs, it is unsurprising that professional clubs and anti-racist football organizations are often out of touch with the identities, attitudes and desires of young British Asian footballers.

What has become clear is that engaging with dominant personnel and institutions, such as the police, religious groups and the media, is not necessarily an appropriate method for trying to increase the participation of British Asians in professional football. In some cases, it can actually have negative repercussions. Instead, consulting all sections of the local community and empowering them socially and politically – by involving them in dialogue and decision-making, and by facilitating a sense of project ownership – is arguably the best approach. However, it is evident that many initiatives and organizations continue to adopt the former approach. This is partly the result of a lack of appropriate knowledge, insufficient communication, adherence to stereotypical images of 'Asianness', and ignorance about relations between young British Asians and dominant social institutions, whether it be the police or their own community organizations. It is also a consequence of the membership of these agencies, the structures that govern and the power relations that permeate them, and the way that they interact with local communities. In other words, the preferred approach arises from an increasing tendency for the anti-racist football movement to engage in what Carrington and McDonald (2003: 138) label 'bureaucratic managerialism'. Whilst anti-racism in English soccer was originally established by protest and activist groups, approaches are increasingly formalized, hierarchical and bureaucratic. Indeed, it can be argued that the anti-racist football movement now forms part of the establishment that it was originally designed to challenge. Its sources of funding, the manner in which it exchanges and disseminates information – through steering groups, task forces, conferences and glossy brochures – and the additional personnel involved – the police, teachers and social workers – increasingly reflect a changing approach to, and status and relations with, its target groups. As long as this remains the case, it appears that the distance between anti-racist football organizations/professional club schemes and minority ethnic groups will inevitably remain, whilst the capacity for consultation with, and involvement of, young British Asians will become more remote.

8 Concluding remarks

British Asians and football: so what?

A possible response to the issues raised and analysed in this book might be, 'So what?' 'Why is football considered to be so important?' and 'What is the crucial significance of British Asians in this context?'

There is still a tendency in academic and popular discourses to overlook the critical role that sport – and especially football – plays in the construction and reproduction of social divisions, ethnic identities, and a whole range of prejudices and inequities. Accordingly, a monograph on the relationship between British Asians and football may appear trivial and peripheral to more imperative concerns within ethnic and racial studies, such as questions of discrimination and racism in the police and criminal justice, education or healthcare systems. In addition, whilst British Asians are under-represented as professional footballers, in the popular imagination they are perceived to be over-represented in other professional roles, for example, as doctors and lawyers and in remunerative trades and businesses, putatively signifying that racism is no longer a problem in British society. Critical voices might also challenge the significance of football, arguing that gainful employment in the elite professions is more important than playing professional football and more likely to increase the political and economic power of British Asians, so crucial to overcoming entrenched structural racism and promoting social mobility.

Such views are erroneous in different ways: for example, for failing to address the social significance of football in contemporary Britain; for an overly benign portrait of British 'race relations'; for assuming that one can generalize about other recruitment practices from one employment sphere; for the essentialization of, and failure to distinguish between, different sections of British Asian communities in relation to access to the professions and economic success.

One example of an account that embodies the 'so what' approach is an essay by Geoffrey Wheatcroft, published in the *Guardian* (Wheatcroft 2001). Illuminatingly titled, 'This misguided campaign for Asians to play football', Wheatcroft's analysis demonstrates a fundamental failure to appreciate the cultural sensibilities of young British Asians and an ignorance of the ways that contemporary racisms manifest themselves in the world of professional football.

Wheatcroft's objection to campaigns and scholarship that strive to overcome the exclusion of British Asians is premised on the belief that it should be of no more or less concern that there are very few British Asians in the game than that there are large numbers of African-Caribbeans. He suggests that 'whether any ethnic group should be excluded from a sport is a question which answers itself. But is there any reason why a particular group should be encouraged – or merely expected – to play any particular sport?' (Wheatcroft 2001: 26). His second misunderstanding is embodied in the statement that: 'Clubs want to win. Manchester United are not going to turn away a match-winning player because of the colour of his skin or his name – and that goes when the player is brown-skinned and called Singh or Patel' (ibid.). He concludes his argument with the question: 'And so if there is no "Asian" footballer at a high level, does that actually matter in itself?' (ibid.).

First, Wheatcroft clearly fails to understand the importance of football to many young British Asian men, both as a leisure activity and as a desirable career choice. As this book has shown, the game is hugely popular amongst, and played by large numbers of, British Asians throughout the country, and many would relish the opportunity to become professional players. Clearly, Wheatcroft does not appreciate that attempts to overcome their exclusion from the professional game are not being forged purely for the sake of it or without considerable justification. Likewise, British Asians are not being encouraged or expected to play against their desires. On the contrary, these campaigns represent a means of challenging the dominant discourses and practices that have discouraged and expected British Asians not to play *despite* their desire and commitment to participate. The wider project – in both an academic and activist sense – to increase the inclusion of British Asian footballers in the professional game is not, therefore, about trying to drum up participation and support amongst those British Asians who have no interest in the game, either as players or spectators; it is about providing equality of opportunity for those who enjoy the game as much as their contemporaries from other ethnic backgrounds, but have been restricted from being included in it to a similar degree. It is for this reason that, in an analytical sense, the term 'exclusion' is prioritized in this book ahead of 'under-representation'. When a particular social group is under-represented in an activity that is popular with them, valued by them and in which they wish to be involved, this amounts to exclusion. It then becomes not just a footballing issue, but also a wider social problem, and thus deserves to be a significant area of study within ethnic and racial studies. Wheatcroft also assumes that the over-representation of black footballers is based on unequivocally positive perceptions about their physical and cultural traits, and ignores the wider social, economic and political ramifications of the way that black men are stereotyped in dominant sporting discourses.

Second, Wheatcroft is probably accurate in his claim that a professional club would not turn away a talented player simply because he is British Asian, although evidence suggests that this does sometimes occur in amateur sport (Carrington and McDonald 2001c). However, what he fails to appreciate are the complex, subtle and nuanced ways that racism operates in English football. As this book has argued, there are a variety of factors, from the ways that professional clubs represent themselves to the processes and procedures through which players are recruited, that mean that British Asian players often do not even get to the stage at which professional clubs decide whether to sign them as full-time professionals. Finally, Wheatcroft's question that, 'If there is no "Asian" footballer at a high level, does that actually matter in itself?', warrants no further discussion. It should be clear by now that the answer to this is, and must continue to be, unequivocally a 'Yes'. In short, the campaign for British Asians to play football is clearly not, as Wheatcroft (2001: 26) suggests, 'misguided'.

Integration: what is it, who wants it and what do they want it for?

This book has been published during a period when the citizenship and identities of British Asians – especially Muslims – have been at the forefront of intense public and political debate. In particular, British Asians have become central figures in relation to two enduringly contentious issues: multiculturalism and integration. These issues have been discussed and argued over ever since Britain made its first claims to be a 'multi-ethnic' nation, but have become particularly salient again at the beginning of the twenty-first century. Since 7/7, they have featured regularly on the pages of the nation's newspapers and in television news bulletins, and they have been incorporated as key 'buzz words' in the discourses and vote-chasing policies of all sections of the political spectrum. As Britain seeks to make sense of the events of 7/7, and various agencies strive to make the necessary provisions for a future of racial tolerance and peaceful co-existence for multi-ethnic Britain, multiculturalism and integration represent the fields in which political battles surrounding 'race', ethnicity, citizenship and national identity are fought.

   Issues surrounding multiculturalism were discussed in Chapter 6. The analysis demonstrates the importance of moving away from a dichotomous model of multiculturalism, where it is viewed as being unequivocally positive or negative, good or bad, as is often posited in dominant discourses. Instead, its uses, abuses, benefits and disadvantages in attempting to promote understanding of minority ethnic groups, facilitating interaction and combating racism need to be considered in relation to its divergent manifestations and the different contexts in which it operates. For example, in professional football, multiculturalism in a generic sense is an important strategy in celebrating the increasing ethnic diversity of the professional game and in attempting to challenge normative 'whiteness' within clubs and governing bodies. Yet when multiculturalism becomes 'official' and institutionalized, discourses and practices often end up reproducing reified notions of 'race' and culture, and marginalizing issues of power and racism from the analysis of exclusion. In this regard, official multiculturalism fails to challenge triumphalist and supremacist discourses surrounding 'race' and ethnicity (Kim 2004).

For the purposes of this concluding chapter, it is the related concept of integration that warrants specific attention, for it is inexorably connected to debates around both the existing participation of British Asians in amateur football and their future inclusion in the professional sphere. Integration has been increasingly heralded by New Labour as the most efficacious way of overcoming the 'parallel lives' (Home Office 2001b) believed to be experienced by Britain's white and British Asian (particularly Muslim) communities. As Ted Cantle, author of one of the governmental inquiries into the 2001 urban unrest states, 'These "parallel lives" do not meet at any point, with little or no opportunity to explore the differences and to build mutual respect, let alone to see them as enriching our communities' (Cantle 2005: 86). In short, a lack of integration is seen not only to have hampered inter-ethnic understanding and interaction, but also to have accentuated the factors that contributed to the urban unrest in Bradford, Burnley, Leeds and Oldham in 2001, and allowed Islamic extremism to develop unabated and unmonitored in Britain's Muslim communities. Parallel to multiculturalism, integration is a phrase that is frequently employed, but often lacks specific definition. Such an important and contentious concept requires clearer and more coherent explanation, not simply for purposes of clarity, but also for understanding the context in, and the premise on, which it is being used. In public debates and political discourses, there is considerable confusion about the differences in meaning between integration and assimilation which requires critical reflection. An excellent contribution in this regard is Gary Younge's essay in the *Guardian* on issues of integration and equality (Younge 2005). Written two months after the 7/7 bombings, he provides a thoughtful analysis of the contemporaneous political clamour for increased ethnic and racial integration. The application of Younge's arguments to the issue of inclusion of British Asians in professional football is considered below.

This book has argued that integration is an inexorably central component in overcoming the exclusion of British Asians at professional level. Put simply, with a single governing body and competitive structure in the game, integration in a general sense is the only means by which British Asians will be able to play the game in a professional capacity. In this regard, integration represents something that should be strongly encouraged. However, as was noted in Chapter 3, support for integration in the professional game should not be conflated with wider political calls for enforced integration between British Asian and white communities *per se*. Fundamentally, it is the prerogative of individual players to decide who they want to play the game with, just as it is (or should be) their right to live with and socialize with whomsoever they wish. Yet it becomes an issue when playing football exclusively with members of one's own ethnic group or separate from the ethnic majority is: i) not desired; ii) enforced due to discrimination and racism in 'mainstream' sport; and/or iii) prevents progression to elite level and access to the highest levels of achievement and rewards. In such instances, integration represents a desirable outcome – one that is not based on a political aspiration to inculcate minorities into a consensus of 'shared values', but on a moral belief in providing equality of opportunity and eradicating discrimination.

Further questions must also be posed in relation to the present analysis: what does integration look like? Can it be measured and, if so, when will we recognize that it has occurred? What are its wider consequences and implications? For some, integration is something that will/should evolve naturally. An oft-cited lay explanation for the lack of British Asians in the professional game is that it is simply a matter of time and that the career trajectories of black British players will eventually be replicated by British Asians. For others, legislation should be introduced to make integration mandatory, as epitomized by the implementation of a quota system in South African sport. Both arguments have their supporters yet, as this book has argued, sitting back and waiting for integration to occur represents an overly utopian and 'colour-blind' approach which ignores the entrenched structures of exclusion that currently exist in football, whilst the contrived South African policy is arguably just a superficial advance that seeks to mask racism in a society that is still, in many areas, as divided as it was under apartheid. In institutions such as the police, integration is assumed when a particular force is numerically reflective of the various local communities that it serves. If this model was applied to football, what would be expected? Will integration have occurred when the overall number of British Asian professional players reflects national statistics, or should the specifics of local populations be more important? Should we be less concerned with levels of representation at a club such as Torquay United (from a town with negligible minority ethnic communities) and more interested in ensuring that a quarter of the squad at Leicester City, for example, is one-quarter British Indian? The approach favoured by the police ignores racial power dynamics in the game and the importance of British Asians not simply becoming players, but also reaching positions of power in management and governance. Irrespective of the number of British Asians playing for professional clubs, the fact that not a single person on the FA's ninety-two member council is black or British Asian (Black Information Link 2006; Bradbury and Williams 2006) will always be an impediment to true equality. Furthermore, taking into account the issues discussed in Chapter 4, can integration be said to have occurred if those British Asians present in the professional sphere continue to consciously underplay their ethnic identities and do not display outward symbols of what would traditionally be interpreted as 'Asianness'? One would not, for example, see any of the current crop of players play a match wearing a turban or turn up for training dressed in *shalwar kameez*. The notion of integration at amateur level is equally open to debate. At what level would we expect to see it occur – integrated teams, leagues, local associations? What is the role towards integration played by tournaments such as the Unity Cup in England or the Amsterdam World Cup in the Netherlands? By having teams that reflect distinct ethnic and national identities, does this serve to produce interaction and understanding or end up reifying and concretizing ethnic boundaries? This book does not propose that there is, or should be, a single measure by which integration can be judged or observed; rather it calls for critical analysis of the notion of integration and an awareness of different interpretations and desired outcomes. It is crucially important that integration does not just become a 'numbers game' or a 'tick-box' exercise: British Asian player? Yes. British Asian steward. Yes? British Asian coach? Yes. Pat on the back, job done. If it is viewed in such a way, changes to the game in terms of overcoming the exclusion of British Asians will only be a superficial advancement and will consequently fail to subvert the underlying structures of privilege and exclusion.

Younge (2005) poignantly points out that the black Huyton teenager Anthony Walker was ostensibly integrated in the most-widely used sense of the word: he had a white girlfriend and school friends, he was a prominent member of his local church, and he had often expressed his desire to become a lawyer. Yet this level of integration did not prevent his motiveless, brutal, racist murder in the summer of 2005 by individuals who, simply because of the colour of their skins – and despite having carried out such a depraved act – would be regarded in dominant political discourses to be fully integrated members of society. One can consider a variety of other examples. When a British Asian shopkeeper is assaulted in a racist attack, do the perpetrators pause to consider whether s/he can speak fluent English, lives in a community of white neighbours, or encourages her/his children to have a love marriage? Clearly not. Black professional footballers are considered to be exemplars of integration *par excellence*, within both teams and player subcultures, but this evidently does not prevent them from experiencing racism in the game. Then there is the case of the boxer Amir Khan, widely heralded in popular, political and media discourses as exemplifying Pakistani Muslim integration in Britain. Yet this did not stop him being racially abused whilst watching his brother box in Liverpool (Britton 2006) or his supporters – other British Asians, articulating a similar sense of hybrid identity – being pelted with missiles and subjected to chants of 'BNP' and 'Pakis go home' after celebrating his victory at a fight in Glasgow (Taylor 2005). Not only is it evident that integration does not directly correlate with social cohesion, but also that embodying what are perceived to be 'shared values' or what David Blunkett dubbed 'norms of acceptability' clearly does not preclude experiencing prejudice, discrimination, exclusion and violence.

As Younge (2005: 23) states, 'The value of integration is contingent on whom you are asking to integrate, what you are asking them to integrate into and on what basis you are asking them to do so'. When politicians make statements that British Asians should speak English at home or should marry a British-born partner, these are often not simply requests – they are expectations or demands. If one considers debates about segregation in amateur football, it is British Asians (or blacks, Poles, Kurds, Venezuelans, etc.) that are held to be accountable, rather than all-white teams or the leagues/associations themselves. The notion of integration is thus heavily loaded and inextricably related to power relations and racial dynamics in contemporary British society. As Younge states:

> When a group of white people gather, they call it a country club, board room or – for most of the last century – the House of Commons. But when

non-white people reach a critical mass in any area, they always hit the G-spot – the point at which policymakers scream.

(Ibid.)

Consequently, the contemporary emphasis on integration, 'shared values' and 'norms of acceptability' is evidently often a euphemism for assimilation. The pursuit of integration in football is not simply about facilitating minority groups to participate with others; it must necessarily involve significant action by all parties and changes within key institutions, such as clubs, leagues and governing bodies. It is not (i.e. should not be) purely a case of British Asians adapting to the white 'mainstream'. In other words, integration must be two-way and mutual. At both amateur and professional levels this would require significant structural and attitudinal change, in order to overcome entrenched institutional barriers. Younge (ibid.) argues that 'unless integration is coupled with the equally vigorous pursuit of equality and anti-racism, it does not go very far'. This is what the goal must be in football: not simply integration, but also equality of opportunity. If one major trend emanated from talking to the British Asian players included in this book, it is not the wish to be seen as different or to receive special treatment; it is the desire to be treated equally and equitably.

The final point in relation to integration concerns the increasing tendency for football to become implicated in wider debates about community cohesion, 'shared values' and, by association, notions of 'Britishness'. Chapter 6 noted the increasing trend for football to be linked to issues of community cohesion and, in particular, an expanding focus on British Asians within this. A distinct, yet closely related component within this shift has been references to football in discourses surrounding young British Muslims that have been involved in, or have been accused of involvement in, terrorism. For example, Werbner (2004) refers to Shafiq Rasul and Asif Iqbal, young British Pakistani men from Tipton in the West Midlands who, along with Ruhel Ahmed, were imprisoned at Camp X-Ray in Guantanamo Bay on suspicion of terrorist activities. The men had travelled to Pakistan for a wedding, but after visiting Afghanistan, had been detained on mistaken suspicion of Taliban/al-Qaeda membership. Werbner states that, 'All these young men were relatively educated, *soccer players for local teams*, and apparently integrated into British society, although two had belonged to Asian youth gangs earlier in their lives. Why did they join the Taliban?' (ibid.: 461, emphasis added). In the media, newspaper reports eagerly pointed out that both young men were big football fans, played for local teams, and supported Liverpool and Manchester United, respectively (see e.g. Morris and Vasagar 2002). The same sport-focused discourse emerged after the 7/7 bus and tube bombings in London when, in trying to uncover the motives of the four bombers, much of the investigation focused on Shehzad Tanweer from Leeds, who was widely described as being a dedicated sport lover, particularly of football and cricket (see e.g. Laville and Cobain 2005; see Rai 2006 for further analysis).

Central to these media reports is the belief that these young men *spontaneously* turned to terrorism. For example, in customary style for his paper (a right-wing tabloid), *Daily Mail* journalist David Jones described Tanweer's life route as 'a chilling metamorphosis, from cricket-mad chip shop assistant to suicide terrorist' (Jones 2005). It is significant that being a sport fan and a terrorist are seen to be mutually exclusive. In this and other examples, the authors appear incredulous that young men might love football, but also hold extreme views and/or engage in violent or terrorist acts, serving to position football (and sport more generally) as part of 'the West', i.e. developed, good, desirable, and in opposition to 'the rest', i.e. under-developed, bad, undesirable (S. Hall 1992c: 277). The sport/terrorism opposition supports the notion that 'British' and 'Muslim' values and cultures are antithetical, and through the suggestion that Rasul, Iqbal, Tanweer and others went *from* football lovers *to* extremists/terrorists, rather than indulging in them concurrently (as appears to be the case with Tanweer, the only one whose involvement in terrorism is conclusive), football becomes a prominent player in the 'shared values'/integration debate that is central to this distinction.

Following the 'parallel lives' thesis proposed in the Cantle Report (Home Office 2001b), calls have come from New Labour, and associated agencies such as the CRE – including people who are British Muslim themselves, such as MP Shahid Malik (Shahid Malik 2005) – that British Muslims must become more involved in 'mainstream' British life and politics. For example, the government has stated that there is a need for 'the minority, largely non-white community, to develop a greater acceptance of, and engagement with, the principal national institutions' (Home Office 2001b: 19). As Alexander points out, in the eyes of the government:

> The blame for 'bad communities' lies in their possession of traditional 'culture', which seemingly prevents their participation in wider society. The remedy is to break down these traditions and values and replace them with the appropriate 'core values', which can be seen to underpin the attainment of 'citizenship'.
>
> (2005: 206)

This rhetoric enables the government to claim that it has been a lack of engagement with core values, rather than racism, Islamophobia and double-standards in foreign policy in Afghanistan, Chechnya, Iraq, Kashmir, Kosovo and Palestine, that has contributed to unrest, extremism and terrorism amongst British Muslim men. In this regard, Gilroy labels New Labour's position as 'diversity management' in separating 'good' and 'bad' Muslims (Gilroy and Ouseley 2005). Sport has already become implicated in this debate, for example, through political and media usage of Amir Khan to demonstrate dominant opinions of how one must behave or what one must do to be a 'good', 'integrated' British Muslim (Burdsey 2005a). Football is increasingly becoming regarded as one of the principal national institutions that reproduces desired core values, without questioning whose values football should be expected to endorse, and without recognition that the claims of multiculturalism espoused by the government simply reinforce hegemonic, exclusionary models of what it means to be British.

The drive to overcome the exclusion of British Asians from professional football must not, therefore, become implicated in a wider political project of trying to enforce minority communities, and British Muslims in particular, to connect with 'principal national institutions'. Such a policy would only serve to reproduce the exclusion that British Asians have experienced in relation to the game and reinforce the problems that are already believed to characterize many anti-racist initiatives.

A game of two halves but multiple identities

This book does not seek to make the case that exclusion from football is any worse or more significant than exclusion from other institutions. Nor does it suggest that the patterns and trends identified in football are any more prominent or revealing that in other social and cultural spheres. It does, however, represent a call for football (and sport in general) to be taken seriously and given adequate focus in sociological investigations into identity, racism and the lifestyles of young British Asians in the early twenty-first century.

In seeking to understand the contemporary position of young British Asian footballers it is necessary to examine both the *structural* constraints that they endure and their role as *agents* in developing their own careers. There is a need to focus on the effects of racism in society and within the structures of professional football, together with players' abilities to actively create and modify their own identities in a manner that will facilitate their inclusion and provide the grounding for their subsequent achievements in the game. In seeking to further analyse the identities of young British Asian footballers, it is pertinent to return to the player with whom the book started. As a young boy Michael Chopra was as likely to be watching his beloved Newcastle United at St James' Park, accompanied by his Indian father, as attending the local Hindu temple. Such patterns have been reflected in his career as a player. Throughout various interviews Chopra has often said that he is proud of, and comfortable with, his dual ethnicity, and he refuses to prioritize either his 'Indianness' or the white components of his heritage. In fact, the Newcastle-born player has often remarked that it is his local 'Geordie' background that is the most significant aspect of his identity (e.g. Harrison 2003). Notably, there are no significant minority ethnic populations in Chopra's hometown and the popular celebration of his 'Geordie' identity has a strong correlation with white, northern English masculinity (Nayak 2003), yet Chopra's comments represent a conscious reflection on the potentialities of a 'post-racial' (S. Ali 2003) identity. Furthermore, off the field, Chopra has attitudes, preferences, aspirations and lifestyle choices linked, in particular, to the commercialization of youth culture – to fashion, music and other leisure pursuits – which he shares with white, British Asian and black youths alike. In other words, his identity is multiple and complex, resulting in the construction of a specifically British Asian male youth identity, rather than an insular 'Asian' or 'British' one. Chopra is by no means unique. For many other British Asian footballers, professional or otherwise, the culture of football provides an important context for the construction of British Asian identities. Similar multiple identifications as articulated by Chopra can also be found among young British Asian *amateur* footballers. Importantly, this sense of hybridity applies not simply to those of dual ethnicity, but also to those with two British Asian parents. In other words, the complexities of Chopra's specific sense of British 'Asianness' are increasingly common among young British Asian men throughout Britain. As this book demonstrates, they have been articulating and reflecting on the complexities of their hybrid identities long before Home Office Minister Hazel Blears suggested that such a form of identity politics was permitted or desired.

In recent years, increasing recognition has been given to the fact that British Asians live their lives according to both the cultural traditions of the subcontinent *and* the social practices of Britain and beyond. Traditionally young British Asians were popularly and academically seen as being 'caught between two cultures'. In other words, they were seen to operate within a 'culture clash' between the constraining influence of their parents on one hand and either the permissive attitudes of British society (Anwar 1976; Watson 1977) or discriminatory social practices (C. Ballard 1979) on the other. As Alexander (2006: 260) points out, 'The conflict model was underscored by an anthropological understanding of "culture" and "cultural identity" as an unchanging essence possessed by discrete and homogenous "communities" or "ethnic groups"' (see also Brah 1996). For example, Ghuman (1999: 11) has gone as far as to suggest that, as a result of their marginality, British Asian adolescents face an 'identity crisis'. He argues that they 'are likely to find identity exploration and formation a real challenge because of dual socialization and racial prejudice' (Ghuman 2003: 35–6). However, as Ramji (2003: 229) argues, 'by framing questions of culture as dichotomous and oppositional, traditional or Western, the clash of culture thesis fails to come to grips with the complex realities of South Asian [people's] everyday lives'. Similarly, Kathleen Hall (1995) argues that notions of 'biculturalism' and 'cultural conflict' have become increasingly inadequate in trying to understand the lives of British Asians. She suggests that the way young British Asians shift between different cultural spheres signifies the possession of a 'fragmented consciousness' and, in her ethnography of Sikh schoolchildren in Leeds, argues that the dominant perception amongst these youngsters is that there is 'a time to act Indian [home] and a time to act English [at school and in town]' (K. Hall 1995: 254). Nonetheless, whilst Hall suggests that young Sikhs possess the agency to switch between cultures at will and without confusion or disorientation, she actually implies an essentialist and dichotomous model of 'Indian' and 'British' cultures. Therefore, both interpretations – that of cultural conflict and the postmodern notion of cultural fragmentation – are problematic in their representations of British Asian lifestyles and identities. Both approaches polarize subcontinental and British 'cultures' as mutually exclusive entities: the former posits that British Asians are positioned between them and equally excluded by, and marginal to, each, whilst Hall's model argues that identities and lifestyles are articulated solely in relation to one or other culture, and that individuals shift completely from one to other without inhabiting any cultural border zones or traversing boundaries. Basically, these approaches fail to appreciate the possibility for fusions or creolizations of subcontinental and British cultural forms. As this book has argued, a hybrid sense of being is an increasingly prominent and influential aspect of young British Asian identities at the beginning of the twenty-first century.

Whilst recognition of, and adherence to, the religions and traditional practices of the subcontinent remain intrinsic elements in the identities and lifestyles of many British Asians, the balance between these and what might loosely be labelled 'Western' practices is increasingly shifting. Hutnyk (2005: 247) points out that 'to assume that caste, kinship, arranged marriages and religious tradition are the main keys to comprehension of the social and political experience of South Asians in Britain is a common delusion'. Instead, in many cases, the lifestyles and identities of young British Asians are being articulated in relation to the sensibilities of late modern, urban Britain and consequently 'new' identities and ethnicities (S. Hall 1996) are being actively created. For many young British Asian footballers, these processes are undertaken with reference to their lives in Rusholme, Southall or Stepney rather than, in the case of previous generations, to the 'imagined' lives of friends and relations in Rawalpindi, Srinagar or Sylhet. Amalgamating the cultures of their own ethnic communities with elements of local and global popular culture, young footballers are able to form identities that are specifically British Asian. They are promoting a sense of 'Asianness' that takes increasing reference from globally mediated spheres such as sport, music, fashion, style and consumption, combined with a localism based in their personal and urban landscapes. Modood (2005: 195) points out that 'ethnic identification is no longer necessarily connected to personal participation in distinctive cultural practices, such as those of language, religion, or dress. It is fair to say a new conception of ethnic identity has emerged' (see also Nazroo and Karlsen 2003). In this regard, one thing is increasingly clear – being British Asian is not the same as being Asian in Britain. The hybridization of British and South Asian identities thus represents a 'third space' (Bhabha 1990) from which new forms and articulations of British 'Asianness' develop. These British Asian youth identities are 'formed in the encounter between (individual and collective) agency and historical and social process' and thus represent 'a state of "becoming" rather than "being" (Alexander 2006: 270–1). This book has demonstrated that football is a key site for the construction and emergence of these new identities.

A further common orthodoxy that this book has sought to challenge is the reproduction of stereotypical interpretations of British Asian life choices and career paths. As Appiah (2005: 110) states, in dominant discourses minority groups are expected to follow certain 'life-scripts'. However, as this book has illustrated, the early twenty-first century is witnessing a generation of young British Asian men resisting stereotypical conceptions of 'Asianness' and what it means to be young, male and of South Asian heritage in contemporary Britain. Their definitions, articulations, experiences and expectations of being British Asian in the contemporary epoch are clearly different from – although not necessarily a source of conflict with – those of previous generations. Consequently, they are challenging traditional South Asian social structures and dominant ideas with regard to the family, religious practices, financial prudence, and career aspirations. Equally importantly, young British Asians, and particularly footballers, are generating resistance to processes of labelling, stereotyping and being channelled towards 'traditional' paths with regard to leisure and employment.

This book has demonstrated that young British Asians footballers possess lifestyles that are similar in many ways to those of their team-mates of different ethnicities, including whites and African-Caribbeans. In many instances they have more in common with their sporting contemporaries who have different backgrounds than with members of their own ethnic communities from different generations or in other socio-economic strata. In other words, they share with other footballers a particular sporting or cultural habitus. British Asian players are clearly proud of their ethno-cultural backgrounds and the differences that these engender, but they also stress that their interest in football is commensurate with the interest of other groups. Put simply, in football, young British Asians are asserting their right to celebrate both their 'sameness' and their 'difference' to the game's dominant (sub)cultures and identities. Theoretically, this represents a challenge to the dominant tendency for cultural differences to be viewed as more pertinent or problematic than age or class differences in social relations (K. Malik 2005a: 362) yet, in practice, arbitrary ideological boundaries that continue to construct British Asian footballers as 'Other' and inexorably alien to professional football cultures have been much harder to subvert. Perceived differences between ethnic groups still remain more salient than similarities. Taking these patterns into consideration helps to establish a most significant request that British Asian players are making with regard to their exclusion from the professional game. They are not expecting or asking for allowances to be made for them simply because of their ethno-cultural backgrounds or to receive special treatment. What they really desire is a simple human right: equality and the chance to prove their abilities just like their non-Asian contemporaries.

The final whistle

The interviews and informal conversations that I had with British Asian players for this book revealed their deep and sensitive reflections about their under-representation in professional football. Although various organizations and agencies – and, indeed, academics – have only relatively recently begun to focus seriously on this topic, the issues raised in this book are by no means new to British Asian players themselves. Playing football is tremendously important to them and they are especially troubled about their exclusion from the professional game.

If the situation is to improve, complacency must be challenged and the idea that problems of exclusion and racism are being adequately addressed must be rejected. In November 2005, at a conference entitled, *The Future for Asians in British Football* held at Leicester City FC, a series of keynote speakers repeated the frustrating and erroneous mantra that, 'We know what the issues are so I won't go over them again'. At the same conference, references to the role of racism in excluding British Asians from the game were worryingly conspicuous by their absence. Yet what the research for this book has uncovered is that the dominant ideologues of British football clearly do not fully understand what all the issues are and cannot afford to ignore any of them. Racism in particular must be kept on the agenda and the experiences and opinions of British Asian players themselves should be integral to all deliberations, and should result in concrete action, not hollow promises. Momentum also needs to be maintained to keep discussions alive and productive.

Any impact that this book might make will arguably be felt mostly within the walls of academe. However, many of the players involved in the research did not want just to participate in it; they wanted to read the finished product. It is important that they are able to do so. Players were generous in their support for my project, shared with me their very personal thoughts about sensitive, difficult topics, and showed me very rare items, such as documents about trials with professional clubs and photographs of team squads. One of the players gave me some precious photographs of himself playing for his professional club. When I asked him why he was prepared to part with them, his response was, 'Because *you* can tell our story, Dan'. His sentiments embody the feelings of all the players involved in the project, who clearly felt that they had been denied the opportunity to speak out in the past. This book has provided the chance for them to express their frustrations, feelings, hopes and desires. All the British Asian players that I spoke to understood that they did not have the power to change their circumstances on their own and wanted, at the very least, for their voices to be heard. This book provides that opportunity and is a small means of repaying them for their generous contribution to my research. Clearly, their story is not the whole of the British Asian football story, but represents a substantial chapter of it.

Notes

1 Introduction

1 The *langar* is the meal served at every *gurdwara* to ensure that the needy are always able to eat and as a way of emphasizing that all people, regardless of caste, can consume their food communally.

2 Myths, stereotypes and discourses surrounding the exclusion of British Asian professional footballers

1 For example, in the BBC's profile of London APSA, a predominantly British Pakistani amateur club, a large proportion of the programme was spent focusing on the furniture business owned by one of the players (BBC TV 2001b). Similarly, the *Express* newspaper published a sizeable article noting only the fact that the players in the Sikh Hunter New Boys club in the West Midlands all shared the surname Singh (Stote 2002).

2 Pakistan and Bangladesh did not exist as nation-states until 1947 and 1971, respectively.

3 'We shall fight like lions' was the rallying cry of Southall's (predominantly Punjabi) British Asian population during their protests against racism, discrimination in housing and employment, and police harassment in the late 1970s to early 1980s (Campaign Against Racism and Fascism/Southall Rights 1981).

4 As K. Hall (2002: 130) states, 'through the taking of *amrit* (nectar), Sikhs become Singhs; they are converted from lamb to lion (the literal meaning of "Singh"). They are imbibed with the spirit of the Guru and adapt themselves to his living and his form'.

5 The ninth month of the Muslim year (lasting thirty days), during which individuals must fast – consuming neither food nor water – between sunrise and sunset.

6 This incident had some positive consequences, however, as at the start of the 2005–06 season, the FA instructed local amateur leagues to arrange fixtures so that, where necessary, they do not clash with non-Christian religious and cultural festivals.

7 For example, a letter from a British Indian reader to the *Guardian* newspaper regarding an article on British Asian footballers argued that 'Asians are intimidated by football but also see it as a proletarian sport and Asians (particularly Indians) don't see themselves as proles' (*Guardian* 2001).

8 In the South Asian sport of kabaddi, players from each of the two competing teams take turns to make a 'raid' on the opposition's territory and return to their side of the court without being 'captured'. The time each 'raider' is permitted to make a 'raid' is limited by the length of time they are able to hold their breath. The 'raider' demonstrates this to the umpire by continuously chanting 'kabaddi' (see Alter 2000).

3 Racial discrimination and white privilege in English football

1 In the summer of 2006, Bowyer rejoined West Ham, potentially reigniting the debate.

2 This latter event occurred a month after teenage British Asian rugby player Ushanth Kantharuban, hooker for the Saracens under-15 side, was racially abused, kicked and punched so severely during a match against Bath that the game was abandoned and the player vowed never to play rugby again (Chaudhary 2002).

3 The 'Bradford Twelve' were a group of young British Pakistani men who were charged with possession of petrol bombs. The group claimed that they were simply planning to defend themselves against a threatened attack by racists. Between 1982 and 1984, New Right ideologue Honeyford wrote a number of articles in the *Salisbury Review* that made derogatory references to local British Pakistani communities.

4 For example, former Home Secretary, David Blunkett, and Labour MP Ann Cryer have cited problems that they perceive to be associated with the entrenched 'Islamic ghetto culture' of British Muslims. Blunkett suggested that only by speaking English, as well as other languages, in their home environments could Muslims overcome the 'schizophrenia which bedevils generational relationships' (cited in Pallister 2002). Cryer, MP for Keighley in West Yorkshire, argued that Muslim migrants who cannot speak English should be refused entry to England because they are 'importing poverty' (cited in Dodd 2001). In November 2003, Europe Minister Denis MacShane was forced to withdraw a speech in which he proposed to challenge British Muslims to choose between the 'British way' or the 'way of terrorists' (Hall and Taylor 2003).

5 Relations between England and Pakistan reached their nadir during the late 1980s to early 1990s with the re-emergence of English accusations of cheating by Pakistani players and umpires. In particular, full-scale scandals developed over allegations of 'ball tampering' – altering the condition of a cricket ball in an illegal manner, such as adding sweat, grease or dirt to influence the movement of a delivery – by Pakistan bowlers and the on-pitch confrontation between England captain Mike Gatting and Pakistani umpire, Shakoor Rana, during a match in Faisalabad in 1987. Rana allegedly accused Gatting of cheating, whilst Gatting labelled Rana a 'shit awful umpire' (cited in Williams 2001: 138). The following day's play was suspended as Rana refused to take the field until Gatting apologized to him, which he did in a letter written on a piece of scrap paper.

6 In an interesting comparison, a match between Cameroon and Morocco at Evry-Bondoufle, south of Paris, in November 2005, was postponed amid security concerns in the wake of widespread rioting involving predominantly (but not exclusively) African and Arab youths in the Paris area.

4   Ethnicity, hybridity and cultural capital

1 There are notable exceptions. For example, a major part of the work of Football Unites Racism Divides (FURD) is constructing and touring an exhibition that details the historical contribution of minority ethnic players in British professional football.

2 *Bend It Like Beckham* is a British movie written by Gurinder Chadha (also the film's director), Paul Mayeda Berges and Guljit Bindra. The film revolves around a British Asian girl and her aim, against the wishes of her parents, to play football. In October 2002 it won the Hitchcock L'Argent audience award at the *Festival du Film Britannique* at Dinard, France. Also that year, Parminder Nagra, who plays Jess, the main character in the film, was somewhat bizarrely chosen to be FIFA's Football Personality of the Year.

3 In April 2001, Robin Cook, the Foreign Secretary, made a speech to the Social Market Foundation political think-tank stressing the multicultural composition of Britain. He stated that 'the British are not a race, but a gathering of countless different races, the vast majority of which are not indigenous to these islands.. ..Chicken tikka masala is now Britain's true national dish, not only because it is the most popular, but because it is a perfect illustration of the way Britain absorbs and adapts external influences' (cited in Wintour 2001).

4 The term 'Asian Underground' (also known as the 'New Asian Kool') was coined by the British music press in relation to a collection of late-twentieth-century British Asian musicians, such as T. J. Rehmi, Radical Sista, Bally Sagoo, Nitin Sawnhey and Talvin Singh. These artists formed part of a London-based club scene, at venues such as *Anokha*, *Sitarfunk*, *Outcaste* and *Swaraj* (see Banerjea 2000). This musical genre achieved popularity amongst the capital's young, upwardly mobile, white club-goers. Hutnyk and Sharma (2000: 59) argue that 'there is perhaps currently no better illustration of how ethnicity as a marker of (exotic) otherness has entered into the realms of a European popular music culture than the example of the "New Asian Dance Music"'.

5 Exceptions are Monsoon (aka Sheila Chandra), who reached number 12 in the British music charts in 1982 with the track *Ever So Lonely*, and Bally Sagoo, whose track *Dil Cheez* made the Top 20 in 1996.

6 In 2003, *Mundian To Bach Ke*, a four-year-old track by Birmingham-based artist Panjabi MC reached the Top 10 after it was remixed with a hip-hop beat and samples from 1980s American television show *Knightrider*. A reversal of this process has also occurred with Timbaland sampling a *tumbi* drum to create Missy Elliott's *Get Ur Freak On* (2001) and Dr. Dre sampling the vocals of bhangra superstar Lata Mangeshkar for Truth Hurts' *Addictive* (2002). Furthermore, many 'mainstream' pop artists are now seeking to have their music remixed with a bhangra influence. For example, young British Asian producers Rishi Rich, Juggy D and Jay Sean have worked with Mary J Blige, Craig David, Liberty X, Jennifer Lopez, Ricky Martin, Mis-teeq, Britney Spears and Sugababes, whilst Panjabi Hit Squad have remixed material by Ashanti and Mariah Carey. Talvin Singh fuses electronic dance music with traditional South Asian instruments such as the *tabla* drum. In 1999 he won the Mercury Music Prize – an annual award given to the artist(s) recording the best album – for his album *Okay*.

7 *Goodness Gracious Me!* is a sketch show that ran between 1998 and 2001. It is estimated that the first series was watched by an audience that was 85 per cent white (Malik 2002: 103). *The Kumars at No. 42* (2001–present) involves the spoof Kumar family interviewing real-life celebrity guests, the majority of whom are white. Indeed, in 2003, Elaine Sihera, founder of the annual British Diversity Awards and the Windrush Achievement Awards stated that, 'I am unhappy with the fact that *The Kumars at No. 42* only seems to welcome white guests, and never has a single black person on it... .I don't think it is good enough to stand on its own without white celebrities' (cited in M. Ahmed 2003).

8 A similar process occurred in the summer of 2005 with the coterminous consumption of what was marketed as 'Gypsy' fashion and widespread media and public vilification of Gypsies and Travellers (Hughes 2005).

9 Bisson, James and Mistri all starred in the 1990s British movie *East is East*. Set in 1960/70s Salford, the story follows a family headed by a Pakistani father and a white mother, and focuses on the issues faced by the children in coming to terms with their dual ethnicities. Bisson also appeared in *Coronation Street*, whilst James and Mistri have had roles in *Eastenders*.

10 For an analysis of the sporting successes achieved by Anglo-Indians during British rule in India see M. Mills (2001).

11 The dual ethnicity Scottish-Indian Paul Wilson played for Celtic in the 1970s. Other players of South Asian background to have played in Scotland are Salim Bachi-Khan (Celtic) in the 1930s, and Rashid Sarwar (Kilmarnock) and Jas Juttla (Rangers and Greenock Morton) in the 1990s.

12 There are notable exceptions. During the 1980s, the Bhatti brothers were directors at Wolverhampton Wanderers and the Kumar brothers held similar positions at Birmingham City and Cardiff City. In 2003, Raj Bhatia was part of a consortium that attempted to take over Notts County.

13 These included African American tennis star Serena Williams and players from the New York Knicks basketball team.

14 Woods personally constructed the label 'Cablinasian' as an amalgam of the terms Caucasian, black, Indian and Asian. He is one-quarter Thai, one-quarter Chinese, one-quarter white, one-eighth Native American and one-eighth African American (see Rockquemore 2004).

5   Identity, diaspora and citizenship

1 In 1978, the year before she became Prime Minister, Margaret Thatcher stated that, because of insufficient immigration controls, Britain was being 'swamped' by an 'alien culture'.

2 Sivanandan (2001: 2) argues that, to some extent, the notion of cultural racism has been superseded by a *xeno*-racism, which 'is racism in substance but xeno in form – a racism that is meted out to impoverished strangers even if they are white'. It is based on neither colour nor culture, but a fear of the homogenizing effects of the European Union and the consequences emanating from the destruction of international barriers, for example, an increase in the number of people seeking political asylum.

3 Such a claim is ironic, considering that it was BNP chairman Nick Griffin who suggested constructing a 'peace wall' in Oldham to separate white and British Asian communities.

4 Despite this trend, there are still individuals and groups that wish to maintain the flag's right-wing associations. For example, in 2005, at a match between Brentford and Oldham, a section of the latter's supporters unfurled a St George flag embossed with the words 'Born in England, Live in England, Die in England'. Debates about whether the flag was racist continued for a number of weeks until it was eventually withdrawn by its owner who, despite not believing it to be racist, was concerned about the publicity it had created. However, before the clubs were due to meet in an FA Cup replay, the BNP's website published a message urging fans to take St George flags to the game, as a display of patriotism (Turner 2006).

5 During the mid-1990s, David Baddiel and Frank Skinner found fame as co-hosts of *Fantasy Football League*, a television show that provided an ironic and irreverent analysis of the game and championed, somewhat superficially, football nostalgia. Broadcast on BBC2 late on Friday nights – in the 'post-pub' slot – the show promoted a form of (white) 'New Laddism' closely associated with drinking, football, jokes about women and Britpop music. Although there are notable exceptions, this guitar-based rock-pop genre, drawing liberally on 1960s modernist groups, such as the Small Faces, the Kinks and the Who, and post-punk favourites including Madness and the Jam, was performed by white, male artists (see Carrington 1998 for a full analysis).

6 In 2000, whilst the attendance for the match between West Bromwich Albion and India exceeded 12,000, only 5,000 people watched the Fulham versus India game. Just 3,000 people watched Bangladesh play India in Leicester. In 2001, 1,292 fans attended the match between Bury and Pakistan. The following year, India played two matches against Jamaica in England. Only 1,200 people watched the first match at Vicarage Road, Watford whilst only 4,000 spectators attended the second fixture at Wolverhampton Wanderers' Molineux stadium.

7 In 2000, India lost 2–0 to Fulham and drew 0–0 with West Bromwich Albion. In 2001, they lost 3–0 to Brentford, 2–0 to Walsall, 2–0 to Nottingham Forest and drew 1–1 with Leyton Orient. Also that year, Pakistan lost 3–0 to Bury and 2–0 to Coventry City.

8 In contrast, Delhi-born Simran Singh, who plays in Denmark for AB Copenhagen was called up to the India under-18 training camp in 2003 (Chaudhari and Daniel 2003).

9 Bangladesh only achieved Test status in the 1990s.

6 British Asians and anti-racism in English football I: strategies and symbolism

1 According to Bloom (2003), the term 'Paki-bashing' originated in the media in April 1970, after a group of British Asian workers were attacked at the London Chest Hospital in Bethnal Green.

2 Note, for example, the chant of 'Cahill is a Paki' by West Ham supporters towards Everton's Tim Cahill, a Samoan-Australian, during a match in March 2006 (field notes, 4 March 2006).

3 In 1992, the mosque which occupied the site was razed to the ground by tens of thousands of Hindu extremists who claimed that the site is the birthplace of the god Lord Ram. Since then, disputes between Hindus and Muslims over the designation of the site have resulted in widespread riots and massacres. In February 2002, fifty-nine Hindu activists died after the train bringing them home from a visit to Ayodhya was deliberately set alight by a group of Muslims. Over one thousand Muslims died in the resulting riots and anti-Muslim pogroms, primarily in Ahmedabad, in the state of Gujarat.

4 I am grateful to Steve Bradbury for this information.

7 British Asians and anti-racism in English football II: case studies and critique

1 This does not, however, explain why African-Caribbeans, who are well-represented as professional players, face discrimination in reaching the higher positions of management. There are contrasting schools of thought regarding the reason for this discrepancy, but it is undoubtedly influenced by dominant views by club managers and directors on black physicality and intellect (Moran 2001; King 2004a).

2 For example, in February 2001, plans to turn the Al Hijrah school in Bordesley Green, Birmingham into Britain's first state-funded Islamic secondary school were labelled 'a question of apartheid in education' by Conservative councillor James Hutchings (Smithers 2001).

3 These include Winston Silcott, wrongly convicted (as part of the 'Broadwater Three') for the murder of PC Keith Blakelock in Tottenham in 1985; Duwayne Brooks, who was inexplicably treated as a suspect rather than a victim/witness in the murder of his friend Stephen Lawrence; and Christopher Alder, Francisco Borg, Sylbert Farquharson and Darren Hoole who were assaulted, mistreated and/or unlawfully imprisoned by the police. The Metropolitan Police have paid compensation to Dal Babu, Ali Dizaei, Gurpal Virdi and Leroy Logan, their own minority ethnic officers who were either subjected to racial or religious discrimination, or incorrectly accused of committing misdemeanours.

4 After their pictures were distributed by the police, a large number of British Asians who were involved in the urban unrest in Bradford during the summer of 2001 voluntarily gave themselves up. Many of them had no previous convictions and provided good character references in court, yet were sentenced to prison terms of between four and six years. In a court of appeal verdict in January 2003, Michael Mansfield QC decreed that the sentencing of these men was 'manifestly excessive' and claimed that the original trial judge had ignored the 'matrix of fear' present amongst British Asians in the city (Dodd 2003a). A number of sentences were subsequently reduced.

5 Tickets for the matches between India and Jamaica in 2002 were priced £20 for adults and £10 for children, a considerable sum for a friendly match.

6 For example, in 1998, as a consequence of their matches against the KFF, Millwall signed goalkeeper Amritpal Sidhu on schoolboy forms.

References

Abbas, T. (2005) *Muslim Britain: Communities under Pressure*, London: Zed Books.
—— (2006) 'Introduction', in A. Malik (ed.) *The State We Are In: Identity, Terror and the Law of Jihad*, Bristol: Amal Press.
Ahmed, M. (2003) 'Kumars is a "cul de sac for blacks"', *Eastern Eye*, 10 January.
Ahmed, S. (1997) '"It's a sun-tan, isn't it?": autobiography as an identificatory practice', in H.S. Mirza (ed.) *Black British Feminism: A Reader*, London: Routledge.
—— (2004) 'Declarations of whiteness: the non-performativity of anti-racism', *Borderlands*, 3, 2. Available online at <http://www.borderlandsejournal.adelaide.edu.au/issues/vol3 no2.html>, accessed 16 February 2006.
Alexander, C. (2000) *The Asian Gang: Ethnicity, Identity, Masculinity*, Oxford: Berg.
—— (2002) 'Beyond black: re-thinking the colour/culture divide', *Ethnic and Racial Studies*, 25, 4: 552–71.
—— (2004a) 'Imagining the Asian gang: ethnicity, masculinity and youth after "the riots"', *Critical Social Policy*, 24, 4: 526–49.
—— (2004b) 'Writing race: ethnography and the imagination of *The Asian Gang*', in M. Bulmer and J. Solomos (eds) *Researching Race and Racism*, London: Routledge.
—— (2005) 'Embodying violence: "riots", dis/order and the private lives of the "Asian gang"', in C. Alexander and C. Knowles (eds) *Making Race Matter: Bodies, Space and Identity*, Basingstoke: Palgrave.
—— (2006) 'Imagining the politics of BrAsian youth', in N. Ali, V.S. Kalra and S. Sayyid (eds) *A Postcolonial People: South Asians in Britain*, London: Hurst.
Alexander, C. and Knowles, C. (2005) 'Introduction', in C. Alexander and C. Knowles (eds) *Making Race Matter: Bodies, Space and Identity*, Basingstoke: Palgrave.
Ali, N., Kalra, V.S. and Sayyid, S. (eds) (2006) *A Postcolonial People: South Asians in Britain*, London: Hurst.
Ali, S. (2003) *Mixed-race, Post Race: Gender, New Ethnicities and Cultural Practices*, Oxford: Berg.
Alibhai-Brown, Y. (2001a) *Mixed Feelings: The Complex Lives of Mixed-race Britons*, London: Women's Press.
—— (2001b) 'The fear and alienation that lie behind the explosion of violence', *Independent*, 10 July.
Allen, C. (2005) 'From race to religion: the new face of discrimination', in T. Abbas (ed.) *Muslim Britain: Communities under Pressure*, London: Zed Books.
Alter, J. (1994) *The Wrestler's Body: Identity and Ideology in North India*, Berkeley, CA: University of California Press.
—— (2000) 'Kabaddi, a national sport of India: the internationalism of nationalism

and the foreignness of Indianness', in N. Dyck (ed.) *Games, Sports and Cultures*, Oxford: Berg.

Andersen, M. (1993) 'Studying across difference: race, class and gender in qualitative research', in J. Stanfield and R. Dennis (eds) *Race and Ethnicity in Research Methods*, London: Sage.

Anderson, B. (1991) *Imagined Communities*, London: Verso.

Ansari, H. (2004) *The Infidel Within: Muslims in Britain since 1800*, London: Hurst.

Anthias, F. (1998) 'Evaluating "diaspora": beyond ethnicity?', *Sociology*, 32, 3: 557–80.

—— (2001) 'New hybridities, old concepts: the limits of "culture"', *Ethnic and Racial Studies*, 24, 4: 619–41.

Anthias, F. and Lloyd, C. (2002) 'Introduction: fighting racisms, defining the territory', in F. Anthias and C. Lloyd (eds) *Rethinking Anti-racisms: From Theory to Practice*, London: Routledge.

Anwar, M. (1976) 'Young Asians between two cultures', *New Society*, 38: 563–65.

—— (1998) *Between Cultures: Continuity and Change in the Lives of Young Asians*, London: Routledge.

Appiah, K.A. (2005) *The Ethics of Identity*, Princeton, NJ: Princeton University Press.

Appignanesi, L. and Maitland, S. (eds) (1989) *The Rushdie File*, London: Fourth Estate.

Armstrong, G. (2002) 'Talking up the game: football and the reconstruction of Liberia, west Africa', *Identities: Global Studies in Culture and Power*, 9: 471–94.

Asad, T. (1990) 'Multiculturalism and British identity in the wake of the Rushdie affair', *Politics and Society*, 18, 4: 455–80.

Asian News (2004) 'Soccer bosses to act over Muslim "ban"', 30 November.

Asians in Football Forum (2005) 'Asians can play football', Asians in Football Forum.

Back, L. (1996) *New Ethnicities and Urban Culture: Racisms and Multiculture in Young Lives*, London: UCL Press.

—— (2005) '"Home from home": youth, belonging and place', in C. Alexander and C. Knowles (eds) *Making Race Matter: Bodies, Space and Identity*, Basingstoke: Palgrave.

Back, L., Crabbe, T. and Solomos, J. (1998) 'Racism in football: patterns of continuity and change' in A. Brown (ed.) *Fanatics! Power, Identity and Fandom in Football*, London: Routledge.

—— (2001a) '"Lions and black skins": race, nation and local patriotism in football', in B. Carrington and I. McDonald (eds) *'Race', Sport and British Society*, London: Routledge.

—— (2001b) *The Changing Face of Football: Racism, Identity and Multiculture in the English Game*, Oxford: Berg.

Bagguley, P. and Hussain, Y. (2005) 'Flying the flag for England? Citizenship, religion and cultural identity among British Pakistani Muslims', in T. Abbas (ed.) *Muslim Britain: Communities under Pressure*, London: Zed Books.

Bailey, A. (2003) 'The blame game', *When Saturday Comes*, 196, June.

Bains, J. and Johal, S. (1998) *Corner Flags and Corner Shops: The Asian Football Experience*, London: Gollancz.

Bains, J. and Patel, R. (1996) *Asians Can't Play Football*, Birmingham: Asian Social Development Agency.

Balibar, E. (1991a) 'Is there a "neo-racism"?' in E. Balibar and I. Wallerstein (eds) *Race, Nation, Class: Ambiguous Identities*, London: Verso.

—— (1991b) 'Racism and nationalism', in E. Balibar and I. Wallerstein (eds) *Race, Nation, Class: Ambiguous Identities*, London: Verso.

Ballard, C. (1979) 'Conflict, continuity and change: second generation South Asians', in V.S. Khan (ed.) *Minority Families in Britain: Support and Stress*, London: Macmillan.

Ballard, R. (ed.) (1994a) *Desh Pardesh: the South Asian Presence in Britain*, London: Hurst.

—— (1994b) 'Introduction: the emergence of Desh Pardesh', in R. Ballard (ed.) *Desh Pardesh: The South Asian Presence in Britain*, London: Hurst.

Banerjea, K. (2000) 'Sounds of whose underground? The fine tuning of diaspora in an age of mechanical reproduction', *Theory, Culture and Society*, 17, 3: 64–79.

Bans, K. (2001) 'Hooligans of cricket', *Eastern Eye*, 25 May.

Banton, M. (1998) *Racial Theories*, Cambridge: Cambridge University Press.

Barker, M. (1981) *The New Racism*, London: Junction Books.

Basu, S. (2003) *Curry: The Story of the Nation's Favourite Dish*, Stroud: Sutton Publishing.

Bauman, Z. (1988) 'Exit visas and entry tickets: the paradoxes of Jewish assimilation', *Telos*, 77: 45–77.

Baumann, G. (1996) *Contesting Culture: Discourses of Identity in Multi-ethnic London*, Cambridge: Cambridge University Press.

—— (1999) *The Multicultural Riddle: Rethinking National, Ethnic and Religious Identities*, London: Routledge.

BBC Radio (2002) 'On the line', BBC Radio Five Live, 15 July.

—— (2005a) 'Don't call me Asian!', BBC Radio Four, 11 January.

—— (2005b) 'Taking on Tehran', BBC Radio Four, 9 December.

—— (2006) 'Worricker on Sunday', BBC Radio Five Live, 19 March.

BBC TV (2001a) 'Islamophobia', BBC2, 18 August.

—— (2001b) 'They think it's all Islam', BBC2, 16 August.

—— (2003a) 'Network East Late', BBC2, 19 February.

—— (2003b) 'The secret policeman', BBC1, 21 October.

Becker, H. (1970) *Sociological Work*, Chicago, IL: Aldine.

Bell, V. (2002) 'Reflections on "The End of Antiracism"', in P. Essed and D.T. Goldberg (eds) *Race Critical Theories*, Oxford: Blackwell.

Bennett, A. (2000) *Popular Music and Youth Culture: Music, Identity and Place*, Basingstoke: Palgrave.

Benson, S. (1997) 'The body, health and eating disorders', in K. Woodward (ed.) *Identity and Difference*, London: Sage.

Berthoud, R. and Beishon, S. (1997) 'People, families and households', in T. Modood, R. Berthoud, J. Lakey, J. Nazroo, P. Smith, S. Virdee and S. Beishon, *Ethnic Minorities in Britain: Diversity and Disadvantage*, London: PSI.

Bhabha, H. (1990) 'The third space – interview with Homi Bhabha', in J. Rutherford (ed.) *Identity: Community, Culture, Difference*, London: Lawrence and Wishart.

Bhatia, S. (2003a) 'Bowyer brings baggage of hate', *Guardian*, 8 January.

—— (2003b) 'Harpal is ready to make huge step', *Eastern Eye*, 17 January.

—— (2003c) 'Harpal thanks family fortunes', *Eastern Eye*, 24 January.

Bhatt, C. (1997) *Liberation and Purity*, London: UCL Press.

Bhattacharyya, G. (2005) 'Born on the second of July', *Guardian*, 8 October.

Birt, Y. (2006) 'Islamic citizenship in Britain after 7/7: tackling extremism and preserving freedoms', in A. Malik (ed.) *The State We Are In: Identity, Terror and the Law of Jihad*, Bristol: Amal Press.

Black Information Link (2006) 'Ouseley flags FA offside on race'. Available online at <http://www.blink.org.uk/pdescription.asp?key=10600&grp=53&cat=152>, accessed 23 February 2006.

Blackshaw, T. and Crabbe, T. (2005) 'Leeds on trial: soap opera, performativity and the racialization of sports-related violence', *Patterns of Prejudice*, 39, 3: 327–42.

Blake, I. (2002) 'The further trials of Lee Bowyer', *When Saturday Comes*, 180, February.
Bloom, C. (2003) *Violent London: 2000 Years of Riots, Rebels and Revolts*, Basingstoke and Oxford: Sidgwick & Jackson.
Blunkett, D. (2005) 'A new England: an English identity within Britain', speech given at the Institute for Public Policy Research, London, 14 March 2005.
Bonnett, A. (2000) *Anti-racism*, London: Routledge.
Bourdieu, P. (1977) *Outline of a Theory of Practice*, Cambridge: Cambridge University Press.
—— (1978) 'Sport and social class', *Social Science Information*, 17, 6: 819–40.
—— (1984) *Distinction: a Social Critique of the Judgement of Taste*, Cambridge, MA: Harvard University Press.
—— (1986) 'The forms of capital', in J. Richardson (ed.) *Handbook of Theory and Research for the Sociology of Education*, Westport, CT: Greenwood Press.
—— (1988) 'Program for a sociology of sport', *Sociology of Sport Journal*, 5, 2: 153–61.
—— (1990) *The Logic of Practice*, Stanford, CA: Stanford University Press.
—— (1993) *The Field of Cultural Production: Essays on Art and Literature*, New York: Columbia University Press.
Bourdieu, P. and Wacquant, L. (2002) *An Introduction to Reflexive Sociology*, Chicago, IL: Chicago University Press.
Bradbury, S. (2001a) '*Football Unites, Racism Divides*: an evaluation of the period 1998–2000', Sir Norman Chester Centre for Football Research, University of Leicester.
—— (2001b) 'The new communities: a survey of professional football clubs on issues of community, ethnicity and social inclusion', Sir Norman Chester Centre for Football Research, University of Leicester.
Bradbury, S. and Williams, J. (2006) 'New Labour, racism and "new" football in England', *Patterns of Prejudice*, 40, 1: 61–82.
Brah, A. (1996) *Cartographies of Diaspora: Contesting Identities*, London: Routledge.
Branigan, T. (2001) 'The effete east', *Guardian*, 12 November.
Brentford, Chiswick and Isleworth Times (1995) 'Asian boys close to Bees breakthrough', 16 February.
Britton, P. (2006) 'Amir race abuse shock', *Manchester Evening News*, 25 February.
Brodkin, J. (2003a) 'Fans unite to protest against new recruit and racism', *Guardian*, 11 January.
—— (2003b) 'Victim's family condemn West Ham move for Bowyer', *Guardian*, 8 January.
Brown, M. (2006) 'Leeds united', *Times Educational Supplement*, 24 February.
Brown, T., Jackson, J., Brown, K., Sellers, R., Keiper, S. and Manuel, W. (2003) '"There's no race on the playing field": perceptions of racial discrimination among white and black athletes', *Journal of Sport and Social Issues*, 27, 2: 162–83.
Brubaker, R. (2005) 'The "diaspora" diaspora', *Ethnic and Racial Studies*, 28, 1: 1–19.
Bulmer, M. and Solomos, J. (2004) 'Introduction: researching race and racism', in M. Bulmer and J. Solomos (eds) *Researching Race and Racism*, London: Routledge.
Bunting, M. (ed.) (2005) *Islam, Race and Being British*, London: Guardian/Barrow Cadbury Trust.
Burdsey, D. (2004a) 'Obstacle race? "Race", racism and the recruitment of British Asian professional footballers', *Patterns of Prejudice*, 38, 3: 279–99.
—— (2004b) '"One of the lads"? Dual ethnicity and assimilated ethnicities in the careers of British Asian professional footballers', *Ethnic and Racial Studies*, 27, 5: 757–79.
—— (2005a) '"Role with the punches": "race", representation and the construction of

Amir Khan as a role model for multiethnic Britain', paper presented at *Lost in transl-Asian? British Asians, Sport, Leisure and Popular Culture* study workshop, University of Brighton, 19 November 2005.

—— (2005b) '(White man) in Bangla Town: grappling with conundrums of ethnography, ethics and ethnicity', *Leisure Studies Newsletter*, 70, March.

—— (2006) 'No ball games allowed? A socio-historical examination of the development and social roles of British Asian football clubs', *Journal of Ethnic and Migration Studies*, 32, 3: 477–96.

—— (forthcoming) '"I don't want to go to a football match for an onion bhaji!": anti-racist campaigns, multiculturalism and English football', in M.D. Alleyne (ed.) *Anti-racist Discourses: Theory and Comparison*.

Burgess, R. (1984) *In the Field: an Introduction to Field Research*, London: Allen & Unwin.

Burlet, S. and Reid, H. (1995) 'Co-operation and conflict: the South Asian diaspora after Ayodhya', *New Community*, 21, 4: 587–97.

Burnett, J. (2004) 'Community, cohesion and the state', *Race and Class*, 45, 3: 1–18.

Burnley Task Force (2001) 'Burnley speaks, who listens . . .? Burnley Task Force report on the disturbances in June 2001', Burnley: Burnley Task Force.

Caglar, A. (1997) 'Hyphenated identities and the limits of "culture"', in T. Modood and P. Werbner (eds) *The Politics of Multiculturalism in the New Europe: Racism, Identity and Community*, London: Zed Books.

Campaign Against Racism and Fascism (2001) 'CARF 63', August/September.

—— (2002) 'CARF 66', February/March.

Campaign Against Racism and Fascism/Southall Rights (1981) *Southall: Birth of a Black Community*, London: Institute of Race Relations/Southall Rights.

Campbell, D. (2001a) 'Football's new star rises from the East', *Observer*, 9 September.

—— (2001b) 'Hussain lashes British Asians as unpatriotic', *Observer*, 27 May.

Cantle, T. (2005) 'England: a segregated country?', in M. Bunting (ed.) *Islam, Race and Being British*, London: Guardian/Barrow Cadbury Trust.

Carmichael, S. and Hamilton, C. (1967) *Black Power: The Politics of Liberation in America*, London: Jonathan Cape.

Carrington, Ben (1998a) '"Football's coming home" but whose home? And do we want it? Nation, football and the politics of exclusion', in A. Brown (ed.) *Fanatics! Power, Identity and Fandom in Football*, London: Routledge.

—— (1998b) 'Sport, masculinity and black cultural resistance', *Journal of Sport and Social Issues*, 22, 3: 275–98.

—— (2000) 'Double consciousness and the black British athlete', in K. Owusu (ed.) *Black British Culture and Society*, London: Routledge.

—— (2004a) 'Cosmopolitan Olympism, humanism and the spectacle of "race"', in J. Bale and M.K. Christensen (eds) *Post-Olympism? Questioning Sport in the Twenty-first Century*, Oxford: Berg.

—— (2004b) 'Introduction: race/nation/sport', *Leisure Studies*, 23, 1: 1–3.

Carrington, Ben and McDonald, I. (2001a) 'Introduction: "race", sport and British society', in B. Carrington and I. McDonald (eds) *'Race', Sport and British Society*, London: Routledge.

—— (2001b) *'Race', Sport and British Society*, London: Routledge.

—— (2001c) 'Whose game is it anyway? Racism in local league cricket', in B. Carrington and I. McDonald (eds) *'Race', Sport and British Society*, London: Routledge.

—— (2003) 'The politics of "race" and sports policy', in B. Houlihan (ed.) *Handbook of Sport and Society*, London: Sage.

Carrington, Bruce, Chivers, T. and Williams, T. (1987) 'Gender, leisure and sport: a case study of young people of South Asian descent', *Leisure Studies*, 6: 265–79.

Carroll, B. and Hollinshead, G. (1993) 'Ethnicity and conflict in Physical Education', *British Educational Research Journal*, 19, 1: 59–76.

Carvel, J. (2000) 'The rise of the little Englanders', *Guardian*, 28 November.

Chadband, I. and Low, V. (2003) 'East end fears Bowyer could split community', *Evening Standard*, 10 January.

Charlton Athletic Race Equality (2000) *Equaliser*, 4, Spring.

Chaudhari, A. and Daniel, C. (2003) 'Finally it's happening...'. Available online at <http://www.indianfootball.com/article/article154.html>, accessed 19 October 2005.

Chaudhary, V. (1996) '"Asians can't play" barrier', *Guardian*, 10 February.

—— (2001) 'A question of support', *Guardian*, 29 May.

—— (2002) 'Bath under fire after "racist" assault on boy', *Guardian*, 16 March.

Clifford, J. (1986) 'Introduction: partial truths', in J. Clifford and G. Marcus (eds) *Writing Culture: the Poetics and Politics of Ethnography*, Berkeley and Los Angeles: University of California Press.

—— (1994) 'Diasporas', *Cultural Anthropology*, 9: 302–38.

Cohen, P. (1992) '"It's racism what dunnit": hidden narratives in theories of racism', in J. Donald and A. Rattansi (eds) *'Race', Culture and Difference*, London: Sage.

—— (1996) 'Homing devices', in V. Amit-Talai and C. Knowles (eds) *Re-situating Identities: The Politics of Race, Ethnicity and Culture*, Hadleigh: Broadview.

Cohen, P. and Bains, H. (eds) (1988) *Multi-racist Britain*, London: Macmillan.

Cohen, R. (1999) *Global Diasporas: An Introduction*, London: UCL Press.

Cole, C. and Andrews, D. (2001) 'America's new son: Tiger Woods and America's multiculturalism', in D. Andrews and S. Jackson (eds) *Sport Stars: The Cultural Politics of Sporting Celebrity*, London: Routledge.

Commission for Racial Equality (1995) 'Kick it – again: uniting football against racism', London: CRE.

—— (2004) 'Racial equality in football: a survey', London: CRE.

Cowan, R. and Hyder, K. (2005) 'Met calls on Asian firms to hire "at risk" youths', *Guardian*, 31 May.

Crabbe, T. and Wagg, S. (2000) '"A carnival of cricket?": the cricket world cup, "race" and the politics of carnival', *Culture, Sport and Society*, 3, 2: 70–88.

Crumley, B. (2005) 'Personal goals', *Time*, 10 October.

Dagkas, S. and Benn, T. (2006) 'Young Muslim women's experiences of Islam and physical education in Greece and Britain: a comparative study', *Sport, Education and Society*, 11, 1: 21–38.

Dalmage, H. (ed.) (2004) *The Politics of Multiracialism: Challenging Racial Thinking*, Albany, NY: SUNY Press.

Dasgupta, S. (2005) 'Indian or otherwise: PIO footballers are just a couple of strikes away', *Soccer and Society*, 6, 1: 34–48.

De Knop, P., Theeboom, M., Wittock, H. and De Martelaer, K. (1996) 'Implications of Islam on Muslim girls' sport participation in western Europe: review and policy recommendations for sport promotion', *Sport, Education and Society*, 1, 2: 147–64.

Delgado, R. (1989) 'Storytelling for oppositionists and others: a plea for narrative', *Michigan Law Review*, 87, 2411–41.

Dench, G., Gavron, K. and Young, M. (2006) *The New East End: Kinship, Race and Conflict*, London: Profile Books.

Dimeo, P. (2001a) 'Contemporary developments in Indian football', *Contemporary South Asia*, 10, 2: 251–64.

—— (2001b) 'Football and politics in Bengal: colonialism, nationalism, communalism', in P. Dimeo and J. Mills (eds) *Soccer in South Asia: Empire, Nation, Diaspora*, London: Frank Cass.

—— (2002a) 'Colonial bodies, colonial sport: "martial" Punjabis, "effeminate" Bengalis and the development of Indian football', *International Journal of the History of Sport*, 19, 1: 72–90.

—— (2002b) 'The local, national and global in Indian football: issues of power and identity', *Football Studies*, 5, 2: 74–87.

Din, I. and Cullingford, C. (2004) 'Boyzone and bhangra: the place of popular and minority cultures', *Race, Ethnicity and Education*, 7, 3: 307–20.

Dodd, V. (2001) 'Calls to reprimand race row MP', *Guardian*, 14 July.

—— (2003a) 'Bradford riot sentences "too harsh"', *Guardian*, 30 January.

—— (2003b) 'Police could face action over stop and search', *Guardian*, 21 March.

—— (2004) 'Four out of 10 whites do not want black neighbours, poll shows', *Guardian*, 19 January.

—— (2005a) 'Asian men targeted in stop and search', *Guardian*, 17 August.

—— (2005b) 'Racial integration increasing, study shows', *Guardian*, 15 November.

Dodd, V. and Travis, A. (2005) 'Muslims face increased stop and search', *Guardian*, 2 March.

Donegan, L. (2002) 'Old father shrine', *Observer Sport Monthly*, 24, April.

Donovan, M. (2003) 'Twenty questions with Albion loan star Zesh Rehman', *Brighton and Hove Sports Argus*, 18 October.

Duneier, M. (1999) *Sidewalk*, New York: Farrar, Straus & Giroux.

Dwyer, C. and Crang, P. (2002) 'Fashioning ethnicities: the commercial spaces of multiculture', *Ethnicities*, 2, 3: 410–30.

Dyer, R. (1997) *White*, London: Routledge.

Eade, J. (1994) 'Identity, nation and religion: educated young Bangladeshi Muslims in London's east end', *International Sociology*, 9, 3: 377–94.

Eastern Eye (2002a) 'Asian football kicks off at Wembley', 12 July.

—— (2002b) 'Leicester show comic the red card', 10 May.

Eisenstein, H. (1984) *Contemporary Feminist Thought*, London: Allen & Unwin.

Entine, J. (2000) *Taboo: Why Black Athletes Dominate Sports and Why we're Afraid to Talk about it*, New York: Public Affairs.

Esbé (2005) 'Riots plunge France into crisis', *Searchlight*, 366, December.

Essed, P. (1991) *Understanding Everyday Racism: an Interdisciplinary Theory*, London: Sage.

Falzon, M-A. (2003) '"Bombay, our cultural heart": rethinking the relation between homeland and diaspora', *Ethnic and Racial Studies*, 26, 4: 662–83.

Fanon, F. (1967) *Towards the African Revolution*, New York: Monthly Review Press.

—— (1986) *Black Skin, White Masks*, London: Pluto Press.

Feagin, J. and Vera, H. (1995) *White Racism*, London: Routledge.

Fiske, S. (1993) 'Controlling other people: the impact of power on stereotyping', *American Psychologist*, 48, 6: 621–8.

Fleming, S. (1994) 'Sport and South Asian youth: the perils of false universalism and stereotyping', *Leisure Studies*, 13: 159–77.

—— (1995) *Home and Away: Sport and South Asian Male Youth*, Aldershot: Avebury.

—— (2001) 'Racial science and South Asian and black physicality', in B. Carrington and I. McDonald (eds) *'Race', Sport and British Society*, London: Routledge.

Football Association (1999) 'Asians and football: providing opportunities for excellence – evidence of research and good practice', London: Football Association.

—— (2005) 'Rehman chooses Pakistan'. Available online at<http://www.thefa.com/TheFA/Ethics AndSportsEquity/NewsAndFeatures/Postings/2005/11/Rehman_chooses_pakistan.htm>, accessed 1 February 2006.

—— (no date) 'Asians in football', London: Football Association.

Football Unites Racism Divides (2000) 'Calendar of racist incidents/anti-racist initiatives in the United Kingdom 1900–2000'. Available online at <http://www.furd.org/archive-/calendar.html>, accessed 16 November 2000.

—— (2001) 'Annual report 2000–2001', Sheffield: FURD.

—— (2004) 'Review 2003', Sheffield: FURD.

Fortier, A-M. (2005) 'Pride politics and multiculturalist citizenship', *Ethnic and Racial Studies*, 28, 3: 559–78.

Frampton, P., Michie, J. and Walsh, A. (2001) 'Fresh players, new tactics: lessons from the Northampton Town supporters' trust', a report for the Football Governance Research Unit, Birkbeck, University of London for Supporters Direct.

Frankenburg, R. (1993) *White Women, Race Matters: The Social Construction of Whiteness*, London: Routledge.

Freeman, S. (1996) 'Ooh, aah . . . Jaginder!', *Independent*, 17 August.

Friedman, J. (1997) 'Global crises, the struggle for cultural identity and intellectual porkbarrelling: cosmopolitans versus locals, ethnics and nationals in an era of de-hegemonization', in P. Werbner and T. Modood (eds) *Debating Cultural Hybridity: Multi-cultural Identities and the Politics of Anti-racism*, London: Zed Books.

Gardner, K. and Shukur, A. (1994) '"I'm Bengali, I'm Asian and I'm living here": the changing identity of British Bengalis', in R. Ballard (ed.) *Desh Pardesh: The South Asian Presence in Britain*, London: Hurst.

Garland, J. and Rowe, M. (1996) 'Football, racism and xenophobia in England: challenging racism and xenophobia', in U. Merkel and W. Tokarski (eds) *Racism and Xenophobia in European Football*, Aachen: Meyer & Meyer.

—— (2001) *Racism and Anti-racism in Football*, Basingstoke: Palgrave.

Ghuman, P. (1999) *Asian Adolescents in the West*, Leicester: BPS.

—— (2003) *Double Loyalties: South Asian Adolescents in the West*, Cardiff: University of Wales Press.

Giardina, M. (2003) '"Bending it like Beckham" in the global popular: stylish hybridity, performativity and the politics of representation', *Journal of Sport and Social Issues*, 27, 1: 65–82.

Gilchrist, P. (2005) 'Local heroes and global stars', in L. Allison (ed.) *The Global Politics of Sport: The Role of Global Institutions in Sport*, London: Routledge.

Gillan, A. (2005) 'Ghettoes in English cities "almost equal to Chicago"', *Guardian*, 23 September.

Gilroy, P. (1987) *There Ain't no Black in the Union Jack: The Cultural Politics of Race and Nation*, London: Routledge.

—— (1992) 'The end of anti-racism', in J. Donald and A. Rattansi (eds) *'Race', Culture and Difference*, London: Sage.

—— (1993) *Small Acts: Thoughts on the Politics of Black Cultures*, London: Serpent's Tail.

—— (2004) *After Empire: Melancholia or Convivial Culture?*, London: Routledge.

Gilroy, P. and Ouseley, H. (2005) 'Is faith redefining the race equality project', in M. Bunting (ed.) *Islam, Race and Being British*, London: Guardian/Barrow Cadbury Trust.

Glynn, S. (2002) 'Bengali Muslims: the new east end radicals? *Ethnic and Racial Studies*, 25, 6: 969–88.

Goldberg, D.T. (1996) 'In/visibility and super/vision', in L. Gordon, T. Sharpley-Whiting and R. White (eds) *Fanon: A Critical Reader*, Oxford: Blackwell.

—— (2006) 'Racial Europeanization', *Ethnic and Racial Studies*, 29, 2: 331–64.

Goodey, J. (2001) 'The criminalization of British Asian youth: research from Bradford and Sheffield', *Journal of Youth Studies* 4, 4: 429–50.

Guardian (2001) 'Asians kick around a few ideas about football', 9 March.

—— (2002) 'Decision on "riot" officer', 1 May.

Gunaratnam, Y. (2003) *Researching 'Race' and Ethnicity: Methods, Knowledge and Power*, London: Sage.

Gupta, R. (ed.) (2003) *From Homebreakers to Jailbreakers: Southall Black Sisters*, London: Zed Books.

Hall, K. (1995) '"There's a time to act English and a time to act Indian": the politics of identity amongst British-Sikh teenagers', in S. Stephens (ed.) *Children and the Politics of Culture*, Princeton, NJ: Princeton University Press.

—— (2002) *Lives in Transition: Sikh Youth as British Citizens*, Philadelphia, PN: University of Pennsylvania Press.

Hall, Sarah and Taylor, M. (2003) 'Minister's call to choose outrages British Muslims', *Guardian*, 22 November.

Hall, Stuart (1990) 'Cultural identity and diaspora', in J. Rutherford (ed.) *Identity: Community, Culture, Difference*, London: Lawrence and Wishart.

—— (1991) 'Old and new identities, old and new ethnicities', in A. King (ed.) *Culture, Globalization and the World System*, Basingstoke: Macmillan.

—— (1992a) 'New ethnicities', in J. Donald and A. Rattansi (eds) *'Race', Culture and Difference*, London: Sage.

—— (1992b) 'The question of cultural identity', in S. Hall, D. Held and T. McGrew (eds) *Modernity and its Futures*, Cambridge: Polity Press.

—— (1992c) 'The west and the rest: discourses and power', in S. Hall and B. Gieben (eds) *Formations of Modernity*, Cambridge: Polity Press.

—— (1996) 'New ethnicities', in D. Morley and K-H. Chen (eds) *Stuart Hall: Critical Dialogues in Cultural Studies*, London: Routledge.

—— (1997) 'The centrality of culture: notes on the cultural revolutions of our time', in K. Thompson (ed.) *Media and Cultural Regulation*, London: Sage.

—— (1998) 'Aspiration and attitude . . . reflections on black Britain in the nineties', *New Formations*, 33: 38–46.

—— (2000a) 'Frontlines and backyards', in K. Owusu (ed.) *Black British Culture and Society*, London: Routledge.

—— (2000b) 'Old and new identities, old and new ethnicities', in L. Back and J. Solomos (eds) *Theories of Race and Racism*, London: Routledge.

—— (2001) 'The multicultural question', Pavis Papers in Social and Cultural Research, No. 4, Faculty of Social Sciences, Open University.

Hare, G. (2003) *Football in France: A Cultural History*, Oxford: Berg.

Hargreaves, J. (2000) *Heroines of Sport: The Politics of Difference and Identity*, London: Routledge.

Harrison, D. (2003) 'I'm proud of my Asian roots but really I'm a Geordie all the way through', *News of the World*, 13 April.

Hawkey, I. (2002) 'Hitting back at racism on the home pitch', *Sunday Times*, 20 October.

Hayes, S. and Sugden, J. (1999) 'Winning through "naturally" still? An analysis of the perceptions held by physical education teachers towards the performance of black pupils in school sport and in the classroom', *Race, Ethnicity and Education*, 2, 1: 93–107.

Henderson, B. (1995) 'Is it in the blood?, *Wisden Cricket Monthly*, July.

Herbert, I. and Burrell, I. (2002) 'Dossier reveals a massive rise in attacks on British Muslims', *Independent*, 4 January.

Herman, M. (2001) 'Anwar aims high', *East End Life*, 1–7 October.

Hewitt, R. (2005) *White Backlash and the Politics of Multiculturalism*, Cambridge: Cambridge University Press.

Hoberman, J. (1997) *Darwin's Athletes: How Sport has Damaged Black America and Preserved the Myth of Race*, New York: Mariner Books.

Hobsbawm, E. (1990) *Nations and Nationalism since 1780: Programme, Myth, Reality*, Cambridge: Cambridge University Press.

Holland, B. (1995) 'Kicking racism out of football: an assessment of racial harassment in and around football grounds', *New Community*, 21, 4: 567–86.

Home Office (2001a) 'Building cohesive communities: a report of the ministerial group on public order and community cohesion', London: HMSO.

——(2001b) 'Community cohesion: a report of the independent review team', London: HMSO.

hooks, b. (1992) 'Representing whiteness in the black imagination', in L. Grossberg, C. Nelson and P. Treichler (eds) *Cultural Studies*, London: Routledge.

Howard, M. (2001) 'Running battles as fans clash', *Stoke Sentinel*, 30 April.

Hughes, K. (2005) 'The meaning of espadrilles', *Guardian*, 14 July.

Huntingdon, S. (1997) *The Clash of Civilizations and the Remaking of World Order*, New York: Simon and Schuster.

Hussain, T. (2001a) 'Eriksson's brown and white army', *Eastern Eye*, 28 September.

——(2001b) 'Tipped to be shear class', *Eastern Eye*, 21 September.

Hussain, Y. and Bagguley, P. (2005) 'Citizenship, ethnicity and identity: British Pakistanis after the 2001 "riots"', *Sociology*, 39, 3: 407–25.

Hutnyk, J. (2000) *Critique of Exotica*, London: Pluto Press.

——(2005) 'The dialectic of here and there: anthropology "at home" and British Asian communism', *Social Identities*, 11, 4: 345–61.

Hutnyk, J. and Sharma, S. (2000) 'Music and politics: an introduction', *Theory, Culture and Society*, 17, 3: 55–63.

Hylton, K. (2005) '"Race", sport and leisure: lessons from critical race theory', *Leisure Studies*, 24, 1: 81–98.

Ifekwunigwe, J. (1999) *Scattered Belongings: Cultural Paradoxes of Race, Nation and Gender*, London: Routledge.

——(ed.) (2004) *'Mixed Race' Studies: A Reader*, London: Routledge.

Independent Football Commission (2004) 'Annual report 2003: a call for unity of purpose', Middlesbrough: Independent Football Commission/University of Teeside.

Indianfootball.com (2006) 'Profile of "players of Indian origin"'. Available online at <http://www.indianfootball.com/pio.html>, accessed 8 February 2006.

Ismond, P. (2003) *Black and Asian Athletes in British Sport and Society: A Sporting Chance?* Basingstoke: Palgrave.

Jacob, G. (2005) 'Mido taunted by West Ham fans', *Times*, 21 November.

Jacobson, J. (1997) 'Religion and ethnicity: dual and alternative sources of identity among young British Pakistanis', *Ethnic and Racial Studies*, 20, 2: 238–56.

Jazeel, T. (2005) 'The world is sound? Geography, musicology and British Asian soundscapes', *Area*, 37, 3: 233–41.

Jenkins, R. and Kennedy, D. (2001) 'Asians vent anger at "police inaction"', Times, 28 May.

Johal, S. (2001) 'Playing their own game: a South Asian football experience', in B. Carrington and I. McDonald (eds) 'Race', Sport and British Society, London: Routledge.

Jones, D. (2005) 'What drove these young Muslims to become suicide bombers?', Daily Mail, 18 July.

Jones, R. (2002) 'The black experience within English semiprofessional soccer', Journal of Sport and Social Issues, 26, 1: 47–65.

Kalra, V.S. (2000) From Textile Mills to Taxi Ranks: Experiences of Migration, Labour and Social Change, Aldershot: Ashgate.

—— (2003) 'Police lore and community disorder: diversity in the criminal justice system', in D. Mason (ed.) Explaining Ethnic Differences: Changing Patterns of Disadvantage in Britain, Bristol: Policy Press.

Kapadia, N. (2001) 'Triumphs and disasters: the story of Indian football, 1889–2000', in P. Dimeo and J. Mills (eds) Soccer in South Asia: Empire, Nation, Diaspora, London: Frank Cass.

Kapadia, N. and Kundu, A. (2001) 'Chima Okorie's "passage to India"', Contemporary South Asia, 10, 2: 265–72.

Karis, T. (2004) '"I prefer to speak of culture": white mothers of multiracial children', in H. Dalmage (ed.) The Politics of Multiracialism: Challenging Racial Thinking, Albany, NY: SUNY Press.

Kaur, R. and Hutnyk, J. (eds) (1999) Travel Worlds: Journeys in Contemporary Cultural Politics, London: Zed Books.

Kaur, R. and Kalra, V.S. (1996) 'New paths for South Asian identity and musical creativity', in S. Sharma, J. Hutnyk and A. Sharma (eds) Dis-orienting Rhythms: the Politics of the New Asian Dance Music, London: Zed Books.

Kaur Grewal, H. (2003a) 'Hammer horror', Eastern Eye, 10 January.

—— (2003b) 'Racists stick the boot in', Eastern Eye, 17 January.

Keely, A. (2005) 'Bowyer makes out-of-court settlement to student', Guardian, 30 November.

Keith, M. (2005) After the Cosmopolitan? Multicultural Cities and the Future of Racism, London: Routledge.

Kelso, P. (2002) 'Black Britons prefer Nigeria to England in cup poll', Guardian, 28 May.

—— (2003) 'Fans facing sanctions after violence', Guardian, 3 April.

—— (2005) [untitled], Guardian, 27 August.

Kick It Out (1998a) 'Annual report: 1997–98', London: Kick It Out.

—— (1998b) 'Asians in football newsletter', Autumn/Winter, London: Kick It Out.

—— (1999) 'Newsletter', Autumn/Winter, London: Kick It Out.

—— (2000a) 'Asians in football', London: Kick It Out.

—— (2000b) 'Racism and xenophobia in English football', A paper for the Secretary of State for the Home Office, London: Kick It Out.

—— (2001) 'Kick it out magazine (3)', London: Kick It Out.

—— (2005) 'Newsletter', Autumn/Winter, London: Kick It Out.

Kim, C.J. (2004) 'Imagining race and nation in multiculturalist America', Ethnic and Racial Studies, 27, 6: 987–1005.

King, C. (2004a) Offside Racism: Playing the White Man, Oxford: Berg.

—— (2004b) 'Race and cultural identity: playing the race game inside football', Leisure Studies, 23, 1: 19–30.

Kumar, K. (2003) The Making of English National Identity, Cambridge: Cambridge University Press.

Kundnani, A. (2000) '"Stumbling on": race, class and England', Race and Class, 41, 4: 1–18.

—— (2001) 'From Oldham to Bradford: the violence of the violated', Race and Class, 43, 2: 105–10.

—— (2002a) 'An unholy alliance? Racism, religion and communalism', Race and Class, 44, 2: 71–80.

—— (2002b) 'The death of multiculturalism', Race and Class, 43, 4: 67–72.

—— (2003) 'Nine months for white racist thugs who sparked the Oldham riots'. Available online at <http://www.irr.org.uk/2003/june/ak000009.html:>, accessed 19 June 2003.

Kundu, A. (1994) 'The Ayodhya aftermath: Hindu versus Muslim violence in Britain', Immigrants and Minorities, 13, 1: 26–47.

Kureishi, H. (2005) The Word and the Bomb, London: Faber & Faber.

—— (2006) 'When Hanif met Amir', Observer Sport Monthly, 70, February.

Laville, S. (2004) 'White shirt, no shame for British Asians', Guardian, 21 June.

Laville, S. and Cobain, I. (2005) 'From cricket-lover who enjoyed a laugh to terror suspect', Guardian, 13 July.

Leicester City FC (2004) 'Community backs Indian links'. Available online at <http://www.lcfc.premiumtv.co.uk/page/NewsDetail/0,,10274~483140,00.html>, accessed 4 February 2004.

Lentin, A. (2004) Racism and Anti-racism in Europe, London: Pluto Press.

Lewis, P. (1997) 'Arenas of ethnic negotiation: cooperation and conflict in Bradford', in T. Modood and P. Werbner (eds) The Politics of Multiculturalism in the New Europe: Racism, Identity and Community, London: Zed Books.

—— (2002) 'Between Lord Ahmed and Ali G: which future for British Muslims?', in W. Shadid and P. van Koningsveld (eds) Religious Freedom and the Neutrality of the State: the Position of Islam in the European Union, Leuven: Peeters.

Licudi, A. (2003) 'West Ham sign Singh', Eastern Eye, 31 January.

Lindsey, E. (1997) 'The hateful game in Essex', Observer, 23 February.

—— (1999) 'The player', Observer, 7 March.

Long, J. (2000) 'No racism here? A preliminary examination of sporting innocence', Managing Leisure, 5: 121–33.

Long, J. and Hylton, K. (2002) 'Shades of white: an examination of whiteness in sport', Leisure Studies, 21: 87–103.

Long, J. and McNamee, M. (2004) 'On the moral economy of racism and racist rationalizations in sport', International Review for the Sociology of Sport, 39, 4: 405–20.

Long, J. and Spracklen, K. (1996) 'Positional play: racial stereotyping in rugby league', Bulletin of Physical Education, 32, 1: 18–23.

Long, J., Carrington, B. and Spracklen, K. (1997a) '"Asians cannot wear turbans in the scrum": explorations of racist discourse within professional rugby league', Leisure Studies, 16, 4: 249–59.

Long, J., Hylton, K., Welch, M. and Dart, J. (2000) 'Part of the game? An examination of racism in grassroots football', Kick It Out/Centre for Leisure and Sport Research, Leeds Metropolitan University.

Long, J., Nesti, M., Carrington, B. and Gilson, N. (1997b) 'Crossing the boundary: a study of the nature and extent of racism in local league cricket', Leeds Metropolitan University.

Long, J., Robinson, P. and Spracklen, K. (2005) 'Promoting racial equality within sports organizations', *Journal of Sport and Social Issues*, 29, 1: 41–59.

Lowles, N. (2005a) 'Fascism, racism and the English disease', *Searchlight*, 365, November.

—— (2005b) 'Stoke BNP pushes Islamophobia', *Searchlight*, 365, November.

Lusted, J. (2005) 'Can Asians play football? Sports equity policy, British Asians and local football', paper presented at *Lost in transl-Asian? British Asians, Sport, Leisure and Popular Culture* study workshop, University of Brighton, 19 November 2005.

McDonald, I. (2002) 'Critical social research and political intervention: moralistic versus radical approaches', in J. Sugden and A. Tomlinson (eds) *Power Games: A Critical Sociology of Sport*, London: Routledge.

McDonald, I. and Ugra, S. (1998) 'Anyone for cricket? Equal opportunities and changing cricket cultures in Essex and East London', University of East London.

Macey, M. (2002) 'Interpreting Islam: young Muslim men's involvement in criminal activity in Bradford', in B. Spalek (ed.) *Islam, Crime and Criminal Justice*, Cullompton: Willan Publishing.

McGhee, D. (2005) 'Patriots of the future? A critical examination of community cohesion strategies in contemporary Britain', *Sociological Research Online*, 10, 3. Available online at <http://www.socresonline.org.uk/10/3/mcghee.html>, accessed 19 January 2006.

McGuire, B. and Collins, D. (1998) 'Sport, ethnicity and racism: the experience of Asian heritage boys', *Sport, Education and Society*, 3, 1: 79–88.

McGuire, B., Monks, K. and Halsall, R. (2001) 'Young Asian males: social exclusion and social injustice in British professional football?' *Culture, Sport, Society*, 4, 3: 65–80.

Mackay, D. (2005) 'Revealing track outfit "not normal Bahraini clothing"', *Guardian*, 5 August.

McLoughlin, S. (2005) 'Mosques and the public space: conflict and cooperation in Bradford', *Journal of Ethnic and Migration Studies*, 31, 6: 1045–66.

Macpherson, W. (1999) *The Stephen Lawrence Inquiry: Report of an Inquiry made by Sir William Macpherson of Cluny*, London: Home Office, Cm 4262-I.

Magee, J. and Olsson, C. (2005) 'Burnley football club, ethnic diversity and the Asian community: an analysis of leisure and community programmes and youth player recruitment', International Football Institute, University of Central Lancashire.

Maguire, J. (1991) 'Sport, racism and British society: a sociological analysis of England's elite male Afro/Caribbean soccer and rugby union players', in G. Jarvie (ed.) *Sport, Racism and Ethnicity*, London: Falmer Press.

Majumdar, B. (2003) 'Forwards and backwards: women's soccer in twentieth-century India', *Soccer and Society*, 4, 2/3: 80–94.

Malcolm, D. (1997) 'Stacking in cricket: a figurational sociological reappraisal of centrality', *Sociology of Sport Journal*, 14: 263–82.

Malik, A. (ed.) (2006) *The State We Are In: Identity, Terror and the Law of Jihad*, Bristol: Amal Press.

Malik, K. (1996) *The Meaning of Race: Race, History and Culture in Western Society*, Basingstoke: Macmillan.

—— (2005a) 'Making a difference: culture, race and social policy', *Patterns of Prejudice*, 39, 4: 361–78.

—— (2005b) 'Multiculturalism has fanned the flames of Islamic extremism', *Times*, 16 July.

Malik, Sarita (2002) *Representing Black Britain: Black and Asian Images on Television*, London: Sage.

Malik, Shahid (2005) 'Isolated young men must join the mainstream', *Observer*, 24 July.

Malik, Shiv (2005) 'The conveyor belt of extremism', New Statesman, 18 July.

Mangan, J. (1998) The Games Ethic and Imperialism: Aspects of the Diffusion of an Ideal, London: Frank Cass.

Mason, D. (2003) 'Changing patterns of ethnic disadvantage in employment', in D. Mason (ed.) Explaining Ethnic Differences: Changing Patterns of Disadvantage in Britain, Bristol: Policy Press.

Miles, R. (1989) Racism, London: Routledge.

Mills, J. (2006) '"Manipur rules here": gender, politics and sport in an Asian border zone', Journal of Sport and Social Issues, 30, 1: 62–78.

Mills, J. and Dimeo, P. (2003) '"When gold is fired it shines": sport, the imagination and the body in colonial and postcolonial India', in J. Bale and M. Cronin (eds) Sport and Postcolonialism, Oxford: Berg.

Mills, M. (2001) 'A most remarkable community: Anglo-Indian contributions to sport in India', Contemporary South Asia, 10, 2: 223–36.

Mirza, H. S. (2003) '"All the women are white, all the blacks are men – but some of us are brave": mapping the consequences of invisibility for black and minority ethnic women in Britain', in D. Mason (ed.) Explaining Ethnic Differences: Changing Patterns of Disadvantage in Britain, Bristol: Policy Press.

Modood, T. (1988) '"Black", racial equality and Asian identity', New Community, 14, 3: 397–404.

—— (1992a) 'British Asian Muslims and the Rushdie affair', in J. Donald and A. Rattansi (eds) 'Race', Culture and Difference, London: Sage.

—— (1992b) Not Easy being British: Colour, Culture and Citizenship, Stoke-on-Trent: Runnymede Trust and Trentham Books.

—— (1994) 'Political blackness and British Asians', Sociology, 28, 4: 858–876.

—— (1997a) 'Culture and identity', in T. Modood, R. Berthoud, J. Lakey, J. Nazroo, P. Smith, S. Virdee and S. Beishon Ethnic Minorities in Britain: Diversity and Disadvantage, London: PSI.

—— (1997b) '"Difference", cultural racism and anti-racism', in P. Werbner and T. Modood (eds) Debating Cultural Hybridity: Multi-cultural Identities and the Politics of Anti-racism, London: Zed Books.

—— (1997c) 'Qualifications and English language', in T. Modood, R. Berthoud, J. Lakey, J. Nazroo, P. Smith, S. Virdee and S. Beishon, Ethnic Minorities in Britain: Diversity and Disadvantage, London: PSI.

—— (2005) Multicultural Politics: Racism, Ethnicity and Muslims in Britain, Edinburgh: Edinburgh University Press.

Moran, R. (2000) 'Racism in football: a victim's perspective', in J. Garland, D. Malcolm and M. Rowe (eds) The Future of Football: Challenges for the Twenty-first Century, London: Frank Cass.

Morris, S. and Vasagar, J. (2002) 'How two football-mad Tipton lads ended up in chains at Camp X-Ray', Guardian, 28 January.

Muir, H. (2005) 'Far right and football gangs plot "revenge"', Guardian, 15 July.

Muir, H. and Butt, R. (2005) 'A rumour, outrage and then a riot. How tension in a Birmingham suburb erupted', Guardian, 24 October.

Nayak, A. (2003) Race, Place and Globalization: Youth Cultures in a Changing World, Oxford: Berg.

Nazroo, J. and Karlsen, S. (2003) 'Patterns of identity among ethnic minority people: diversity and commonality', Ethnic and Racial Studies, 26, 5: 902–30.

Neiyyar, D. (2001) 'Survey shows war damaged race relations', Eastern Eye, 23 November.

Nicholls, A. (2002) Scally: Confessions of a Category C Football Hooligan, Ramsbottom: Milo.

Observer (2002) 'Will they never learn?', 6 January.

—— (2005) 'Using intelligence', 3 August.

Office for National Statistics (2004) Office for National Statistics website. Available online at <http://www.statistics.gov.uk/cci/nugget.asp?id=459>, accessed 8 January 2004.

Ofsted (2005) 'Citizenship poll', London: Ofsted.

Oldham Independent Review (2001) 'One Oldham, one future: panel report', Oldham: Oldham Independent Review.

Oliver, A. (2003) 'I'm no racist', Evening Chronicle, 22 August.

Ouseley, H. (2001) 'Community pride not prejudice: making diversity work in Bradford', Report presented to Bradford Vision, Bradford: Bradford Vision.

Pallister, D. (2002) 'Anger at new advice to Asians', Guardian, 16 September.

Parekh, B. (2000) 'National identity in a multicultural society', in M. Anwar, P. Roach and R. Sondhi (eds) From Legislation to Integration? Race Relations in Britain, Basingstoke: Macmillan.

Parker, A. (2001) 'Soccer, servitude and sub-cultural identity: football traineeship and masculine construction', Soccer and Society, 2, 1: 59–80.

Parker, D. and Song, M. (eds) (2001) Rethinking 'Mixed Race', London: Pluto Press.

Parker, L. and Lynn, M. (2002) 'What's race got to do with it? Critical Race Theory's conflicts with and connections to qualitative research methodology and epistemology', Qualitative Inquiry, 8, 1: 7–22.

Patel, P. (2002) 'Back to the future: avoiding déjà vu in resisting racism', in F. Anthias and C. Lloyd (eds) Rethinking Anti-racisms: From Theory to Practice, London: Routledge.

Pearson, G. (1976) '"Paki-bashing" in a north east Lancashire cotton town: a case study and its history', in G. Mungham and G. Pearson (eds) Working-class Youth Culture, London: Routledge & Kegan Paul.

Perryman, M. (2006) Ingerland: Travels with a Football Nation, London: Simon & Schuster.

Phillips, C. (2002) 'United we stand?', Guardian, 22 June.

Pickering, M. (2001) Stereotyping: the Politics of Representation, Basingstoke: Palgrave.

Pilkington, A. (2003) Racial Disadvantage and Ethnic Diversity in Britain, Basingstoke: Palgrave.

Pinto, T., Drew, D. and Minhas, N. (1997) 'Sheffield divided or united?: a study of "race" and football', Survey and Statistical Research Centre, Sheffield Hallam University.

Prior, L. (1997) 'Following in Foucault's footsteps', in D. Silverman (ed.) Qualitative Research: Theory, Method and Practice, London: Sage.

Puwar, N. (2005) Space Invaders: Race, Gender and Bodies out of Place, Oxford: Berg.

Rai, M. (2006) 7/7: The London Bombings, Islam and the Iraq War, London: Pluto Press.

Raj, D.S. (2000) '"Who the hell do you think you are?": promoting religious identity among young Hindus in Britain', Ethnic and Racial Studies, 23, 3: 535–58.

Ramdin, R. (1999) Reimagining Britain: 500 years of Black and Asian History, London: Pluto Press.

Ramesh, R. (2005) 'Fatwa orders Indian tennis star to cover up', Guardian, 10 September.

Ramji, H. (2003) 'Engendering diasporic identities', in N. Puwar and P. Raghuram, P. (eds) South Asian Women in the Diaspora, Oxford: Berg.

Ratna, A. (2005) 'Flying the flag for England?: national and social identities amongst British Asian female football players', paper presented at Lost in Transl-Asian? British

Asians, Sport, Leisure and Popular Culture study workshop, University of Brighton, 19 November.

Rattansi, A. (1992) 'Changing the subject? Racism, culture and education', in J. Donald and A. Rattansi (eds) *'Race', Culture and Difference*, London: Sage.

Raval, S. (1989) 'Gender, leisure and sport: a case study of young people of South Asian descent – a response', *Leisure Studies*, 8: 237–40.

Ray, L. and Reed, K. (2005) 'Community, mobility and racism in a semi-rural area: comparing minority experience in East Kent', *Ethnic and Racial Studies*, 28, 2: 212–34.

Redhead, S. (1997) *Post-fandom and the Millennial Blues: the Transformation of Soccer Culture*, London: Routledge.

Renton, D. (2006) *When We Touched The Sky: The Anti-Nazi League 1977–1981*, Cheltenham: New Clarion Press.

Robertson, R. (1995) 'Glocalization: time–space and homogeneity–heterogeneity', in M. Featherstone, S. Lash and R. Robertson (eds) *Global Modernities*, London: Sage.

Rockquemore, K. (2004) 'Deconstructing Tiger Woods: the promise and the pitfalls of multiracial identity', in H. Dalmage (ed.) *The Politics of Multiracialism: Challenging Racial Thinking*, Albany, NY: SUNY Press.

Ross, K. (1996) *Black and White Media*, Cambridge: Polity Press.

Runnymede Trust (1997) *Islamophobia: a Challenge for us all*, London: Runnymede Trust.

Saeed, A., Blain, N. and Forbes, D. (1999) 'New ethnic and national questions in Scotland: post-British identities among Glasgow Pakistani teenagers', *Ethnic and Racial Studies*, 22, 5: 821–44.

Said, E. (1985) *Orientalism: Western Conceptions of the Orient*, London: Penguin.

—— (1997) *Covering Islam: How the Media and the Experts Determine how we see the Rest of the World*, London: Vintage.

Samad, Y. (1992) 'Book burning and race relations: political mobilisation of Bradford Muslims', *New Community*, 18, 4: 507–19.

—— (1998) 'Imagining a British Muslim identification', in S. Vertovec and A. Rogers (eds) *Muslim European Youth: Reproducing Ethnicity, Religion, Culture*, Aldershot: Ashgate.

Sampson, E. (1993) *Celebrating the Other*, Boulder, CO: Westview Press.

Sayyid, S. (2006) 'Introduction: BrAsians – postcolonial people, ironic citizens', in N. Ali, V.S. Kalra and S. Sayyid (eds) *A Postcolonial People: South Asians in Britain*, London: Hurst.

Scraton, S., Caudwell, J. and Holland, S. (2005) '"Bend it like Patel": centring "race", ethnicity and gender in feminist analysis of women's football in England', *International Review for the Sociology of Sport*, 40, 1: 71–88.

Scruton, R. (2005) *The West and the Rest: Globalization and the Terrorist Threat*, London: Continuum International.

Shah, A. (2004) 'The "partial insider": power relations in the interview situation', in G. Craig (ed.) *'Race' and Social Research: Five Case Studies*, University of Hull.

Shah, D. and Das Gupta, I. (2001) 'British Muslims hold emergency talks over threats', *Evening Standard*, 14 September.

Shah, H. (2004) 'Reading and using mass communication research on the "other": whiteness, "folk wisdom" and objects of research', *Multicultural Perspectives*, 6, 2: 10–16.

Sharma, S. (1996) 'Noisy Asians or "Asian noise"?', in S. Sharma, J. Hutnyk and A. Sharma (eds) *Dis-orienting Rhythms: the Politics of the New Asian Dance Music*, London: Zed Books.

—— (2003) 'The sounds of alterity', in M. Bull and L. Back (eds) *The Auditory Culture Reader*, Oxford: Berg.

Sharma, S., Hutnyk, J. and Sharma, A. (eds) (1996) *Dis-orienting Rhythms: the Politics of the New Asian Dance Music*, London: Zed Books.

Shaw, A. (2000) *Kinship and Continuity: Pakistani Families in Britain*, Amsterdam: Harwood Academic Publishers.

Show Racism the Red Card (2000) 'Annual review 1999–2000', London: Unison.

—— (2002) 'Red Card', Whitley Bay: Show Racism The Red Card.

Shukla, S. (2003) *India Abroad: Diasporic Cultures of Postwar America and England*, Princeton, NJ: Princeton University Press.

Singer, J. (2005) 'Understanding racism through the eyes of African-American male student-athletes', *Race, Ethnicity and Education*, 8, 4: 365–86.

Singh, P. (1999) *The Sikhs*, New York: Doubleday.

Siraj-Blatchford, I. (1993) 'Ethnicity and conflict in physical education: a critique of Carroll and Hollinshead's case study', *British Educational Research Journal*, 19, 1: 77–82.

Sivanandan, A. (1981/2) 'From resistance to rebellion: Asian and Afro-Caribbean struggles in Britain', *Race and Class*, 23, 2/3: 111–52.

—— (2001) 'Poverty is the new black', *Race and Class*, 43, 2: 1–5.

Sky Sports (2006) 'Rehman's Pakistan aim'. Available online at <http://home.skysports.com/list.asp?hlid=320331&CPID=219&CLID=&lid=549&title=Rehman's+Pakistan+aim&channel=asia>, accessed 1 March 2006.

Smithers, R. (2001) 'Apartheid claim over Islam school', *Guardian*, 10 February.

Solomos, J. and Back, L. (1996) *Racism and Society*, London: Macmillan.

Song, M. (2003) *Choosing Ethnic Identity*, Cambridge: Polity.

—— (2004) 'Racial hierarchies in the USA and Britain: investigating a politically sensitive issue', in M. Bulmer and J. Solomos (eds) *Researching Race and Racism*, London: Routledge.

—— (2005) 'Global and local articulations of Asian identity', in C. Alexander and C. Knowles (eds) *Making Race Matter: Bodies, Space and Identity*, Basingstoke: Palgrave.

Spivak, G. (1990) *The Post-colonial Critic: Interviews, Strategies, Dialogue*, London: Routledge.

Spracklen, K. (2001) '"Black pearl, black diamonds": exploring racial identities in rugby league', in B. Carrington and I. McDonald (eds) *'Race', Sport and British Society*, London: Routledge.

—— (2003) 'Setting a standard? Measuring progress in tackling racism and promoting social inclusion in English sport', in A. Ibbetson, B. Watson and M. Ferguson (eds) *Leisure, Sport and Social Inclusion: Potential, Participation and Possibilities*, Eastbourne: Leisure Studies Association.

St Louis, B. (2003) 'Sport, genetics and the "natural athlete": the resurgence of racial science', *Body and Society*, 9, 2: 75–95.

—— (2004) 'Sport and common-sense racial science', *Leisure Studies*, 23, 1: 31–46.

—— (2005) Brilliant bodies, fragile minds: race, sport and the mind/body split', in C. Alexander and C. Knowles (eds) *Making Race Matter: Bodies, Space and Identity*, Basingstoke: Palgrave.

Stear, H. (2002) 'Knowing the score?', *Inclusion*, 3, Autumn.

Stote, M. (2002) 'Singh when you're winning', *Express*, 14 November.

Talbot, I. (2000) *India and Pakistan*, London: Arnold.

Taylor, D. (2005) 'Boxing racists hunted', *Scottish Mail*, 13 November.

Thomas, P. (1995) 'Kicking racism out of football: a supporter's view', *Race and Class*, 36, 4: 95–101.

Thorpe, M. (2002) 'Leeds called to task over racist abuse', *Guardian*, 26 March.

Times (2002) 'Skinheads "attacked Asian footballers"', 12 April.

Tizard, B. and Phoenix, A. (2002) *Black, White or Mixed Race? Race and Racism in the Lives of Young People of Mixed Parentage*, revised edition, London: Routledge.

Travis, A. (2002) 'Sport schemes urged to soothe refugee tensions', *Guardian*, 12 December.

Turnbull, S. (2003) 'A reluctant symbol keeps low profile', *Independent on Sunday*, 8 June.

Turner, D. (2006) 'Flagged down', *When Saturday Comes*, 228, February.

Turner, T. (1993) 'Anthropology and multiculturalism: what is anthropology that multi-culturalists should be mindful of it?', *Cultural Anthropology*, 8, 4: 411–29.

van Dijk, T. (2002) 'Denying racism: elite discourse and racism', in P. Essed and D.T. Goldberg (eds) *Race Critical Theories*, Oxford: Blackwell.

van Zoonen, L., Müller, F. and de Roode, L. (2005) 'Accidental racists: experiences and contradictions of racism in local Amsterdam soccer fan culture', unpublished paper, Amsterdam School of Communication Research, University of Amsterdam.

Vasagar, J., Ward, D., Etim, A. and Keating, M. (2001) '"No go for whites" in race hotspot', *Guardian*, 20 April.

Vasili, P. (2000) *Colouring over the White Line: The History of Black Footballers in Britain*, Edinburgh: Mainstream Publishing.

Vertovec, S. (1998) 'Young Muslims in Keighley, West Yorkshire: cultural identity, context and "community"', in S. Vertovec and A. Rogers (eds) *Muslim European Youth: Reproducing Ethnicity, Religion, Culture*, Aldershot: Ashgate.

Visram, R. (2002) *Asians in Britain: 400 years of History*, London: Pluto Press.

von der Lippe, G. (2000) 'Heresy as a victorious political practice: grass-roots politics in Norwegian sports 1972–1975', *International Review for the Sociology of Sport*, 35, 2: 181–98.

Wainwright, M. (2001) 'Church initiative after Oldham stand-off', *Guardian*, 7 May.

—— (2003) 'Racist shadow falls over village cricket', *Guardian*, 6 August.

Walker, D. (2002) 'Study reveals job plight of Muslims', *Guardian*, 20 February.

Walker, M. (2003a) 'Robson: I would not sign a racist', *Guardian*, 31 January.

—— (2003b) 'Roeder tiptoes through the moral minefield as Bowyer storm intensifies', *Guardian*, 11 January.

—— (2003c) 'Touré comes out fighting with his back to the wall', *Guardian*, 20 September.

Walsh, D. (2005) 'Mullahs target women runners', *Guardian*, 12 April.

Walton-Roberts, M. (2004) 'Globalization, national autonomy and non-resident Indians', *Contemporary South Asia*, 13, 1: 53–69.

Watson, J. (ed.) (1977) *Between Two Cultures: Migrants and Minorities in Britain*, Oxford: Basil Blackwell.

Wazir, B. (2001) 'Born in Manchester but loyal to Lahore', *Observer*, 24 June.

Werbner, P. (1996a) 'Fun spaces: on identity and social empowerment among British Pakistanis', *Theory, Culture and Society*, 13, 4: 53–79.

—— (1996b) '"Our blood is green": cricket, identity and social empowerment among British Pakistanis', in J. MacClancy (ed.) *Sport, Identity and Ethnicity*, Oxford: Berg.

—— (1997) 'Essentialising essentialism, essentialising "silence": ambivalence and multi-culturalism in the constructions of racism and ethnicity', in P. Werbner and T. Modood (eds) *Debating Cultural Hybridity: Multi-cultural Identities and the Politics of Anti-racism*, London: Zed Books.

178   References

—— (2002) *Imagined Diasporas among Manchester Muslims: the Public Performance of Pakistani Transnational Identity Politics*, Oxford: James Currey.

—— (2004) 'The predicament of diaspora and millennial Islam: reflections on September 11, 2001', *Ethnicities*, 4, 4: 451–76.

—— (2005) 'The translocation of culture: "community cohesion" and the force of multiculturalism in history', *Sociological Review*, 53, 4: 745–67.

West, C. (1999) 'The new cultural politics of difference', in S. During (ed.) *The Cultural Studies Reader*, second edition, London: Routledge.

Wheatcroft, G. (2001) 'This misguided campaign for Asians to play football', *Guardian*, 8 March.

White, M. (2001) 'Tory rapped for saying Enoch Powell was right', *Guardian*, 28 March.

—— (2004) 'Try boxing test, says Lady Amos', *Guardian*, 27 October.

Williams, J. (2000) 'Asians, cricket and ethnic relations in northern England', *Sporting Traditions*, 16, 2: 39–53.

—— (2001) *Cricket and Race*, Oxford: Berg.

—— (2003) '"Paki cheats!": postcolonial tensions in England–Pakistan cricket', in J. Bale and M. Cronin (eds) *Sport and Postcolonialism*, Oxford: Berg.

Wintour, P. (2001) 'Chicken tikka Britain is new Cook recipe', *Guardian*, 19 April.

Young Jr, A. (2004) 'Experiences in ethnographic interviewing about race: the inside and outside of it', in M. Bulmer and J. Solomos (eds) *Researching Race and Racism*, London: Routledge.

Younge, G. (2005) 'Please stop fetishising integration. Equality is what we really need', *Guardian*, 19 September.

Index